THE URBAN AND REGIONAL TRANSFORMATION OF BRITAIN

CW00420979

THE URBAN AND REGIONAL TRANSFORMATION OF BRITAIN

edited by J. B. Goddard
and A. G. Champion

METHUEN LONDON AND NEW YORK

First published in 1983 by
Methuen & Co. Ltd
11 New Fetter Lane,
London EC4P 4EE
Published in the USA by
Methuen & Co.
in association with Methuen, Inc.
733 Third Avenue, New York,
NY 10017

Typeset by
Scarborough Typesetting Services
and printed in Great Britain at
The University Press,
Cambridge

British Library Cataloguing
in Publication Data

The Urban and regional transformation
of Britain.
1. Anthropo-geography – Great Britain
I. Goddard, J. B.   II. Champion, A. G.
304.2'0941   GF551

ISBN 0–416–30900–3

Library of Congress Cataloging
in Publication Data
Main entry under title:

The Urban and regional transformation
of Britain.
Bibliography: p.
Includes index.
1. Great Britain – Economic conditions
– 1945–
– Addresses, essays, lectures.
2. Great Britain – Social conditions
– 1945–
– Addresses, essays, lectures.
3. Urban economics – Addresses,
essays, lectures.
4. Regional economics – Addresses,
essays, lectures.
5. Social change – Addresses,
essays, lectures.
I. Goddard, J. B.
II. Champion, A. G. (Anthony Gerard)
HC256.6.U72 1983   330.942'0858
83–7952

ISBN 0–416–30900–3

Contents

vi *Contents*

List of tables

List of figures

List of contributors

A. G. CHAMPION is Lecturer in Geography at the University of Newcastle upon Tyne. His research interests are in recent trends in population distribution in advanced industrial societies and in land-use planning. He is co-author of *Facts about the British New Towns* (with K. Clegg and R. L. Davies) and co-editor of *The Future of the City Centre* (with R. L. Davies).

PETER DICKEN is Senior Lecturer at the University of Manchester and former co-director of the North West Industry Research Unit. His primary research interest lies in the geography of transnational enterprises and in inward and outward direct investment in UK manufacturing industry. His major publications have been concerned with the spatial behaviour of business enterprises, the geography of foreign direct investment and the role of business enterprises in urban–regional industrial change. He is co-author (with Peter Lloyd) of *Location in Space* and *Modern Western Society*.

STEPHEN FOTHERGILL is a Research Associate in the Department of Land Economy, University of Cambridge. He previously worked at the Centre for Environmental Studies, where he and Graham Gudgin undertook the research on which chapter 2 is based. His other publications include *Unequal Growth: Urban and Regional Employment Change in the U.K.* (with Graham Gudgin).

M. E. FROST is Lecturer in Geography at King's College London. He has been responsible for directing a number of government and research council projects upon which some of the research contained in this volume is based. He is author of *The Impact of Regional Policy* and *Unemployment, Structural Economic Change and Public Policy in British Regions* (with N. A. Spence).

A. E. GILLESPIE is a Research Associate at the Centre for Urban and Regional Development Studies at the University of Newcastle upon Tyne, with current research interests in local labour market restructuring and in the delivery of industrial policy. He was previously a Research Officer on the Urban Change in Britain project at the London School of Economics, with responsibility for the analysis of journey-to-work change, the results of which form the basis for his contribution in this volume.

J. B. GODDARD is Director of the Centre for Urban and Regional Development Studies and Head of the Department of Geography at the University of Newcastle upon Tyne. He was previously a lecturer at the Department of Geography at the London School of Economics, where he was co-director with N. A. Spence and J. R. Drewett of the study of Urban Change in Britain, financed by the Department of the Environment and on which several chapters in this volume are based.

GRAHAM GUDGIN is a Senior Research Officer in the Department of Applied Economics at the University of Cambridge and is a member of the Cambridge Economic Policy Group. Previous publications include *Industrial Location Processes and Regional Employment Growth*, 'Non-production activities in UK manufacturing industry' (with R. Crum), *Seats Votes and the Spatial Organization of Elections* (with P. J. Taylor) and *Unequal Growth* (with S. Fothergill).

STEPHEN KENNETT is currently Senior Research Officer in the Inner Cities Directorate of the Department of the Environment. He was previously Research Officer at the London School of Economics on the Urban Change in Britain project and, subsequently, the SSRC-sponsored 'Inner Cities in Context Review Study' under the direction of Peter Hall and Derek Diamond. His contribution to this volume is largely based on his Ph.D. work, which was undertaken at the London School of Economics and investigated 'Population Decentralisation and Deconcentration in England and Wales 1961–78 and some implications for local authorities'.

PETER LLOYD is Reader in Geography at the University of Manchester and Director of the North West Industry Research Unit. He has contributed to published work on the development problems of Merseyside, the characteristics of new small firms in conurbation cores, and the impact of industrial incentives in Southern Ontario. He is co-author (with Peter Dicken) of *Location in Space* and *Modern Western Society*.

JUDITH MARQUAND is Head of the Training Economics and Statistics Branch in the Manpower Services Commission and was Head of

Regional Economics and Statistics at the Department of Industry until the end of 1981. During 1977–8, as a Research Fellow at the University of Lodvain-la-Neuve, she co-ordinated a nine-nation EEC D.G.XVI research project on behalf of the Centre for Environmental Studies. Publications arising from this study included 'The service sector and regional policy in the United Kingdom' and 'The role of the tertiary sector in regional policy: a comparative study'.

S. P. PINCH is Lecturer in Geography at the University of Southampton. A graduate of Sussex University, he obtained his doctorate from the London School of Economics where he also worked as a research officer with the Urban Change Project. His research is concerned with the influence of the local state upon service provision in cities, and the social consequences of structural and geographical changes in local economies.

N. A. SPENCE is Lecturer in Geography at the London School of Economics and Political Science. He has been responsible for directing a number of government and research council projects upon which some of the research contained in this volume is based. He is author of *Unemployment, Structural Economic Change and Public Policy in British Regions* (with M. E. Frost), *The Evolving Metropolitan Area* (Open University) and editor of *British Cities: Analysis of Urban Change*.

ALLAN M. WILLIAMS graduated from University College Swansea in 1972 with a Joint Honours Degree in Geography and Economics, and he obtained his doctorate from the London School of Economics in 1976 for his work on 'Social change and residential differentiation'. During 1975–6 he was a Research Officer at the London School of Economics and worked on socio-economic changes in British cities, as part of the Urban Change in Britain project. He is now Lecturer in Geography at Exeter University and his research interests include rural housing and employment markets in the UK and urban and regional development in Iberia. He is co-author of *Rural Housing and the Public Sector* and *British Cities: Analysis of Urban Change*.

Acknowledgements

The authors, contributors and publishers gratefully acknowledge the following for permission to reproduce copyright material:

Heinemann Educational Books for illustrations and material in chapter 2 from S. Fothergill and G. Gudgin, *Unequal Growth: Urban and Regional Employment Change in the U.K.*;

The Cambridge University Press and Regional Studies Association for figure 3.1 from P. E. Lloyd and D. E. Reeve, 'North West England 1971–77: a study in industrial decline and economic restructuring', *Regional Studies* 16.5, 345–59, and for figure 3.3 from P. Dicken and P. E. Lloyd, 'Inner metropolitan industrial change, enterprise structures and policy issues: case studies of Manchester and Merseyside', *Regional Studies* 12.2, 181–97;

J. A. S. Robertson for table 5.3 from *The Structure and Employment Prospects of the Service Industries*, Department of Employment Research Paper 30, table 28;

The Directorate-General for Regional Policy, Commission of the European Communities (D.G.XVI), for table 5.6 from R. E. Crum and G. Gudgin, *Non-production Activities in U.K. Manufacturing Industry*, Collection Studies, Regional Policy Series 3;

Pergamon Press for table 4.3 and part of table 4.4 from N. A. Spence and M. E. Frost, *Unemployment, Structural Economic Change and Public Policy in British Regions*, Progress in Planning Vol. 16, part 1.

The Controller of Her Majesty's Stationery Office for figures 4.1, 6.1, 6.2, 9.2, 9.3, 9.4 and tables 4.1, 4.2, 6.1–6.6, 7.1–7.6 and 9.1–9.3, based wholly or in part on material researched for the Urban Change Project which was carried out at the London School of Economics under the sponsorship of the Department of the Environment.

The editors also gratefully acknowledge the assistance of Eric Quenet and Olive Teasdale in redrawing some of the figures, John Knipe for other cartographic advice and Dorothy Osler for helping with editing.

Preface

The essays in this volume are concerned with various aspects of recent economic and social changes recorded across the cities and regions of Britain. The contributions are distinctive because with one exception the analyses which they present cover the country as a whole at a level of spatial resolution below that of the ten major standard regions for which most official statistics are produced. Such comprehensive coverage is important because the experiences of different areas are frequently interlinked; for example, in terms of population losses in one locality and gains in another, with the two areas being linked by migration streams. While there are important and long-standing differences between the major regions of Britain, particularly between the south-east core region and more peripheral areas, many of the recent processes of change appear to have operated at a more local scale, within rather than between regions. The importance of the labour market in shaping processes of economic and social change is widely acknowledged and, although there are considerable difficulties involved in translating this non-spatial concept into a geographical one, there can be little doubt about the significance of the local labour market *area* in the organization of society. For example, it is the area within which individuals tend to search for and change jobs without changing residence. Many of the contributions in this volume therefore seek to bring together change at the regional and local labour market scales.

Several of the chapters in this volume have their origin in a research project on urban change in Britain commissioned by the Department of the Environment and carried out at the Department of Geography at the London School of Economics. That project sought to describe and analyse patterns of economic and social change in Britain over the period between 1951 and 1971 for a set of consistently defined functional urban areas – basically urban centres and their commuting hinterlands. This framework facilitated the simultaneous examination of trends at the intra- and inter-urban scale over the entire country, not just for the largest cities which have been the focus of most research attention. Preliminary analyses of population and employment change for these areas were published by the Department of the Environment (1976a), with the more detailed factual statements appearing in Spence *et al.* (1982). In this volume the contributions by Spence and Frost on employment change, Pinch and Williams on social change, Gillespie on journey-to-work patterns and Kennett on migration highlight some of the major findings of the Urban Change study and then go on to examine their background and policy implications.

Whilst it has been possible to extend some of the population statistics for these urban areas to 1974, the reorganization of local government in that year created a fundamental discontinuity in the statistical series. In order to update the picture as well as to incorporate other statistics, particularly covering employment and unemployment which are collected for areas incompatible with the census data used in the urban analysis, a number of other contributions have been included in the volume. Thus Fothergill and Gudgin examine long-run manufacturing employment trends for sub-regions, while Frost and Spence analyse unemployment trends in the 1970s. Another scale of analysis, the upper-tier local government areas, is introduced in essays by Marquand and Champion when discussing trends in service sector employment and recent changes in population distribution.

Apart from the difficulties of reconciling information for different areal frameworks, one of the inevitable consequences of adopting a nation-wide perspective is the need to rely on statistically aggregated information. Nowhere is the limitation of this approach clearer than in the study of employment change, where net changes need to be decomposed into their various components – the birth, death, migration, expansion or contraction of manufacturing or service establishments. The micro-data that is necessary for this sort of analysis is available only for selected areas, so one contribution, that by Dicken and Lloyd, exemplifies the insight that can be gained by getting behind the aggregate picture of employment change in the conurbations of Greater Manchester and Merseyside through an analysis of its constituent 'components'. The contribution by Fothergill and Gudgin provides similar data for a more dynamic industrial region – the East Midlands.

Each of the essays in this volume seeks to present the results of original research carried out by the authors. Even in these days of high-speed data-processing, much of this research has involved the laborious manual reclassification of government statistics into a consistent spatial framework for different dates. Only in this way can the generality and true extent of change be documented accurately. Although this desire for consistency may be regarded as pedantic, it can be argued that one of the factors accounting for the failure to appreciate the scale of urban decline occurring during the 1960s was the lack of a definition of cities which adequately represented the process.

As Britain lies in the grip of the most severe recession since the 1930s, the analysis of changes occurring in the more prosperous 1960s and 1970s may seem irrelevant. Nevertheless, past experience suggests that spatial trends are remarkably persistent over long periods of time. Even if in retrospect the significant changes in the distribution of population and economic activity described in the essays in this volume turned out to be unique to the particular thirty-year period collectively covered, the consequences of the changes that have occurred will have to be lived with for some considerable time into the future.

Newcastle upon Tyne   J.B.G

1982   A.G.C.

A note on the spatial representation of urban and regional change

The analyses presented in this volume make use of a number of alternative spatial divisions of Britain. These are mentioned at the appropriate points in the book, but this note provides an overview. It traces the progressive refinement of these statistical reporting units and assesses their strengths and weaknesses in the context of examining urban and regional change.

The broadest level of sub-national generalization is represented by the ten standard regions or economic planning regions: the South East, East Anglia, the South West, the East Midlands, the West Midlands, the North West, Yorkshire and Humberside, the Northern Region, Wales and Scotland (see, for instance, figure 10.2). Prior to local government reorganization in 1974/5 these regions were broken down by government officials into sixty-six subdivisions (sixty-one if the Outer Metropolitan subdivision in the South East is treated as a single unit as shown in figure 4.2 and table 4.4). There does not appear to have been any consistent basis for these definitions. Some of the areas recognized differences in economic structure (e.g. the subdivision Industrial North-East: north) and some the functional significance of major cities (e.g. the London, Manchester and Glasgow subdivisions). These urban subdivisions, however, do not coincide with the conurbations first defined in the 1951 Census, areas which were more or less coterminous with the built-up areas at the time. While the boundaries of some of the large city subdivisions include wide hinterlands (e.g. Glasgow), others (e.g. London) are tightly bounded. Part of London's hinterland is in fact recognized as a subdivision in its own right (the Outer Metropolitan subdivision), but this is the only instance where a complete metropolitan ring is defined.

Up until the early 1970s it was generally believed that the main processes of spatial change in Britain operated at the inter-regional scale, with sub-regional change being generally a local variant of these broader trends. Because the scale and significance of change within and between urban areas was not appreciated, no official attempt was made to produce a consistent definition of urban areas which recognized the functional relationship between urban centres and their surrounding hinterlands. This was in marked contrast to the USA where Standard Metropolitan Statistical Areas have been widely used for statistical reporting purposes even though such areas are not formal units of local administration. It was left to academic geographers to transfer this concept to Britain.

Peter Hall, directing an investigation at Political and Economic Planning on the impact of planning on urban development in Britain, first used the 1961 Census to define Standard Metropolitan Labour Areas in England and Wales (Hall, 1971; Hall *et al.*, 1973). The building blocks for his definition were the old local authority areas (county boroughs, municipal boroughs, urban districts and rural districts) established towards the end of the nineteenth century. In the less densely settled parts of the country, urban districts and their related rural districts recognize the close connection between urban centres and their hinterlands. In the larger urban areas Hall found it necessary to group boroughs and urban districts in order to delineate the high employment density cores of cities. Thus *urban cores* were defined as contiguous local authorities with job densities of over five per acre or a total employment of over 20,000. Around these cores a *metropolitan ring* was identified as comprising those areas from which more than 15 per cent of economically active population commuted to the core. Beyond this an *outer metropolitan ring* was defined as all other contiguous local authority areas having more economically active population commuting to a particular core than to any other core. The core plus the ring was termed the *Standard Metropolitan Labour Area* (SMLA) which had to have, at minimum, a population of 50,000; the addition of an outer ring identified what Hall called the *Metropolitan Economic Labour Area* (MELA). These definitional criteria were subsequently applied to the 1971 Census and extended to Scotland in the London School of Economics study of urban change in Britain, giving a total of 126 areas (Department of Environment, 1976a; Spence *et al.*, 1982).

The SMLAs do not provide the only definition of labour market areas that can be used in a study of urban and regional change. The Department of Employment defines, for its operational purposes, a set of travel-to-work areas (TTWAs) which are composed of aggregations of local employment office areas. Annual employment and unemployment statistics are collected for these local office areas. But because individuals may register as unemployed near their home which might be outside the local office area of their former place of work, the department needs to identify areas which are self-contained with respect to workplace and residence in order to calculate the official unemployment rate (i.e. the number of people seeking work in an area divided by the number of jobs plus work seekers in the TTWA). Unfortunately, journey-to-work data is available only from the census and this relates to local authority areas. As a result the Department of Employment is forced to define groupings of local authority areas within which 75 per cent of population both live and work; the grouping of local employment office areas is then calculated so as best to match these definitions (Smart, 1974). While TTWAs can be grouped approximately into the sixty-one subdivisions of the economic planning regions, there is no way that they can be matched with the SMLAs. This is extremely unfortunate because it means that no employment data are available for functional urban areas beyond 1971.

The reorganization of local government in 1974/5 produced a very fundamental change in areal reporting units, which has affected most sub-regional statistical series except those produced by the Department of Employment. Because they were based upon an aggregation of old local authority areas the subdivisions of the economic planning regions have been discontinued and effectively replaced by the new counties in England and Wales and the new regions in Scotland (see, for instance, figures 5.1 and 8.3). Unfortunately, however, the definition of the new counties pays more respect to tradition (the preservation of shire names), administrative efficiency (minimum and maximum population size) and political expediency (the need to exclude Conservative suburbs from Labour-dominated metropolitan counties) than to local geography and, in particular, tends to ignore the functional relationship between urban centres and their hinterlands. The lower-tier districts suffer from similar deficiencies. Unfortunately, published statistics from the 1981 Census will refer to these units, areas which cannot be directly related to the 1971 local authority, thus precluding easy analysis of intercensal change.

To overcome this difficulty a special set of urban-based functional regions has been developed by the Centre for Urban and Regional Development Studies at the University of Newcastle upon Tyne for use with the 1981 Census (Coombes *et al.*, 1982). This embodies several refinements of the SMLA approach, the principal improvement being the recognition of an upper tier of metropolitan regions based around the largest cities whose sphere of influence contains dominant and subdominant local labour market areas, each with a minimum population of 50,000. Outside the metropolitan regions, the definitions recognize separate free-standing regions with the same minimum population. Each local labour market area is divided into an urban core coterminous with the continuously built-up area and an inner commuting ring from which 15 per cent of the economically active population commute to the core, while outer areas are defined so as to minimize commuting between functional regions. Attempts have been made to minimize the spatial incompatibility between the decennial demographic information from the Census and the annual employment statistics produced by the Department of Employment. This is a critical problem as a full understanding of the working of the labour market in the spatial context requires information on labour supply as well as labour demand.

It is to be hoped that, within the next two years or so, much of the data relevant to the study of urban and regional change in Britain can be set up on the basis of this new set of functional regions. These new areas have already been coded on the base units for the 1981 Census and are compatible with areas that can be built up from the 1971 Census, while their value for socio-economic analyses would improve greatly if the Department of Employment and other major statistical sources could be persuaded to make their data amenable to these areas. In the meantime, this volume explores what is possible with the currently available statistical reporting units and makes observations on developments over the past couple of decades which may be tested and examined further in due course by reference to the more consistently defined functional regions.

1
Structural change in the British space economy

J. B. Goddard

The spatial consequences of de-industrialization

As Britain was the first nation to industrialize it is perhaps not surprising that we are now witnessing various manifestations of a process which has been loosely labelled 'de-industrialization'. Some of the key changes associated with de-industrialization include the shift of employment from manufacturing to service industries especially the public sector, the related growth of female participation in the labour force and of white-collar as opposed to manual occupations, changes which parallel in magnitude the shift out of agricultural production associated with the Industrial Revolution. And just as the Industrial Revolution was associated with fundamental changes in the location of economic activity at both the urban and regional scales, in particular rural decline and the growth of the northern coalfield conurbations, so the process of de-industrialization has come to be associated with large city decline and rural revival, with growth and prosperity shifting further towards the southern part of the country.

While there can be little denying the direction of the economic indicators there is considerable debate about what is cause and what is effect and indeed of the meaning of the term 'de-industrialization'. The Cambridge School of Economists argue that the key process has been the decline in the international competitiveness of British manufacturing industry resulting in a falling share of world markets and rising levels of imports of foreign manufactured goods (Cairncross, 1979). This loss of competitiveness first hit the older staple industries associated with the Industrial Revolution (e.g. steel, shipbuilding, heavy engineering, textiles). Decline has more recently spread to most other manufacturing sectors and has had a particularly marked impact on the larger cities where a substantial proportion of manufacturing capacity is still to be found. Indeed location within the dense built-up area of nineteenth-century cities may have been one of the many factors preventing the adaption to change, especially the introduction of new products and production technologies necessary for industry to remain competitive; so urban decline may be both a cause and an effect of de-industrialization.

However it would be wrong to assume, as the phrase suggests, that there has been a total collapse of manufacturing industry. While manufacturing employment started to decline from 1966 there was a considerable growth of manufacturing output at least for the next ten years; until recently manufacturing investment held up with more goods being produced by fewer workers as the capital intensity of industry increased. This trend has been associated with a major rationalization of production occurring through the elimination of inefficient plants and enterprises and the increasing concentration of the ownership of industry.

Rationalization has had its locational implications with older plants in urban areas being closed down and new plants in small towns and rural areas being opened, although in the process fewer jobs have been created in the new locations than were replaced in the old (Massey and Meegan, 1978). It would therefore be wrong at the subnational scale to associate de-industrialization with uniform declines in manufacturing activity; as several contributions to this volume show, variations in rates of growth as well as decline in manufacturing employment are still central to understanding spatial differences in economic performance within Britain.

What of the service sector? An alternative view of the cause of de-industrialization has been put by Bacon and Eltis (1976), namely that the growth of the service sector, particularly the public services, has starved manufacturing industry of the necessary manpower and financial resources. In quantitative terms the manpower argument is difficult to sustain as the service sector has chiefly grown by the employment of women previously not in the labour force rather than at the expense of manufacturing; equally the level of investment in manufacturing has not indicated a shortage of finance. More cynically one might suggest that it was necessary for governments to allow the expansion of the public services in order to provide employment to a labour force which was expanding because of both demographic factors (i.e. an expanding population in the working age groups) and increasing activity rates (i.e. more people in each age group seeking paid employment).

This last contention should not obscure the fact that a large part of the service sector including major areas in public ownership have experienced significant declines in employment terms, again with particular consequences for cities. In public utilities for example there has been a substantial reduction in employment and a major growth of output.

Similar trends are apparent in transport and communication and in wholesale and retail distribution. Technological change such as the replacement of town gas by natural gas, containerization and the replacement of road by rail transport and automated stock control have contributed to this process. Significantly many of these services have traditionally been urban functions – for example five out of the seven largest cities in Britain (London, Liverpool, Glasgow, Manchester, Newcastle) all have major ports.

The real growth part of the service sector has been insurance, banking and finance, business and professional services and services to individuals provided by the public sector in the form of both central and local governments. With the exception of the financial sector which has seen a significant investment in computers it has not been generally possible until very recently to substitute capital for labour in the service sector; increases in output and the quality of services have therefore only been achievable by increases in employment. While services to industry have tended to grow in cities, services to individuals (such as education and health) have quite naturally followed the movement of population outwards from the largest urban areas. So even the growing parts of the service sector have been contributing to urban decline. Likewise the growth of car ownership which has facilitated outward movement of both people and jobs from cities has indirectly contributed to the decline of the public transport sector.

How these very general trends have worked themselves through the specific conditions prevailing in different cities and regions of Britain is the concern of this collection of essays. Because primacy is given to de-industrialization as a fundamental cause of spatial change it is appropriate to begin discussion with an examination of long-run trends in the regional distribution of manufacturing industry.

Inter- and intra-regional change in the location of manufacturing industry

In describing trends in the inter-regional distribution of manufacturing employment within the period 1952 to 1979, Gudgin and Fothergill highlight in chapter 2 significant patterns of change that do not accord with a simple north/south division of the country. While East Anglia (with a 70.3 per cent increase in manufacturing employment), the South West (+25.7 per cent) and the East Midlands (+11.4 per cent) have all performed well, two of the largest industrial regions, the South East (–9.9 per cent) and the West Midlands (–7.8 per cent) have performed badly. The North West (–24.5 per cent), which is another major industrial region, has also declined dramatically while the North (+7.8 per cent) and Wales (+7.5 per cent) gained significant numbers of manufacturing jobs. However, many of these differences are attributable to the earlier part of this period. With an absolute fall in manufacturing employment in the country as a whole starting in 1966, the relative growth of the North and Wales fell away and the relative decline of the South East ceased.

Gudgin and Fothergill attempt to decompose these changes into four components: that attributable to regional differences in industrial structure (i.e. the tendency for regions to specialize in slow- or fast-growing industries); that due to the urban structure (i.e. the mix of smaller and larger settlements); that due to the size distribution of manufacturing plants as this factor influences differences in birth-rates of new manufacturing establishments; and finally the effect of regional policy constraining industrial expansion in the South East and the Midlands and stimulating it in the peripheral or assisted areas.

With regard to industrial structure, they conclude that this was an important factor in *some regions* prior to the mid-1960s, with positive effects being recorded in the South East and West Midlands arising from their emphasis on fast-growing consumer durable industries and negative effects in the North West and Yorkshire and Humberside with their emphasis on textiles. However, after 1966, with manufacturing decline becoming a ubiquitous feature of all industries, industrial structure ceased to be an important influence.

Having allowed for the effect of national trends and for industrial structure, a large variation in regional manufacturing employment change still remains. The regions that have performed badly appear to have one feature in common: a substantial proportion of their manufacturing activity concentrated in large urban agglomerations. This is particularly the case in the South East (London), the West Midlands (Birmingham) and the North West (Manchester and Liverpool). London, for example, lost 600,000 manufacturing jobs between 1959 and 1975, a 37.5 per cent decrease. In contrast, subdivisions of the planning regions in all parts of the country that Gudgin and Fothergill classify as 'country towns' and 'rural areas' experienced increases of 28.8 per cent and 77.2 per cent respectively over the same period although admittedly starting from a lower base. Thus the regions like the South West and East Anglia that have performed well have very few large urban centres.

This decline of manufacturing in large cities and growth in small towns and rural areas is only partially attributable to the migration of manufacturing plants between the two types of areas. Having allowed for the effect of both industrial structure and movement, Gudgin and Fothergill's analysis suggests that the residual or 'indigenous' manufacturing employment change is inversely related to a hierarchical classification of the subdivisions of the regions (London, the conurbations, free-standing cities, industrial towns, county towns and rural areas). More specifically, the highest rates of indigenous growth are recorded in county towns and rural areas and the most significant losses of indigenous employment are recorded in London and the conurbations. This urban hierarchical distinction is suggested as being more significant than the division of the country into assisted and non-assisted areas.

Fothergill and Gudgin account for these contrasts in terms of differences between large cities and small towns in the ease of physical expansion experienced by manufacturing establishments. They argue that many plants in large urban areas are constrained by their sites; there is little room for the *in situ* expansion necessary to accommodate the new machinery associated with the generally increasing capital intensity of manufacturing industry. In the case of London the accommodation of the national rise in manufacturing floor-space per worker within the existing stock of space would have necessitated a 25 per cent decline of manufacturing employment. In fact, because of demolitions, the amount of space also decreased and to a degree sufficient to account for the observed decline in manufacturing employment. Although there is vacant land in inner urban areas, much of this land is not, in fact, on the market in the form of suitable premises and most firms occupy all of their present sites. Few such problems exist in small towns and rural areas.

Detailed support for this argument comes from micro-data on employment change in manufacturing establishments in one of the more successful manufacturing regions – the East Midlands. Classifying the data according to births, deaths, *in situ* growth or contraction of establishments reveals that the real urban–rural contrast is in the location of growth in the form of both births and *in situ* expansions. The data suggests that this contrast in expansion applies both to establishments which are single-site enterprises and those which are parts of larger concerns.

Another factor favouring the small towns and rural areas has been the size distribution of establishments as it affects the birth-rate of new firms. Again using their micro-data for the East Midlands, Fothergill and Gudgin observe a much lower birth-rate in areas where large establishments predominate. While small firms make only a small contribution to employment growth in the short run (their figures for the East Midlands as a whole over the period 1968–75 suggest +4 per cent), in Leicestershire, where the data goes back much further, manufacturing employment in firms founded since 1947 accounted for a quarter of all employment growth over the next thirty years. Fothergill and Gudgin suggest that this low birth-rate in large plant areas is attributable to the fact that potential entrepreneurs in such plants are remote from management, especially contact with customers, and therefore have little experience or incentive to start up business of their own. In small firm areas the opposite is the case with skilled craftsmen tending to set up in business on their own account in their immediate locality. Extrapolating these findings beyond the East Midlands reveals 'expected' low rates of new firm formation in lagging regions like the North where large plants predominate, a result which appears to be corroborated by more direct evidence on differences in rates of new firm formation in various areas (e.g. Robinson and Storey, 1981).

The final element in Fothergill and Gudgin's explanation of inter-regional trends in manufacturing employment change is the much discussed influence of regional policy. While generally supporting the widely quoted findings of Moore, Rhodes and Tyler (1977), they suggest that the urban–rural shift has reduced the magnitude of this effect. By comparing actual inter-regional employment change with that expected from industrial structure and allowing for the effect of the urban-to-rural shift of jobs, they suggest that between 1966 and 1973 an extra 188,000 jobs in the development areas could be attributable to the effects of regional policies. But after that date, no policy effect is detectable, a possible result of the combined consequence of the relaxation of controls on industrial expansion in the South East and Midlands, the abolition of labour subsidies in development areas (the regional employment premium), the general increasing capital intensity of manufacturing industry and, last but not least, the generally deepening economic recession. From the perspective of the 1980s it could thus appear that the powerful inter-regional dispersal of manufacturing employment, a process reinforced by regional policy, was a phenomenon unique to the late 1960s and early 1970s. More recently, it appears that the main changes are occurring at the intra-regional scale.

While regional policy may no longer be an important influence on the changing distribution of manufacturing activity in Britain, there can be no doubting its past impact on individual cities. This fact is clearly brought out in chapter 3 by Lloyd and Dicken's comparison of the components of employment change in Manchester and Liverpool, with the latter city being profoundly affected by its special development area status. Over the period 1965–75, Merseyside gained 27,000 new manufacturing jobs chiefly in the form of branches of firms based outside the city. Indeed, by the end of the period, 67 per cent of the manufacturing jobs were in plants controlled from outside the area. However, by looking not only at the new openings but also at closures and *in situ* expansions or contractions, Lloyd and Dicken are able to demonstrate a net increase of only 2000 jobs over the period, chiefly because 30,000 jobs were lost in closures. Indeed, if they had been able to take their analysis beyond 1975, they would have found that many of the plants established with the aid of regional policy have now closed or experienced massive labour shedding.

Manchester, without the benefit of substantial regional policy assistance, presents a totally different picture. As a much larger city, it has a more significant share of its employment in indigenously owned manufacturing companies (65 per cent compared with 22.5 per cent in

Liverpool). Here 51,000 jobs were created in plant openings over the period 1966–75 but, unlike Liverpool, the bulk of these were in locally owned establishments. Nevertheless, these gains were more than offset by 143,000 job losses, again chiefly in local companies. So up to 1976, it appears that in both cities local companies were responsible for more job losses than their share of total employment would justify. When all establishments are considered, it seems from this analysis that large multi-plant firms are not the sole cause of employment decline in these cities.

Merseyside appears in this analysis to have been more successful than Manchester in generating manufacturing jobs, but by introducing an ownership dimension into their analysis, Lloyd and Dicken are able to suggest that Merseyside is in the more vulnerable position in that the bulk of its employment is in plants controlled from outside the city. The basis for generating or sustaining employment through civic effort is therefore limited, with the local economy being extremely open to outside influence. These case studies therefore highlight the need to take careful account of the very different conditions prevailing in each of the British conurbations.

Intra-urban employment change

The overall decline in manufacturing employment in large cities documented by Fothergill and Gudgin and by Lloyd and Dicken has also been associated with significant changes in the internal distribution of jobs within the urban area. In the case of Liverpool, most of the employment gains occurred in the outer area, chiefly in externally controlled plants, while the inner area job losses were disproportionately to be found amongst locally owned plants. Regional policy appears therefore to have benefited the suburban areas. The pattern in Manchester is more complex because the outer area contains the centres of a number of older cities (e.g. Rochdale). Nevertheless, the inner areas are still characterized by a high birth-rate of manufacturing establishments, although many are soon registered as closures. Differential rates of opening and closure and *in situ* employment change rather than migration of firms therefore appears to be the principal cause of variations in manufacturing employment change between inner and outer parts of these particular cities.

The analysis of *all* cities presented by Spence and Frost in chapter 4 suggest that overall employment decline (including the service sector) is now a widespread characteristic of urban cores of Metropolitan Economic Labour Areas (MELAs). But this was not the case during the 1950s. Then the decentralization of people was in advance of the decentralization of jobs. Indeed, between 1951 and 1961 the nation's urban cores gained nearly 1 million jobs (an 80 per cent share of the total employment increase in the decade). The next ten years witnessed a

dramatic reversal with urban cores losing over 400,000 jobs and metropolitan rings gaining 700,000 jobs (a 15 per cent increase compared with a
1.7 per cent increase in employment for the country as a whole). It was
this sudden reversal of almost a century of job centralization and the
resulting need for very rapid adjustment of labour supply that has given
rise to the now well-known inner city problem.

Although employment decline began, and is now most pronounced,
in the largest cities, Spence and Frost demonstrate that the process of net
decentralization of jobs is now characteristic of urban Britain as a whole.
Moreover, it has affected all sectors, not just manufacturing, with some of
the largest declines in urban cores occurring in the distributive trades and
miscellaneous services (300,000 out of a total loss of 600,000 jobs between
1966 and 1971). In fact, only insurance, banking and finance and professional and scientific services recorded an increase in urban cores over
this period and then at a lower rate than was recorded in metropolitan
rings.

Spence and Frost's analysis suggests that employment decentralization can be broadly characterized in terms of job losses for men in urban
cores and new job opportunities for women in metropolitan rings. Such
shifts have been associated with significant changes in the proportion of
men and women who are in employment, with the female activity rate
increasing in metropolitan rings from 34.6 per cent in 1961 to 41.5 per
cent in 1971; in contrast, the male activity rate in urban cores declined
from 87.5 per cent to 81.3 per cent. Many of these job opportunities for
women were in office occupations and, contrary to the popular view of
concentration in city centres, Spence and Frost demonstrate that office
employment, particularly in the clerical grades, was also decentralizing,
chiefly within the largest cities, by the end of the 1960s.

Regional and sub-regional trends in the service sector

As one of the most important growth elements, the changing distribution
of office jobs has also had an important impact at the regional and sub-
regional scales. Office occupations can be found in varying degrees in all
sectors of economic activity, including manufacturing and not just in
services like insurance and banking. For example, the proportion of
employment in office occupations ranged from 29.9 per cent in the
capital-intensive chemicals industry to 15.6 per cent in older industries
like shipbuilding.

Detailed figures of industry by occupation are not available at the
sub-regional level. However, by calculating changes in the number of
office workers expected in an area on the basis of its industrial structure
(using the national figures as the control) and comparing that with the
actual changes, Spence and Frost are able to demonstrate that over the

period 1966–71 office jobs were centralizing at the inter-regional scale while decentralizing within regions. Thus the favourable growth of the South East outside London, of East Anglia and the South West, can partly be explained in terms of the way the industrial structure of these areas has favoured those sectors of industry in which the rapidly growing managerial and professional occupations were concentrated.

In chapter 5 Marquand explores further the nature of service sector employment change. An examination of changes in the distribution of employment in insurance, banking and finance over the period 1971–7 reveals the continued favourable growth of the southern half of the country stretching from Hereford in the west and Dorset in the south to Essex and Suffolk in the east. While such services had experienced dramatic employment growth up to 1973, in the next five years a number of services more directly orientated towards individual consumers (such as sport and recreation, medical services and hotels) superseded the so-called 'producer services' in the growth rate league tables. This may be due to such factors as the displacement of labour by computers in the financial sector and the consequences of the general depressed state of the economy after 1973. It remains to be seen whether such trends will affect the consumer services as a result of the increasing use of micro-processor-based capital goods in the home and the marked cut-back in public expenditure on services (Gershuny, 1978).

Whatever the future trends, there are clearly important spatial variations in the level of provision of both producer and consumer services. Marquand relates these to the urban hierarchy, with business services like accountants and lawyers being most highly concentrated in the large cities and personal services like education and health being widely dispersed between urban areas of different size. Such an approach also makes it possible to identify cities which are 'under' or 'over' serviced relative to their size, revealing that it is not only London but also cities throughout the South East as a whole that appear to be well-endowed with a wide range of services. So too, though to a lesser extent, are cities in the South West, East Anglia and Scotland. In contrast cities in the West Midlands, the Northern region, Wales, the East Midlands and Yorkshire and Humberside are poorly endowed with services of almost all kinds. From this analysis, it would appear that areas with an emphasis on manufacturing industry have a poor endowment of both producer and consumer services.

Marquand suggests, however, that differences in the structure of local industry do not form the only explanation of spatial variations in the distribution of service occupations. Account also has to be taken of the ownership structure of business organizations. The evidence on this point suggests that many peripheral regions are characterized by a low level of local ownership of industry and therefore of the occupations associated with head office functions. In the northern region, for example, 78 per cent of manufacturing employment in 1973 was controlled by companies with headquarters outside the region, compared with 57 per cent in 1963 (Smith, 1980). This increase in relative importance has come about partly because of the in-migration of branch plants to the region, assisted by regional policy; but it is also a consequence of the acquisition of local companies by firms based in the core region of the South East. Acquisition tends to result in the centralization of service functions, like accountancy, on the acquiring company (Leigh and North, 1978a). Branch plants created through in-movement or acquisition therefore contain fewer office workers in comparison with independent single-site companies or the headquarters of multi-site firms (Crum and Gudgin, 1977; Marshall, 1979b). In addition, there is some indication that independent firms based in the South East, because they are prepared to devote more resources to activities like research and development and marketing, employ more workers in these functions than their counterparts in peripheral regions. So the growth of white-collar jobs in the South East is both a function of industrial structure *and* organizational structure.

There are important implications of the changing organization of manufacturing industry for the distribution of business service functions provided by independent firms outside the manufacturing sector. While locally owned firms tend to make use of locally provided services, branch plants either do not frequently require these services because their main concern is with production or, when they are required, the services are obtained from company headquarters in another region (Marshall, 1979c). Thus, the relative decline of business services in Manchester noted by Marquand is in part due to the industrial decline of the North West demonstrated by Fothergill and Gudgin and in part due to the increasing external control of industry in that region as noted by Lloyd and Dicken. So while the North West lost fifteen headquarters of companies amongst the thousand largest in the United Kingdom, the South East increased its share from 586 to 622 between 1972 and 1977 (Goddard and Smith, 1978).

Within the South East Marquand demonstrates a considerable degree of intra-regional redistribution of these headquarters functions. Expansion of office activities in the South East outside London is therefore attributable to indigenous growth, inter-regional centralization and intra-regional decentralization from the capital.

Office decentralization has rarely occurred beyond the South East, because the communications costs arising from longer distance movement has seldom outweighed the savings on other items, particularly rent and clerical wages (Goddard and Rye, 1977). Equally, firms based in the South East have much easier access to the wide range of business services available in London than do their counterparts in peripheral regions. Such organizational consideration suggests that there is a subtle inter-relationship between the changing distribution of manufacturing and service activities. The dispersal of manufacturing and the centralization of office functions may therefore be viewed as different facets of the same process of the spatial division of functions within organizations.

It is, therefore, far too simplistic to view the changing distribution of service employment simply as an effect of shifts in the location of manu-facturing activity resulting in positive and negative service multipliers. In the case of multi-site organizations, it is easy to see how manufacturing expansion in the periphery can lead to additional service activity in the South East. What is perhaps less obvious is the reverse effect, namely the influence of regional variations in the distribution of service activity on spatial differences in the performance of manufacturing industry, especially that which is indigenous to different localities.

Such a relationship exists because much service industry outside a company (e.g. market research) and service occupations within com-panies (e.g. research and development) are essential to the process of innovation and diversification within industry. The fact that manufactur-ing firms located in the South East have ready access to business and pro-fessional services does seem to be associated with a better record of product and process innovation. This conclusion is borne out by a study of the location of the first commercial manufacture of significant inno-vations introduced into British industry over the period 1965–76 and quoted by Marquand (Oakey *et al.*, 1980). This study revealed that relative to a national average of 100 the number of innovations per thousand manufacturing workers varied between 152 in East Anglia, 136 in the South West and 130 in the South East to 80 in the North West, 76 in Scotland and 48 in Wales. If, however, the number of innovations is calculated in relation to the number of white-collar workers in each industry inter-regional variations almost totally disappear. In other words, those regions of Britain with large numbers of office workers within manufacturing industry would appear to be the most innovative.

Socio-economic changes and the journey to work

Perhaps the most important corollary of a shift in employment oppor-tunities from the manufacturing to service sector and from manual to white-collar occupations has been changes in the social structure of the country. The spatial consequences of this change are discussed by Pinch and Williams in chapter 6. With their contribution the emphasis of the volume therefore switches from workplace to residence and from pro-duction to consumption, recognizing of course the important links between each pair of relationships. The magnitude of the social changes between 1961 and 1971 are startling, with a 20.5 per cent increase in the managerial and professional socio-economic groups and a 15.9 per cent decrease in the bottom status, semi- and unskilled manual groups. In regional terms it is not surprising to find the South East and the South West recording a rate of increase above the national average for the professional and managerial group, these regions being closely followed by East Anglia and the East and West Midlands. In contrast, peripheral regions like Wales (+11.1 per cent), Yorkshire and Humberside (+12.2 per cent) and the North (+13.9 per cent) lag well behind the national trend towards high-level white-collar occupations. Social change during the 1960s therefore did little to ameliorate the long-standing contrast between a white-collar South and a blue-collar North. Thus by 1971 only 28.2 per cent of the economically active male population in the Northern region worked in non-manual occupations compared with 46.2 per cent in the South East.

At the sub-regional scale it is apparent that the rate of growth of managerial and professional groups has been lower in the larger cities than elsewhere, a reflection in part of the tendency of this group to opt for small town and rural living and to commute long distances into the cities. For example, the London and Manchester Standard Metropolitan Labour Areas (SMLAs) recorded a 14 per cent and 13.1 per cent increase respectively in this group compared with a 27.2 per cent average for cities with a population of less than 1 million. At the intra-urban scale it is clear that the flight from the cities is being spearheaded by the more affluent and that this process is most advanced in the largest cities. Thus as a group the 'Million Cities' experienced an increase in the managerial and professional occupations of only 1.6 per cent in their cores compared with gains of 28.2 per cent in metropolitan rings and 36.4 per cent in outer metropolitan rings. The corresponding figures for the rest of urban Britain were 15.7 per cent in cores, 48.7 per cent in rings and 17.7 per cent in outer rings. The lower-grade white-collar occupations were also participating in decentralization, recording a decline of 1.4 per cent in urban cores of the largest cities compared with increases of 17.7 per cent in the inner and 26.5 per cent in the outer metropolitan rings. Again decentralization was not so advanced in other cities where the rates of change by urban zone were 1.9 per cent, 6.2 per cent and 18.4 per cent respectively.

These figures suggest that the inner parts of cities might have increasing concentrations of the declining manual and unskilled populations. However, Pinch and Williams can find little evidence of this at the scale of urban cores as a whole. The number of skilled manual workers has declined in urban cores at a much faster rate than in the nation as a whole and those who are unskilled at about the same rate. In only one of the largest cities (Liverpool) did the proportion of semi- and unskilled exceed the national average by more than 4 per cent. If concentrations of the most disadvantaged have occurred as a result of selective decentralization then it would appear to exist at a more localized level within cities.

However, before one can come to any definitive conclusion about the consequences of a possible differential decentralization of population in various social groups it is necessary to consider these shifts in the light of changes in the location of jobs and of the commuting journeys linking workplaces and residences. More specifically, if workplaces for the semi-and unskilled are declining in inner city areas faster than the local population qualified to fill only these jobs, or the local jobs are being increasingly filled by residents from outside the inner areas, then unemployment amongst inner city residents will be an inevitable consequence. In chapter 7 Gillespie provides some evidence on these points.

In aggregate it would appear that over the period 1966–71 employed population in the urban cores declined more rapidly than jobs, leading to increased inward commuting. More specifically, the number of resident manual workers in cores declined faster than the number of manual jobs. If jobs were dispersing more rapidly than workers then reverse commuting from cores to rings would have increased. In fact reverse commuting by semi- and unskilled workers from cores to rings declined by 14 per cent between 1966 and 1971. However, there was a small increase in reverse commuting by skilled manual workers. Detailed figures for London suggests that in the inner areas in 1971 there were in fact more jobs than employed workers for eighteen occupation groups.

All of this evidence suggests that decentralization of jobs and population from British cities as a whole has not in aggregate created serious problems of a mismatch between the supply and demand for labour at the city-wide scale. Nevertheless, Gillespie points to a number of other changes in the journey-to-work aspect of the population–job-matching process arising from decentralization which have important social implications. Most significant of these is the switch from public to private transport. Thus in urban Britain as a whole journeys-to-work by bus declined by 1.2 million or 18 per cent between 1966 and 1971 and car journeys increased by 1 million or 16 per cent. Such figures need to be viewed in the light of the additional fact that 86 per cent of professional and managerial socio-economic groups were members of car-owning households in 1971 compared with only 43 per cent of semi- and unskilled manual workers, with 64 per cent of the latter relying on a bus or foot for their journey-to-work compared with only 16 per cent of the latter. Part of the explanation for this decline in the use of public transport can be found in the fact that there was a massive 0.7 million decrease in journeys-to-work within urban cores and it is these journeys which are most suited to public transport. In contrast the greatest increase in the number of journeys has been in those linking residences and workplaces within metropolitan rings; here public transport carried only a third of all passengers compared with nearly 60 per cent of those both beginning and ending in the core.

Gillespie suggests that this switch to private transport is both a cause and a consequence of a changing spatial structure of cities. Journeys in the metropolitan rings characteristically link dispersed residences and dispersed workplaces, trips for which the car is the only suitable means of transport. Increasing car ownership is therefore not the only explanation of the greater use of private transport for the journey-to-work. In fact amongst car-owning households there is evidence of a greater use of the car for the journey-to-work between 1966 and 1971. This switch to the car has been particularly prominent in the smaller towns where car-ownership levels are higher and public transport is less well-developed. Indeed one of the factors contributing to the shift of population towards smaller towns may be the greater freedom such settlements allow for car use.

What are the likely consequences of this pattern of settlement in a situation of increased energy costs? On this point Gillespie suggests that relative to public transport, the costs of using the private car have in fact declined since the oil crisis in 1973. One may therefore anticipate a further decline in the use of public transport for the journey-to-work. In addition, rising unemployment, falling heavily on users of bus transport, is likely to increase unit costs for operators resulting in even higher fares, less patronage and reduced services. And whatever the costs and availability of public transport the dispersed pattern of cities is going to impose serious problems of access to jobs and services for those without use of the car. Thus Gillespie points out that even the Department of Environment's optimistic forecasts suggest that by the year 2010, 30 per cent of households will not own a car and even within car-owning households there will be many without access to private transport.

Population change

Whatever the realities of the situation it could be argued that the perceived higher energy costs will slow down the rate of population decentralization from British cities. The essay by Champion (chapter 8) on population change provides some evidence that the rate of dispersal has indeed declined during the 1970s. There are many factors contributing to this, not just higher energy cost. These include the falling birth-rate, falling household size (particularly the number of households without children), reduction in rates of migration, due to the fact that people do not change jobs in a recession, an end to comprehensive urban renewal including the building of new estates on the urban periphery, and the general reduction in house-building also arising from economic circumstances.

The facts on post-1971 changes in the distribution of population at the urban scale are limited. An extension of the analysis for the constituent zones of MELAs suggests that the rate of population increase in metropolitan rings slowed down in the 1971–4 period. However, the rate of decline in urban cores continued to increase; nevertheless, in the case of the largest cities, extrapolating the figures for the whole of the 1970s would suggest a levelling out of the trajectory of decline compared with earlier periods.

For actual figures on population change after 1974, one has to rely on mid-year population estimates and the preliminary results from the 1981 Census which refer to standard regions, counties and districts rather than MELAs. Nevertheless a number of important conclusions emerge about changing patterns of population redistribution which confirms the influence of the recession on population mobility at both the inter- and intra-regional scale.

A comparison of the more prosperous 1960s with the less prosperous 1970s *as a whole* suggests that there has been a reduction in the net shift of population from the less prosperous North to the more prosperous South. Both the South East and the West Midlands were affected by a reduction of around 7 percentage points in their population growth rates between the two decades. Part of this change could be attributed to an exodus of population from the South East to surrounding southern regions, notably the South West and East Anglia, as well as a reduction in migration from peripheral to core regions as job opportunities declined in the latter areas.

However annual figures suggest that this reversal of the long-established north–south shift of population was only a temporary phenomenon that characterized the period 1971–4. During these years the aggregate population growth rate in the three southern regions (the South East, the South West and East Anglia) was almost overtaken by that of the rest of the country. However, by 1977–80 the gap in growth rates between these three regions and the rest of the country had returned to the level found in the early 1960s. Moreover, in this latest period it was the South East which recorded the improvement in growth rate while rates in the South West and East Anglia declined. Conversely population decline in Scotland, Wales and the Northern region accelerated, as it did also in the North West and West Midlands. So the latest period would seem to suggest a re-emergence of 'core–periphery' contrasts with the North West and Midlands joining the 'periphery' and a reduction in the shift of population to more 'rural' regions like East Anglia and the South West. More direct evidence on these trends comes from migration data derived from National Health Service registration and helps to explain them. This source reveals a decrease in average annual inter-regional migration rates through the 1970s, chiefly because of a reduction of those *leaving* the South East for other parts of the country. Since the major cities dominate the population change figures for each region it is not surprising to see that the net out-migration losses for most metropolitan counties have not continued to accelerate through the 1970s.

These impressions of a marked slowing down of population re-distribution arising from migration in the 1970s stand in marked contrast to the experience of the 1960s described by Kennett (chapter 9). The direct and reasonably reliable data from the 1971 Census used in his analysis reveal startling levels of migration change. In fact, between 1966 and 1971 17.5 million people, a third of the population, moved their place of residence. Of course, the bulk of these moves were very short distances. Nevertheless, 1.9 million moved between urban cores and metropolitan rings and nearly 1 million *in the other direction*. Whilst much of the discussion in migration studies is on net changes it is important to remember these can mask considerable gross flows, including important counter-streams to the general trend of decentralization either within cities or from larger to smaller settlements. Indeed when the gross flow of migrants between cities is examined a clear relationship between in- and out-migration emerges. More specifically, each percentage increase in outward migration is likely to be associated with a more than proportion-ate increase in the rate of inflow. The prosperous parts of the country in the latter part of the 1960s therefore had a high population turnover with inflow exceeding outflow sufficiently to give a net migration balance. In contrast, the less prosperous areas were experiencing a decline based on a low turnover of population. It would therefore seem that inter-urban migration, associated with job change in the labour market, is most characteristic of a dynamic local economy. The reduction in migration observed by Champion for the 1970s is therefore consistent with what one might have expected from an analysis of the experience of the 1960s.

What has been the demographic impact of these very large migration flows on different types of areas? The answer to this question depends, of course, on the characteristics of the population moving into and out of different areas. Kennett reveals that urban cores have ex-perienced a loss of population in all age groups but particularly those in the 15–44-year-old cohort. In contrast, those of pensionable age are less well-represented in migrants from the inner parts of cities. The impli-cation is that the population in these areas is ageing by a process of dif-ferential migration. The metropolitan rings are the chief destination of those in the early years of working life, while the next cohort (45 to retiring age) appears to be moving to the outer metropolitan rings at a later stage in the life cycle. Finally, non-urban areas are gaining popu-lation through retirement migration. Much of this migration is directed to relatively small settlements with consequent problems for the local social infrastructure of welfare facilities.

While the dominant pattern for most age groups is one of decentralization, one cohort demonstrates a net migration balance in favour of the urban cores, and this is the age group 15–29. These figures tend to suggest a life cycle pattern of migration with young adults moving from suburban homes to start their working life in inner areas and then subsequently, at later stages, moving further and further from the city centre. Kennett suggests that this process is not entirely contained within urban areas, with the larger cities playing a particularly key role in articulating the pattern of inter-urban migration. Young migrants from all urban zones in cities of all sizes throughout the country appear to be attracted to London and then subsequently disperse when older to the metropolitan rings of smaller cities in the South East region, thus spreading the process of population shift down the urban hierarchy.

While these trends are of academic interest, the public significance of differential migration arises in connection with changes in the costs of providing local services. Where population is increasing through in-migration of young families with children, there will be additional needs for school provision while elderly migrants will increase the costs of welfare services. In areas of decline the costs of services will be spread over a smaller population, a problem that will be heightened if there is a concentration of the old and young remaining in the locality. Kennett, therefore, concludes his chapter with a discussion of the consequences of migration for local government finance. Because of the significant contribution of central government to local finance, the fiscal consequences of population redistribution away from British cities are not nearly so severe as has been the case in America. Nevertheless, Kennett's comments are particularly relevant in the light of recent changes in the way central government finance is allocated to local authorities. Under the old rate support grant, a 'needs' element in the formula recognized the special problems created by the high costs of services to the elderly and poor, particularly in the inner parts of the larger cities. This system tended to favour the high-spending authorities. In contrast the new block grant arrangement has tended to penalize high-spending authorities. However, many urban authorities have chosen to maintain their services by increasing local rates with the likely consequence that this will encourage a further flight from the cities of wealthier individuals and of industry and commerce. But although population and employment declines, many of the 'fixed' costs, particularly infrastructure managed by the local authority do not fall commensurately. So after a period of stabilization in the rate of population loss from large cities observed by Champion towards the end of the 1970s may be followed by a renewed outflow of people as the cost of living escalates or the level of provision of service deteriorates.

Unemployment

The discussion by Frost and Spence of unemployment has been left to the last chapter in this volume on the grounds that unemployment needs to be seen as a response to changes in both the level of demand for labour (employment trends) and the supply of labour (demographic trends) both of which have been discussed in earlier chapters. Furthermore, unemployment is an important policy indicator. Shifts in the distribution of employment and population are of most concern to policy-makers if the two sorts of change get out of line within the local labour market. If changes in the distribution of jobs are not matched by changes in the distribution of population, labour shortages will arise in some areas and unemployment in others, with consequential losses in economic efficiency and increased public costs in the form of unemployment benefit. It is for these sorts of reasons that levels of unemployment have been a key measure in defining areas for regional industrial assistance and also in measuring the effectiveness of this assistance.

In spite of its importance as a policy measure the points already made suggest that unemployment is an extremely 'fuzzy' indicator because it encapsulates at one and the same time supply and demand factors in the local labour market. This fact has been clearly demonstrated by the Cambridge Economic Policy Review (1980). For the UK as a whole this shows that between 1973 and 1978 the labour supply increased by 853,000 but employment declined by only 18,000 jobs, giving an 871,000 increase in unemployment. This increase in the labour supply can be further broken down into that attributable to the natural increase in the numbers of working age and the proportion of these, particularly women, actually working or seeking work. For example for the longer period 1966–78 the Cambridge Review estimates that there was a 2.6 per cent increase in the labour force as a result of natural change and a further 2.1 per cent increase resulting from a rise in participation in the labour market. Because this 4.7 per cent increase in labour supply coincided with a 1.4 per cent decline in employment there was an employment shortfall of around 6 per cent. However this shortfall was ameliorated by a 4 per cent reduction in labour supply through net emigration from the country.

This migration factor becomes more critical at the sub-national scale. For example in East Anglia over the period 1973–8 the labour force grew by 47,000, chiefly as a result of migration. Since employment increased by only 23,000 the number unemployed grew by 24,000. In contrast, in the East Midlands the labour force grew largely as a result of demographic factors of natural increase and increased participation rates. Here a rise of 77,000 in labour supply was matched by only 26,000 extra jobs giving an increase in employment of 51,000. In another growth region, the South West, a 53,000 increase in labour supply (three-quarters of which could be attributed to migration) unemployment increased by 85,000 because jobs grew by only 15,000. So the rise in unemployment in the once more-prosperous parts of the country described by Frost and Spence needs to be interpreted in the light of these demographic factors.

Notwithstanding the previous caveats the increase in unemployment in regions like the South East and West Midlands that are demonstrated in chapter 10 are dramatic. The South East, whilst still having the lowest relative rate of unemployment, had 350,000 more people unemployed in January 1982 than the whole of Scotland; this should be compared with only 30,000 more for the same month ten years earlier. Even more dramatically, in the West Midlands in January 1982 there were more unemployed people than in all of the development areas in Britain ten years earlier and an unemployment rate of 15.7 per cent, a figure as high as that for Scotland.

Such figures naturally prompt the suggestion that there has been a convergence in unemployment levels between the various parts of the country in the recent past. However Frost and Spence's analysis reveals that one's views on convergence and divergence of unemployment are largely coloured by the particular points in time that are compared. Because of variations in the timing of the response of different areas to peaks and troughs in the national economic cycle, it is possible to demonstrate either convergence or divergence in rates of unemployment between different areas depending on the dates chosen. If, however, one considers unemployment as a continuous series over a long period of time, it seems that regional unemployment rates converge during early periods of a national economic downturn but then diverge during the trough and recovery that follows.

Comparisons of regional and national unemployment rates also raise the question of the degree of sensitivity of particular areas to the macro-economic situation. Frost and Spence's analysis suggests that areas of high unemployment tend to be more sensitive to the national economic situation, a finding which may be related to the types of industry present in such areas. In spite of a regional policy which has succeeded in diversifying the industrial structure of the high unemployment peripheral regions of Britain, it does seem that these areas have not reduced their sensitivity to rises in levels of unemployment nationally. So although there has been a general increase in unemployment in the economy as a whole one must conclude that the picture of a relatively robust core region economy in the South East of England and an unstable economy in a widening peripheral area remains.

The prospects for local economic development

Since most of the research described in this volume was completed, there has been a dramatic increase in the pace of de-industrialization in Britain with a commensurate rise in levels of unemployment. The adverse macro-economic situation facing manufacturing industry has meant that significant job losses have occurred in companies that were, until very recently, highly competitive; moreover, many major redundancies have occurred in the successful county towns of rural England identified by Fothergill and Gudgin in chapter 2 as the growth centres of the 1980s (Townsend, 1981). Nevertheless, the scale of decline in traditional industries such as steel, shipbuilding and textiles, together with the relative buoyancy of the demand for consumer services has meant that the peripheral regions have once again borne the brunt of the recession while the South East has shown the least ill effects. Moreover, the once more prosperous West Midlands region with its heavy dependence on the motor vehicle industry has entered an accelerated decline.

In such a deep and prolonged recession, the scope for regional policies to redress these imbalances is extremely limited. These policies have worked in the past through their impact on new industrial investment but in a recession such investment is low. Analysis of rates of industrial movement through which most new jobs have been created in lagging regions reveals that this movement is closely related to the business cycle. Labour shortages, one of the chief factors responsible for the diversion of industrial investment from more prosperous regions, obviously apply less strongly when unemployment is rising generally; in this situation the policy stick of industrial development controls is more difficult to apply. Thus, the 1970s witnessed a lowering in the number of jobs created in assisted areas as a result of regional policy as compared with the 1960s, approximately 11,000 jobs per annum for the period 1971–6 as compared with 20,000 jobs per annum for the period 1966–71 (Marquand, 1980).

In addition to the cyclical effects of the recession, there may be a number of deeper-seated structural reasons for the inability of regional policy to continue to generate jobs in assisted areas. Most obviously is the tendency for what limited investment there is in manufacturing industry to be capital-intensive rather than labour-intensive and, therefore, to be job-displacing rather than job-creating. Thus, for the period 1973–9, Fothergill and Gudgin in chapter 2 estimated that the employment impact of regional policy was negative. More generally, an upturn in the economy is unlikely to result in many more jobs in existing firms within manufacturing industry; rather firms will be able to expand production by the use of a wide range of process innovations such as computerized numerically controlled machine tools (Goddard, 1980). Another structural factor is the changing international pattern of investment. British companies are increasingly investing in newly industrializing countries where operating costs are lower than in the assisted areas even after taking account of regional policy subsidies (Holland, 1979). One of the former competitive advantages of the assisted areas, namely the low cost of industrialized labour, is no longer a reality in the present international context. At the same time, inward investment to the UK, particularly by US companies, which in the 1960s and 1970s had chiefly taken the form of totally new green-field development in the assisted areas, appears now to be concentrating on the acquisition of successful British companies in the South East region (cf. McDermott, 1977; Smith, 1980).

In the light of these difficulties, increasing emphasis is now being placed on the need to tackle the problems of lagging regions by generating industrial growth in manufacturing plants already located in particular areas and the birth of new enterprises rather than by relying on the transfer of investment from elsewhere (Goddard, 1979). This trend is reinforced by the reduction in the geographical extent of the areas eligible for central government regional assistance and the not unrelated increase in the role of local authorities in promoting economic development. Having said this, the evidence reviewed in this volume suggests that various factors that have a bearing on the performance of industry indigenous to particular localities may combine together in such a way as to create an industrial milieu which may be either highly favourable or totally unconducive to successful local entrepreneurship. The combination of circumstances in a particular locality may create a situation in which 'the whole is more than the sum of the parts', where there is a synergism which either stimulates or hampers the growth of indigenous economic activity.

But at what geographical scale does such a synergism take place? Is the distinction simply one between core and peripheral regions in the space economy? While there are obvious important differences between the major regions of the country like the South East, the Midlands and the North, within these areas there are important local contrasts. It is a basic tenet of this work that the appropriate scale to examine spatial variations in economic development in Britain is not the major regions but the local labour market area – that is the area where the vast majority of people live *and* work, where they can change jobs without changing house. While location with respect to the overall national territory will obviously be important (in the sense that the development potential in otherwise similar areas in core and peripheral regions may be different) it can be argued that insufficient attention has been given in the past to more localized characteristics of places which in certain instances may enable an area to either overcome or fail to capitalize upon its broader regional situation.

There are several reasons for this emphasis on the local labour market. Many studies of the innovation process in manufacturing industry have demonstrated the key role played by individuals either as entrepreneurs or as skilled workers within the company. Researchers such as

Gudgin (1978) have emphasized that founders of new businesses in general set up in areas where they already live and work. In chapter 2 Fothergill and Gudgin show that the size distribution of plants in a local area is a good predictor of rates of new firm formation; areas with a large number of small plants tend to have higher rates of formation than those dominated by a few large employers. The reason for this is that large workplaces often provide a poor training ground for potential entrepreneurs. Workers have little direct experience of managerial decisions. Large plants often tend to be part of a bigger company group and therefore make less use of local subcontracting and it is subcontracting that often provides the first source of business for a new founder.

New firm formation is only one aspect of local indigenous potential; subsequent growth may depend on other factors which may have a different pattern of spatial variation. Again the work of Gudgin suggests that subsequent growth is more likely to occur in firms founded by individuals from professional as opposed to manual working backgrounds. This is because of their greater managerial experience, their ability to raise finance, and their entrepreneurial drive. The spatial division of functions within the multi-site organizations which dominate the UK economy results in professional functions being highly concentrated in the South East with branch plants with a limited range of functions in peripheral regions like the North. At the same time many indigenous companies in peripheral regions do not seem to support such a broad and deep range of professional management as their counterparts elsewhere. While this may be an inevitable characteristic of the industrial structure of such areas, particularly the predominance of heavy engineering, it nevertheless has an important indirect bearing on the local industrial milieu and hence on the potential for indigenous economic development. The existing spatial structure of industry thus may underpin well-established geographical social-class differences within the country described by Pinch and Williams in chapter 6.

The growth of local enterprise will depend not only upon the characteristics of management but also on the work experience of the entire labour force. This is particularly the case in technologically advanced sectors of the economy such as the instrument-engineering and electronics sectors, which depend on a high rate of industrial innovation. On this subject there are a number of seemingly contradictory points. For example, it could be suggested that workers with experience in a number of industries often form the basis of the most successful teams working on a new project. A high level of labour turnover within a particular locality may therefore be an asset. On the other hand successful innovations often depend on maintaining the team for a sufficiently long period to see a project through from inception to completion. A tight labour-market situation with considerable 'poaching' of skilled workers may therefore inhibit successful innovation.

In chapter 9 Kennett has produced evidence of high population turn-over in labour markets in the South East of the country. Areas with significant population growth are also characterized by high in- and out-migration rates while areas in decline have little population turnover. Perhaps there is a point when the rate of mobility of individuals between jobs in a very tight labour market situation begins to inhibit the expansion of indigenous industry. At the other extreme, in stagnant or declining labour markets with employment concentrated in one or two industries or plants, work experience is limited and entrenched labour attitudes may arise which heighten resistance to the sorts of changes that are an essential part of the innovation process. There may be shortages of particular skills required by modern industry but they are of a different kind than those facing the more prosperous localities. Clearly extreme cases at either end of the spectrum may act as a constraint on indigenous industrial development.

Because of their inherited industrial structure many localities in the peripheral regions of the UK possess few of the characteristics necessary for successful self-sustained growth based on indigenous enterprises. The traditional approach to the solution of such a problem has been to intro-duce new industry or managers from outside, initially from the UK but increasingly from overseas, either in the form of the establishment of new manufacturing plants or through the acquisition of indigenous com-panies. While certainly contributing to alleviating immediate employ-ment problems, the qualitative effects of such investments have often been far from positive. Inward investment has often been in large plants using mass production technologies and paying relatively high wages for unskilled work. This has had repercussions on the local labour market, especially for local firms paying lower wages. While in theory the acqui-sition of poorly managed indigenous companies by larger companies from outside the area should improve the performance of a regional establishment there are suggestions that growth rates (at least in terms of employment) have declined; in many instances closures have occurred subsequent to acquisitions (Smith, 1979). Acquisition activity has certainly led to the removal of managerial functions and the reduction of local autonomy with consequent implications for local occupational structure and industrial and service purchasing (Leigh and North, 1978). While there is evidence to suggest that externally controlled industry in the UK peripheral regions does on the whole perform better than its indigenous counterparts there are suggestions that this performance is poorer than the average for their respective industries (Marshall, 1979). There are therefore grave risks that unless such plants also innovate or take up new technologies as rapidly as plants elsewhere in the company or in companies selling competing products, the current spate of closures in such areas may turn into a torrent. These closures may partly reflect

the increasing obsolescence of products or production techniques introduced in plants at the time of their first establishment and now reaching
the end of their useful life.

From a policy point of view the issue of indigenous potential is not
simply a matter relevant to regional development. If many of the constraints on industrial innovation and diversification are local in character,
then macro-economic policy aimed at stimulating entrepreneurship (e.g.
through tax changes) may be frustrated. For example, policy designed to
favour small firms may only have an impact in certain types of areas and
even here various shortages, for example of skills and accommodation,
may act as a constraint on growth. At the same time, in areas where there
is considerable latent potential this may not be realized. The clear implication is that national industrial policies may need to have a regional or
even local element to them if their objectives are to be fulfilled.

Alternative perspectives on local economic development

The preceding discussion, largely based upon conclusions derived from
the papers in this volume, has emphasized the local constraints on economic development. The implication is that by the removal of these
constraints through the efforts of individuals or local and central government these areas can somehow regenerate their economies and thereby
embark on a period of self-sustained economic growth. For example
Fothergill and Gudgin's suggestion that the principal cause of manufacturing employment decline in large cities is one of space constraints
suggests that policies designed to improve the provision of industrial
premises will contribute to overcoming the problems of such job losses.

A recent study by Massey and Meegan (1982) suggests that such
spatial policy recommendations emerge from a mis-specification of the
direction of causality. They argue that to seek causality from analysis of
spatial patterns of economic change overlooks the broader forces at work
in the economy at large, particularly the process by which private industry seeks to accumulate profit at the expense of labour. According to their
analysis urban and regional contrasts in employment growth and decline
are both a response to *and a part of* this process. For example, the shift of
manufacturing industries from cities to small towns may reflect the
desire of certain companies to abandon older plant and machinery
operated by more skilled and highly paid but militant workers in favour
of highly mechanized forms of production operated by more flexible
labour. The former type of factory may happen to be located in the cities
and the latter in smaller towns. The provision of improved accommodation in the urban areas is unlikely to influence such decisions if the
manipulation of labour is the central factor. They argue that it is necessary to have a very clear understanding of the various strategies being

pursued by enterprises in different sectors of the economy, each of which may have very different locational and policy implication.

In analysing structural change in different manufacturing sectors over the period 1973–8 Massey and Meegan make an important distinction between three overlapping types of corporate strategy – production intensification, rationalization and technical change. The example noted above – the introduction of new production techniques in new locations – is representative of the last strategy although it may include elements of rationalization (closure) of excess capacity in the cities arising because of the higher levels of output realizable with new machinery. Such strategies may produce some mobile investment and can therefore be influenced by public incentives of the regional policy type. However the relative importance of each strategy varies with time; in the period since 1978 Massey and Meegan suggest that intensification and rationalization investment have predominated as the world-wide recession has necessitated an elimination of excess capacity by the complete closure of factories wherever they have been situated; at the same time the fear of unemployment has enabled management to intensify production in the remaining sites, employing less labour for the same amount of output.

Massey and Meegan's analysis is particularly concerned with the 'how, why and where' of employment decline. With its emphasis on the power of large private corporations and their utilization of job-displacing *process* technology in production and services, their perspective holds out little hope or scope for action on the part of those concerned with economic development in their own locality. However, it could be argued that while this analysis may be historically correct it ignores the prospect of a technologically led revival of employment opportunities where the emphasis switches to the introduction of totally new *products* and services. Changes in the distribution of population and employment in Britain need to be seen in a longer-term perspective in which major technological advances have played an important role in the past and are likely to play an equally important role in the future. The dispersal of manufacturing to the periphery during the 1950s and 1960s needs to be viewed in the context of the dying phases of an earlier Kondratieff wave of economic expansion based around electro-mechanical technologies with firms seeking to remain competitive in outmoded products through improvement in labour productivity. The so called micro-electronic revolution is already generating a stream of new products which at the moment are primarily benefiting the South East core region in terms of job generation. However the full positive impact of these technologies will not be felt until the necessary telecommunications infrastructure has been installed and the opportunities for new services based around this infrastructure have been widely diffused. How far such developments alter the balance of power between large corporations and small firms and between prosperous and less prosperous areas will depend upon the way in which the potentialities of this new technology are utilized. In this context the opportunities for local initiatives do not seem completely closed.

2

Trends in regional manufacturing employment: the main influences

S. Fothergill and G. Gudgin

Introduction

The British economy depends critically on its manufacturing sector, a base which is now being rapidly eroded. For much of the postwar period the problem was that British industry lagged behind its foreign rivals in terms of the growth of output and productivity, but since the early 1970s output has stagnated and employment has fallen dramatically, and at the beginning of the 1980s the decline in industrial production has become more severe than at any other time this century.

All regions have suffered as a result of these national economic problems, and unemployment has risen even in traditionally prosperous areas. But within this depressing context, trends in manufacturing employment have varied profoundly between different parts of the country. East Anglia, for example, is one of the fastest growing regions in Europe, and the South West has done quite well too, while at the other end of the scale, London and parts of northern England have lost jobs at an unprecedented rate. In regions where the shortage of jobs has been most acute the consequence has been a combination of high and rising unemployment and large-scale out-migration, and where jobs have been more plentiful the steady flow of in-migrants from depressed areas has ensured that the growth in the number of jobs has never been sufficient to eliminate local unemployment.

Traditional economic theories of urban and regional growth offer woefully inadequate explanations for the pattern of employment change. Despite the rapid decline of industry in cities and its growth in small towns and rural areas, which has been going on for at least twenty years, it is still possible to read discussions of 'agglomeration economies' which are supposed to advantage large cities. And despite the manifest un-responsiveness of wages to local labour market conditions, many text-books retain the spurious idea that regional employment problems will be self-correcting because labour surpluses depress wages and improve an area's attractiveness to industry. The irrelevance of these ideas is clear from the way they assume away the very problems we need to under-stand: they describe unreal worlds in which permanently high regional unemployment or urban decline would not arise.

The substantial body of classical industrial location theory does not help much either. This concerns itself with the interaction between profit maximizing firms and an environment in which costs or production and distribution vary from place to place, and argues that factories are sited in the locations where costs are minimized and profits maximized. Peri-pheral regions, for instance, will normally be disadvantaged because of their remoteness. But in a small country with highly developed transport networks the range of cost variation is generally so small as to render these ideas of little relevance except in the case of a handful of industries with particularly high transport costs. Moreover, the conventional emphasis of these theories upon transport costs is hard to reconcile with the empirical finding that manufacturing growth now varies more within regions, between cities and small towns, than between peripheral and centrally located regions.

Much more useful insights have been provided by research which has been essentially non-theoretical. Many of these studies have been detailed and grounded in empirical information about what is actually happening. The impact of government regional policy and the role of industrial movement are now well-understood, and more recently a great deal of research has concentrated upon the influence of the ownership and control of companies. But the main shortcoming of this research from a wider perspective is that it has been piecemeal. Though our knowledge about some influences upon urban and regional employment change has improved, other equally important influences have been neglected, with the consequence that it has been impossible to assess their relative impor-tance, or show how individual factors add up to produce the overall pattern of growth and decline.

Our approach is empirical, but we tackle the pattern of growth and decline as a whole, rather than just one part of it. In this way it is possible to establish which causes of uneven growth are important and which are simply trivial, and how the influences on employment change vary from place to place and from period to period. Also, where hard evidence was previously lacking we have painstakingly assembled new information rather than resort to unsubstantiated speculation or theory. Several popular explanations of urban and regional employment change do not survive confrontation with the detailed facts; other less well-known explanations sometimes emerge as surprisingly important. The evidence upon which our arguments are based is set out in full in Fothergill and Gudgin (1982). This chapter, which summarizes parts of that book, puts forward an explanation of regional growth and decline which is *structural*, by which we mean that manufacturing employment change in all areas is determined by the particular characteristics of industry inherited from the past. These characteristics reflect long periods of investment and change extremely slowly, and they collectively exert a dominant influence on the changing location of manufacturing jobs.

The first structural characteristic is the mix of industries in each region, or *industrial structure* as it is generally known. In the country as a whole different industries experience different rates of employment change. This reflects a number of factors — changes in demand, the growth of labour productivity and import penetration, for example — and gives rise to disparities because the growing and declining industries are not spread evenly across all areas. An area heavily dominated by nationally declining industries, for instance, will tend to experience large job losses.

The second structural characteristic, *urban structure*, has been the dominant influence on the pattern of employment change in recent years. Britain's cities are experiencing a rapid loss of manufacturing jobs, while small towns and rural areas are quite successful in retaining and expanding their industrial base. As a general rule, the larger a settlement the faster its decline. This 'urban–rural shift' is the main influence not only on the uneven growth *within* regions, but also on the differences *between* regions: the most urbanized regions are experiencing the worst falls in industrial employment, while industry is more buoyant in regions dominated by small towns and rural areas.

The third structural element is the *size structure* of factories. This influences employment growth in an area because it is the main cause of disparities in rates of new firm formation. Despite their tiny initial size, new independent firms make an important contribution to employment change, partly through weight of numbers and partly because on average they experience healthy growth during their early years. A disproportionately large share of them are set up by people who have previously worked in small firms, so areas with a substantial heritage of existing small firms experience higher rates of new firm formation than areas dominated by large factories, with beneficial consequences for long-term employment growth.

The worst underlying trends in employment occur in areas with an adverse combination of these three structural characteristics. The North West region, for example, has an unfavourable mix of industries (to a large extent because of its reliance on textiles) in a highly urban setting, and Merseyside, the one part of the region without declining textile and related industries, has one of the highest proportions of employment in very large factories. The consequence has been that the region has lost a quarter of its manufacturing jobs since the early 1950s, a much higher proportion than elsewhere in the country. In contrast, the virtuous combination of a neutral or favourable industrial structure, the lack of a conurbation, and a high proportion of employment in small firms, has pushed East Anglia, the South West and East Midlands towards the top of the growth league.

Where structural disadvantages have caused job losses the resulting problems have generally led to government intervention in the form of *regional policy*, the fourth major influence on the location of employment change but one which differs from the others because it is a response to slow growth rather than an underlying cause of disparities. There is evidence that regional policy has led to a sizeable shift of jobs towards the assisted areas.

These four factors – industrial structure, urban structure, size structure and regional policy – are the focus of this chapter. They are given prominence not because a particular theory asserts that they must explain uneven growth but because there is strong empirical evidence which demonstrates their importance in determining the overall pattern of manufacturing employment change. But before examining each factor in turn it is first useful to look at exactly what that pattern of change has been.

Regional employment change

The most important feature of the regional pattern of change in manufacturing, shown in figure 2.1, is the influence of national trends in manufacturing employment. These make themselves felt in two ways: first through the trade cycle, which can be observed in every region, and secondly through the secular decline in national manufacturing employment which began in the mid-1960s. This second point is exceptionally important, because since 1966 manufacturing employment has grown more slowly (or declined faster) than in earlier years in every UK region. Indeed, in so far as some regions, such as Scotland and the North West, are now suffering exceptionally severe job losses this is not simply because the decline in these places is so much worse than elsewhere, but at least in part because national trends in manufacturing employment are so unfavourable. In these circumstances the number of jobs which regional policies might create in such regions, especially over a short period, is much less than the increase which could be expected from a reversal in the de-industrialization of the British economy – a simple but crucial point which cannot be overstressed.

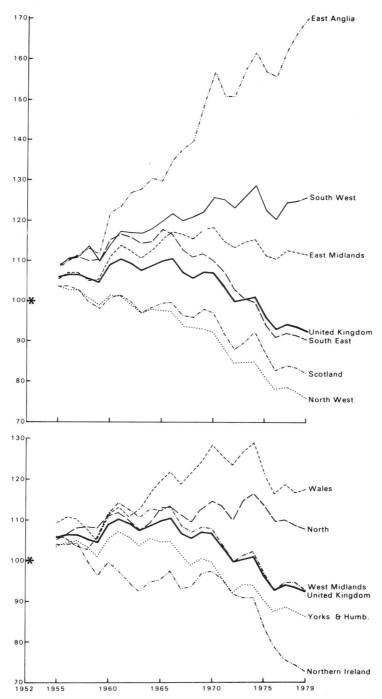

Figure 2.1   Manufacturing employment by region 1952–79 (1952 = 100)

But returning to the regional disparities in growth – the concern of this chapter – the striking feature is the diversity of experience. In particular, the pattern of change does not conform to the simple and widely held 'North versus South' view of Britain. While three regions flanking the South East – East Anglia, the South West and East Midlands – have done quite well, the South East itself has fared *worse* than average over the 1952–79 period as a whole, and the West Midlands, also generally regarded as a 'prosperous' region, has fared little better. It is certainly true that three northerly and peripheral regions – Scotland, Northern Ireland and the North West – have fared worst of all, but in Wales and the Northern region manufacturing growth has been well above average. These figures do not of course indicate that the problems of Wales and the North are illusory, because they exclude the huge decline in coal-mining jobs in these regions, but figure 2.1 does nevertheless indicate that, at least as far as manufacturing is concerned, the simple North–South view of Britain is inappropriate.

The scale of the disparities shown in figure 2.1 should not go unnoticed. At the two extremes, East Anglia increased its manufacturing employment by no less than 70 per cent between 1952 and 1979, and Northern Ireland lost over a quarter of its jobs. In terms of numbers of employees, some of the shifts are very large. The East Midlands, which ranks only fourth among the high-flyers, expanded its manufacturing employment by nearly 20 per cent, or 100,000 jobs more than if it had grown at the national rate. Likewise the relative decline of the North West meant that by 1979 it had 230,000 jobs fewer than if it had grown at the national rate.

Several regions have experienced manufacturing employment growth which has been *consistently* better or worse than in the UK as a whole. This in itself is remarkable given the length of the period (nearly 30 years) and testifies to the strength and stability of some of the underlying causes of growth and decline. Elsewhere there have been changes in trends relative to the rest of the country. From the early 1960s onwards there was a marked improvement in Wales and the North in particular, and a deterioration in the South East and to a lesser extent in the West Midlands. In the second half of the 1970s trends in these regions altered once more: the relative growth of the North and Wales came to an end, and the relative decline of the South East eased too. Northern Ireland is worth singling out for special comment because this region's relative improvement in the 1960s turned into a dramatic collapse in the 1970s which placed it firmly at the bottom of the manufacturing growth league. Since the turnaround in the 1970s in this region has been much sharper than elsewhere it is difficult to escape the conclusion that a major contributory factor has been the province's political troubles.

Industrial structure

As noted earlier, different industries experience different rates of employment change in the country as a whole for a variety of reasons, and this affects the regional pattern of growth because those industries are not evenly represented in each area. A concentration of nationally growing industries favours an increase in employment; a concentration of national declining industries tends to lead to job losses. This is an old-established idea, and the influence of industrial structure can be measured using a simple technique known as 'shift-share analysis'.

Shift-share asks a very basic question: how much employment change would occur in a region if each of its industries grew at the same rate as in the country as a whole? This 'expected' employment change reflects both the mix of industries in the region and their national growth, and can be compared with the actual employment change in that region. More specifically, shift-share disaggregates overall employment change into three components:

A *national component*, which is the change that would have occurred if total manufacturing employment in an area had grown at the same rate as total manufacturing employment in the country as a whole.
A *structural component*, which is the change relative to the country as a whole that can be attributed to an area's particular mix of industries. This is calculated as the change which would have occurred if each industry in the area had grown at the national rate for that industry, less the national component.
A *differential shift*, which is the difference between the expected change (i.e. the sum of the national and structural components) and the actual change in that area.

Some critics of shift-share have suggested that the choice of base year and the level of disaggregation at which the analysis is conducted affect the results, but we have made an exhaustive examination of these points and have concluded that in the context of British regions they make little difference to the results (Fothergill and Gudgin, 1979a).

Table 2.1 presents the results of a shift-share analysis of manufacturing employment change in each region between 1952 and 1979 using employment data which has been fully standardized to permit comparability through time. This shows that industrial structure, as measured by the structural component, has been an important influence in some regions but has had barely any impact in others. The South East has been the principal beneficiary, reflecting the large share of postwar growth industries (such as electrical engineering) found within this region. The West Midlands has also had a favourable structure for employment growth. The most disadvantaged regions have been those in

Table 2.1   Shift-share analysis* of manufacturing employment change by region 1952–79

	1952 manufacturing employment (000s)	as % 1952 employment			
		Actual change	National component	Structural component	Differential shift
East Anglia	138	+70.3	−7.8	+4.1	+74.0
South West	331	+25.7	−7.8	+3.4	+30.1
Wales	268	+17.5	−7.8	−1.0	+26.3
East Midlands	534	+11.4	−7.8	−1.9	+21.1
North	409	+7.8	−7.8	−4.4	+20.0
West Midlands	1119	+7.8	−7.8	+7.3	−7.3
South East	2259	−9.9	−7.8	+15.1	−17.2
Yorks & Humb.	863	−13.7	−7.8	−13.7	+7.8
Scotland	760	−18.4	−7.8	−6.8	−3.8
North West	1414	−24.5	−7.8	−13.2	−3.5
Northern Ireland	186	−27.4	−7.8	−26.7	+7.1

Note: * 1952 base year, 77 industry disaggregation

which textiles are important employers – Yorkshire and Humberside (woollens), the North West (cotton) and worst of all Northern Ireland (linen). But in several regions industrial structure has not had a very great impact on employment change in either direction. It is therefore not surprising that the link between actual manufacturing employment change and the favourability of a region's industrial structure is tenuous. None of the five growing regions owes much to a favourable industrial structure for example, and despite the best industrial structure of all, the South East has actually lost jobs at a slightly faster rate than the country as a whole. In these regions the remaining shifts in employment, measured by the differential shift, are very large indeed.

An important aspect of the role of industrial structure is that its influence has been uneven through time. This is demonstrated by figure 2.2a which shows the structural component by region between 1952 and 1979, but this time including three intermediate dates. In this diagram the structural component has been calculated throughout the whole period using the 1952 mix of industries in each region, but an almost identical pattern emerges even if an allowance is made for the changing mix of industries in each region (by using 1960 as the base year for 1960–6, 1966 as the base year for 1966–73 and 1973 for 1973–9). Figure 2.2a shows that up to 1966 industrial structure was responsible for quite large disparities in growth, but thereafter its influence has been much more modest. The loss of employment due to an adverse structure in Northern Ireland, Scotland, the North West and North eased markedly after 1966. The structural growth in the West Midlands stopped after 1966, and even the high-flying South East has not benefited from a favourable mix of industries since 1973. So despite its continuing popularity as an explanation for regional growth and decline, industrial structure within manufacturing has become relatively unimportant.

The extent to which a region's industrial structure favours employment growth depends on two factors: first, the mix of industries in that region at the start of the period, and secondly the subsequent national employment change in each of those industries. In theory, the demise of industrial structure as an important influence on regional growth could be the result of either or both of these factors. There has certainly been a tendency for the mix of industries in each region to grow more alike. However, in figure 2.2a the mix of industries was held constant (as at 1952) and as we noted, the same pattern emerges even using the mix of industries in other years. The conclusion must therefore be that the demise of industrial structure has been entirely the result of change in national employment trends in individual industries. What occurred, in fact, is that in the years up to 1966, when national manufacturing employment was rising, there were large disparities between growing and declining industries, and since these industries were unevenly distributed across the regions industrial structure accounted for large differences in growth during these years. After 1966, as national decline set in, industrial growth rates became much more alike, and nearly all in a downward direction, and as they became more alike their tendency to generate regional disparities diminished.

Because industrial structure alone does not provide an adequate explanation for contrasts in employment change it is appropriate to take a closer look at the residual disparities in growth, measured by the differential shift. In fact, differential shifts subsume several separate and sometimes conflicting influences on the location of manufacturing jobs, but the pattern through time, in figure 2.2b, is nevertheless interesting. In some regions the trend has been unbroken since the early 1960s: East Anglia, the South West and East Midlands have fared well throughout the period, while there has been a slow but steady decline in the North West and West Midlands. In contrast, Wales, Scotland, Northern Ireland, Yorkshire and Humberside and the North all improved in the 1960s and there was a corresponding deterioration in the South East, though in all these regions earlier trends largely reasserted themselves after 1973.

It has sometimes been suggested that differential shifts represent no more than the second-round or 'multiplier' effect of industrial structure. If a region has a high proportion of its employment in national declining industries, it is argued, this will not only be reflected in an adverse industrial structure but also depress the growth of other industries in the area through local industrial linkages. That this multiplier effect occurs is indisputable, but it has had little influence on the pattern of differential shifts. In no less than seven out of eleven regions the differential shift has been in the *opposite* direction to the structural component, and in several regions the magnitude of the differential shift has been the greater of the two by a large margin. This makes it impossible to explain differential shifts in terms of multipliers from industrial structure. Indeed, all the UK regions are very 'open' economies, selling most of their manufacturing output abroad or to other parts of the country, and we estimate that the regional multiplier within manufacturing is no more than 1.3 to 1.4, which is too small to have much impact on the overall pattern of differential shifts.

Urban structure

The dominant influence on the pattern of differential shifts is the decline of industry in cities and its growth in small towns and rural areas. The

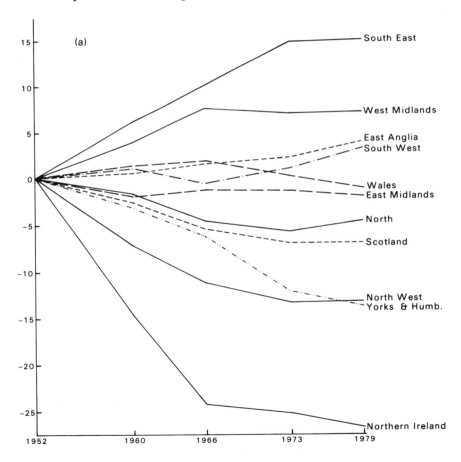

strength of this shift has been quite remarkable during the last two decades. In table 2.2 we have grouped sixty-one sub-regions of Great Britain into six broad headings on the basis of their degree of urbanization and industrialization. The figures (again adjusted to allow comparability through time) show that at one extreme London lost nearly four out of every ten of its manufacturing jobs between 1959 and 1975 – equal to roughly 600,000 jobs – while at the other end of the urban hierarchy, the most rural parts of Britain increased their manufacturing employment by nearly 80 per cent. The shift has been remarkably consistent: the larger a

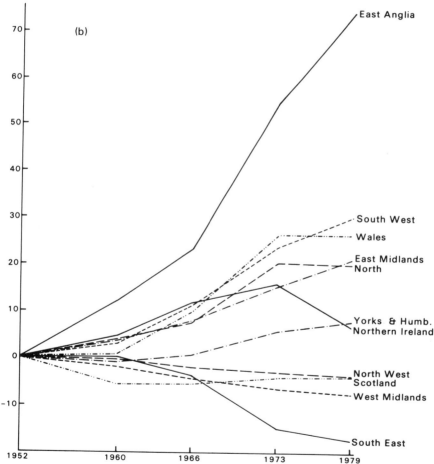

Figure 2.2 Shift-share analysis of manufacturing employment change by region 1952–79: (a) structural component (b) differential shift

Note: Employment at each date is expressed in terms of the percentage change from the 1952 level

Table 2.2   Shift-share analysis* of manufacturing employment change by type of area 1959–75

	1959 manufacturing employment (000s)	Actual change	as % 1959 employment		
			National component	Structural component	Differential shift
London	1551	−37.8	−5.3	+8.3	−40.8
Conurbations	2734	−15.9	−5.3	−4.2	−6.3
Free-standing cities	1647	+4.8	−5.3	+1.0	+9.1
Industrial towns	1568	+16.3	−5.3	−0.4	+21.9
County towns	640	+28.8	−5.3	+1.3	+32.8
Rural areas	95	+77.2	−5.3	−1.6	+84.1

Note: * 1959 base year, 99 industry disaggregation

settlement the faster the average decline. As table 2.2 also shows, none of this dramatic urban–rural shift can be attributed to industrial structure. The full results of this analysis, including the figures for individual sub-regions, have been published elsewhere (Fothergill and Gudgin, 1979b).

The decline of manufacturing in cities and its growth in small towns and rural areas is occurring within every UK region, but it is also important in differentiating whole regions because some regions are more urban than others. For example, the North West is dominated by two conurbations, Manchester and Merseyside, whereas in East Anglia only 15 per cent of the population live in settlements of more than 100,000 people. Therefore as the urban–rural shift has proceeded, the North West, a highly urban region, has been disadvantaged compared to rural East Anglia.

This is a crucial point, and one which explains many contrasts which hitherto have been only dimly understood. But we must look deeper than these superficial figures if we are to provide a satisfactory explanation for this aspect of regional growth. Why is manufacturing employment declining in cities and growing in small towns?

After collating a wide range of evidence on this question we have come to the conclusion that the overriding reason for the decline of manufacturing in cities and its growth elsewhere is the lack of room for physical expansion in major urban areas. Hemmed in by urban development, often at high densities, most *existing* factories in cities are unable to expand in the same way as their rivals in small towns and rural areas, and the relatively high cost of land, restrictions on peripheral growth (such as green belts) and the difficulties of land assembly make the construction of entirely *new* factories in urban areas most unlikely. This lack of room for physical expansion in cities is crucial in two respects.

First, it means that a disproportionately large share of the addition to factory floor-space – and the jobs that go with that floor-space – is located in small towns and rural areas. This is an old-established process which has been spreading industry beyond the confines of cities, and their inner areas in particular, for many years. Recent evidence from Birmingham (Joint Unit for Research on the Urban Environment, 1979), where only 17 per cent of firms have room for expansion within their existing sites, confirms the difficulties in locating new industrial floor-space in a major city.

Secondly, in urban areas the rising capital intensity of production and associated increases in floor-space requirements per employee ensure that in factories with no possibility of extending their existing floor-space, employment falls as new machinery displaces labour on the shop floor. It is this rapid displacement of labour by capital which is the driving force behind the *loss* of manufacturing jobs in cities, and as the rate of increase in capital intensity and floor-space requirements accelerated after 1960 these losses rose dramatically. The same fall in employment occurs on existing floor-space in small towns and rural areas of course, but in these places the job losses are offset by jobs created in factory extensions and new factories.

The full evidence in support of this explanation of the urban–rural shift is presented elsewhere (Fothergill and Gudgin, 1982). Its great strength is that unlike alternative theories of urban decline, this explanation accounts for all the major characteristics of the urban–rural shift which can be identified empirically. This point is worth illustrating.

Let us take the question of the *ways* in which the urban–rural shift is occurring – the role of openings, growth, contractions, closures and factory movement, or the 'components of change' as they have become known. The lack of room for expansion in cities will be felt most acutely by growing firms, who will be forced to relocate or divert some of their additional output into branches in small towns, or even to forgo expansion altogether. In contrast, the lack of room for expansion clearly poses no problem to the firm which contracts or closes for reasons unconnected with location. We would therefore expect the location of additions to employment, in new factories and factory extensions, to differentiate cities and small towns to a greater extent than the location of job losses in contractions and closures.

The experience of the East Midlands confirms this point. Within this region there has been a marked urban–rural contrast in manufacturing employment change typical of trends in the country as a whole. Analysis of a databank containing details of all manufacturing establishments in the East Midlands reveals that between 1968 and 1975 roughly half of the urban–rural contrast reflected the location of the expansion of surviving factories (i.e. factories open at both the start and end of the period).

Almost a further third of the urban–rural contrast could be accounted for by the location of new firms, new branch plants and firms moving into the region from elsewhere. By contrast, the location of job losses through contractions and closures of establishments showed much smaller urban–rural differences (Fothergill and Gudgin, 1982).

The wider generality of conclusions from the East Midlands is confirmed by the comparisons that are possible with the other areas for which establishment data is available. For example, London's loss of jobs in closures has been only marginally higher than that in the cities and small towns of the East Midlands, despite the much greater net decline in London. Similarly, just as factory movement is only a small part of the urban–rural shift in the East Midlands, the same is true over the country as a whole. In table 2.3 'industrial movement' has been defined to include the diversion of jobs from one area to another through the opening of new branch plants in addition to the complete relocation of companies. Nevertheless, the table demonstrates that even though urban decline is popularly attributed to firms 'moving out', industrial movement accounts for no more than a quarter to a third of the overall shift.

Table 2.3   The contribution of industrial movement to the urban–rural shift 1959–75

	as % 1959 manufacturing employment		
	*Industrial movement**	*Other components*	*Net change*
London	−12.1	−25.7	−37.8
Conurbations	+1.5	−17.4	−15.9
Free-standing cities	+1.1	+3.7	+4.8
Industrial towns	+4.2	+12.1	+16.3
County towns	+7.3	+21.5	+28.8
Rural areas	+29.3	+47.9	+77.2

Note: * Estimates based on Department of Industry figures

The lack of room for expansion in urban areas also explains why the urban–rural shift is so pervasive. It is not a phenomenon specific to the British economy, for example, but can also be observed in North America and Western Europe, where the same constraints on urban industrial growth apply. Moreover, the lack of room is a problem which affects a wide range of manufacturing establishments, irrespective of their corporate status, which explains why within the East Midlands we are able to observe poorer growth in the cities among both single-plant and multi-plant firms, and among both locally and non-locally owned firms. The evidence does not support the view that urban manufacturing decline is exclusively the result of the strategies of any one group of firms, such as multinational corporations.

The lack of room for expansion in cities is nevertheless still able to account for two of the more subtle contrasts which can be identified using the East Midlands data. First, very small firms (employing twenty-five or fewer) seem to grow at much the same average rate whether they are located in a city or a small town. This reflects their mobility. Unlike larger establishments, very small firms find it easy to move within urban areas, and frequently do, and in this way they are able to overcome the problem posed by constrained premises. Secondly, the East Midlands data reveals that the urban–rural shift is almost entirely concentrated in industries with high rates of investment. This reflects the fact that the lack of room for expansion in cities poses difficulties only for those firms which need to invest more than can be accommodated within their existing factory sites. Firms in industries with low rates of capital investment will tend not to encounter the same constraint.

But perhaps the most telling pieces of evidence in support of this explanation or urban decline is also one of the simplest. This concerns London. In other towns and cities the proportion of factories with no room for expansion is not known, but in London we can safely assume that the proportion is close to 100 per cent. The density of development, the cost of land and the stringent restrictions on building on the edge of the green belt ensure that few of the capital's firms can undertake substantial physical expansion, and hardly any sizeable sites are available for new factories. Assuming that all London's factories are physically constrained, the national average rise in floor-space per worker could be expected to produce a fall in manufacturing employment of 25 per cent between 1966 and 1975. The actual fall was 34 per cent, but since London's industrial floor-space *fell* during these years (as a result of redevelopment and the encroachment of other uses such as warehousing), the lack of room for expansion, combined with the rising capital intensity of production, comes close to providing a total explanation for the decline of London's manufacturing employment.

Size structure

The size of factories in any area is important because it is the main determinant of the rate at which new independent firms are established. In the short run new firms provide relatively few jobs. The East Midlands establishment data, for example, shows that they added just over 4 per cent to manufacturing employment in their region between 1968 and 1975. But in the long run new firms are considerably more important, partly because large numbers continue to be established and partly because on average they grow quite quickly during their early years.

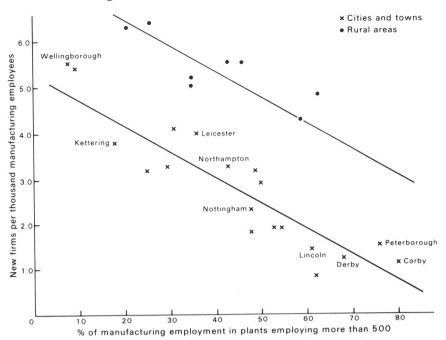

Figure 2.3   New firm foundation by district in the East Midlands, 1968–75

In Leicestershire, for example, the establishment data stretches as far back as 1947 and indicates that almost a quarter of that county's employment is now in firms founded as new independent companies since that date.

The figures for the East Midlands showed that the contribution of new firms to employment growth is higher in rural areas, but a much more important contrast in rates of new firm formation is between areas dominated by large and small manufacturing plants. Towns like Lincoln, Derby, Peterborough and Corby, which have over 60 per cent of their manufacturing employment in plants employing more than 500 workers, have new firm formation rates only a third as high as most of the towns in the region with under 40 per cent in large plants. In the long run this factor undoubtedly contributes towards the poor employment growth of towns dominated by large plants.

Comparable evidence on rates of new firm formation in other parts of the country is hard to come by, but if this relationship between rates of formation and large plant domination holds elsewhere in Britain some of the contrasts are likely to be substantial. In Coventry, for example, where roughly 70 per cent of manufacturing jobs are in factories employing 500 or more, the rate of formation is probably less than a third the rate in

Leicester, twenty miles away, where only 30 per cent are in large plants. The difference represents a relative gain of about 1000 jobs a year to the Leicester area. However, it is in the large-plant towns within the assisted areas that the loss of jobs through low rates of new firm formation is likely to be greatest because some of the towns with the highest proportion of employment in large plants are found here – Teesside, Clydeside, Tyneside and Merseyside. The very low formation rate in Teesside measured by Robinson and Storey (1981) confirms this conclusion.

But if the location of new firms really is important in creating differences in employment growth it should be possible to identify a disparity in the country as a whole between areas dominated by large plants and areas dominated by small plants. To examine this possibility we divided each type of area in the country as a whole – conurbations, free-standing cities, industrial towns and so on – into large and small plant areas. The measure of employment creation we used is 'indigenous performance', which is the employment change after allowing for industrial structure and industrial movement, or in other words the change generated from within each area, which is what we need to look at in order to detect the influence of different rates of new firm formation. As table 2.4 shows, within each type of area indigenous performance has been worse in places dominated by large plants. This is precisely the pattern we would expect, given the association between large-plant towns and low rates of new firm formation.

The higher rate of new firm formation in areas with a sizeable heritage of existing small firms is not occurring because founders are moving to these places to start their businesses. On the contrary, the vast

Table 2.4 Employment generation in large and small plant towns by type of area 1959–75

	Indigenous performance[1] as % of 1959 manufacturing employment	
	Large plant areas[2]	*Small plant areas*
London	n.a.	−28.7
Conurbations	−11.1	−2.7
Free standing cities	+3.5	+15.5
Industrial towns	+12.9	+20.2
County towns	+12.2	+28.9
Rural areas	n.a.	+54.7

Notes: [1] manufacturing employment change after allowing for industrial structure and industrial movement
[2] areas with more than half their manufacturing employment in plants which employ 500 or more (Source: Census of Production 1972)

majority of founders start their firm within their home area. The main reason for the higher formation rate in small-plant areas seems to be that a disproportionately large number of founders are employed by small firms immediately prior to starting their own business – a conclusion supported by the results of a survey of founders which we conducted in the East Midlands, and also by the findings of a similar survey in the Northern region (Johnson and Cathcart, 1979). Quite why large plants inhibit people from setting up in business is not clear, though our survey suggested that the most important problem is probably the limited range of work experience, and in particular the lack of contact with customers. Entrepreneurs need appropriate training it seems, as do people in most skills, and very small firms probably provide the most effective training ground because the owner sets a direct example to his employees. There is also some evidence that the mix of industries and a shortage of suitable subcontract work in large plant towns play minor roles in further depressing rates of formation in these areas.

Taking a long view of employment change, low rates of formation in places such as Tyneside and Clydeside probably help explain why when their traditional industries began to decline they were unable to regenerate their own industrial base, even with substantial government assistance, whereas some other areas with still worse industrial structures, such as West Yorkshire (woollens) and Northamptonshire (footwear), have shown greater resilience. Nevertheless, it must be stressed that the problem is not a lack of entrepreneurial spirit. The problem in Tyneside and Clydeside (or Derby, Corby and Lincoln in the East Midlands for that matter) is that their heritage of large manufacturing plants does not provide a suitable environment for generating entrepreneurs and new firms. Almost as a result of their success in generating large-scale industry in the past, these cities and towns are therefore now locked into a situation of increasing dependence on the fate of their remaining large employers – or on injections of industry from outside.

Regional policy

The injection of industry from outside has been provided mainly by regional policy, the fourth major factor responsible for regional differences in manufacturing employment change. In the immediate postwar years, and then again since about 1960, successive governments have tried to divert jobs into areas of high unemployment, and at times this policy has absorbed large sums of public money.

Considerable advances in measuring the impact of regional policy have been made by Moore and Rhodes (1973) and Moore, Rhodes and Tyler (1977), whose analyses are widely accepted and form the basis of our own estimates. They note that after allowing for the influence of industrial structure, manufacturing employment in the four development area regions (Scotland, Wales, Northern Ireland and the North) declined a little relative to the national average during the 1950s, when regional policy was largely inoperative. In the early 1960s however, at about the same time as policy was intensified, the trend relative to the rest of the country (again allowing for industrial structure) improved dramatically in all four regions. Moore, Rhodes and Tyler assume that if regional policy had not been intensified the downward trend in the development area regions would have been the same as during the 1950s, and after allowing for one or two more minor factors they therefore attribute the improvement to regional policy.

This method of measuring the impact of policy is basically correct but requires an important modification. The major difficulty in measuring the impact of regional policy is that the other influences on employment change must be successfully disentangled. We have argued that there are three underlying causes of regional differences in manufacturing growth – industrial structure, urban structure and size structure. Only the first of these, industrial structure, is fully disentangled in the Moore, Rhodes and Tyler estimates. The other two will affect the estimates of the impact of regional policy if they changed in magnitude before and after 1960 and thus altered underlying regional trends.

In fact the urban–rural shift appears to have accelerated significantly after 1960, for reasons largely unconnected with regional policy, and because the mix of urban and rural areas varies from region to region this consequently altered underlying regional trends. Any comparison of trends after 1960 with trends in earlier years therefore runs the risk that changes brought about by the increased urban–rural shift may be wrongly attributed to regional policy. However, given the change in trend in each type of area in the country as a whole, and the representation of each type of area within each region, it is a comparatively easy step to calculate the change in regional trends attributable to the faster urban–rural shift. We estimate that the decline in the four development area regions resulting from the small deterioration in the conurbations was more than offset by the boost to their employment caused by the sharp improvement in the growth of small towns and rural areas, so that by 1979 manufacturing employment in these regions was 90,000 higher as a result of the increase in the urban–rural shift after 1960. These jobs must be *deducted* from the improvement in the employment trends in the development area regions in order to make an accurate assessment of the impact of regional policy.

Estimates of the impact of policy, incorporating this modification to the Moore, Rhodes and Tyler approach, are shown in table 2.5. Taking the period as a whole, regional policy has raised manufacturing employment in the four development area regions by around 185,000. The impact of policy has therefore been substantial. If recent estimates (Moore, Rhodes and Tyler, 1980) of the jobs created in assisted areas outside these four regions are included, the impact of regional policy has probably been to raise manufacturing employment in all assisted areas in total by around a quarter of a million.

Table 2.5 Estimated impact of regional policy on manufacturing employment 1960–79

	1960–6 (000s)	1966–73 (000s)	1973–9 (000s)	Total	(as % 1960)
North	14	50	−12	52	(11.1)
Scotland	30	25	2	57	(7.4)
Wales	13	35	5	53	(17.8)
Northern Ireland	10	11[1]	1[2]	22	(11.8)
Total	67	121	−4	184	(10.8)

Notes: [1] to 1971 only
[2] employment in 1976 in moves in 1972–6
Methods of estimation are described in full in Fothergill and Gudgin (1982) appendix C

Table 2.5 does nevertheless present one alarming conclusion: after 1973 no regional policy effect can be detected. It could be that this method of estimating the policy effect has simply become inaccurate or inappropriate, but our conclusion is not unique. Keeble (1980) also concluded, from a regression analysis of differential shifts by county between 1971 and 1976 that regional policy 'had ceased by 1976 to exert a measurable impact on the geography of manufacturing employment change in Britain'. It is not difficult to explain why regional policy should now be less effective. Controls on industrial development in more prosperous regions have now been relaxed, and the Regional Employment Premiums, which accounted for about half of all regional policy expenditure, has been abolished. The depressed economic conditions which have prevailed since the early 1970s have reduced the level of potentially mobile investment, so that few new branch plants are available to move to the assisted areas, and even those branch plants which do find their way to assisted areas tend to employ fewer people as manufacturing industry becomes more capital intensive. The declining impact of regional policy does not mean however that regional policy should be abandoned, but rather that traditional policy tools are probably inappropriate in the depressed conditions which now prevail.

Regional employment accounts

'Employment accounts' for each region showing how the four factors contributed to net changes in manufacturing employment between 1960 and 1975 are shown in table 2.6a. The accounts measure the importance of each factor in causing divergences from the national rate of employment change: a negative contribution attributable to new firms, for example, indicates that new firm formation in that region is estimated to be below the national average. While there is inevitably a degree of error in all the estimates, given the information available and the assumptions it has been necessary to make, the accounts do provide a reasonable guide to the main causes of growth and decline in each region.

Three general points should be noted. First, the national decline in manufacturing employment has been an important influence on all regions, and even though some managed to stay well above the average, the pervasiveness of national decline was sufficient to produce a strong downward bias in the pattern of change. Secondly, divergences from the national rate of decline are really only the net result of conflicting influences on growth. Between 1960 and 1975 there was no region in which all four causes of uneven growth worked in the same direction. Thirdly, the four factors vary in magnitude across the country as a whole as well as within individual regions. The urban–rural shift has been the most powerful influence on the pattern of change, reflecting the marked differences in the extent to which each region's industry is concentrated in cities, towns or rural areas, while size structure (which affects rates of new firm formation) has been the least important, principally because some of the sharper contrasts between individual towns are hidden at the regional scale.

The contrast between the East and West Midlands provides a good example of the way in which regional disparities can be explained by the four factors we have outlined. The division of the English Midlands into two regions is often seen as an administrative convenience rather than an economic, social or physical reality, and to some extent this view is justified because both regions have seemed relatively prosperous during the postwar period, with unemployment rates normally a little below the national average. But despite being adjacent regions with much in common, the West Midlands lost over one in eight of its manufacturing jobs between 1960 and 1975 while employment in the East Midlands remained more or less unchanged. Traditional theories of urban and regional growth are at a loss to explain how this contrast arises, but the employment accounts provide an answer. As table 2.6a shows, though the West Midlands' industrial structure boosted its employment by 6–7 per cent relative to its neighbour, this advantage was more than offset by the urban–rural shift, which has benefited regions dominated by medium-sized cities and small towns, such as the East Midlands, at the expense of conurbation-dominated regions such as the West Midlands. The estimated higher rate of new firm formation arising from a more favourable size structure has further boosted the East Midlands' advantage.

Table 2.6 Employment accounts for manufacturing (a) regions 1960–75 (b) two counties 1965–76

	Net change	National change	Differences due to:				
			Industrial structure	Urban structure	Size structure	Regional policy	Residual
(a) REGIONS 1960–75							
East Anglia	+28.6	–12.0	+3.8	+30.8	+1.2	–1.8	+6.6
Wales	+9.5	–12.0	+0.5	+13.6	–2.4	+15.1	–5.3
South West	+7.4	–12.0	–3.4	+18.1	+0.1	+3.2	+1.4
North	+2.5	–12.0	–3.1	+8.6	–4.3	+14.1	–0.8
East Midlands	+0.4	–12.0	–1.8	+10.6	+2.4	–3.4	+4.6
West Midlands	–13.0	–12.0	+4.7	–2.2	–1.6	–3.6	+1.7
Scotland	–14.1	–12.0	–5.9	+8.1	–0.6	+6.5	–10.2
Yorks & Humb.	–14.4	–12.0	–10.4	+3.9	+1.5	–1.1	+3.7
Northern Ireland	–15.9	–12.0	–19.8	+14.7	+1.2	+11.9	–11.9
South East	–18.5	–12.0	+10.1	–18.9	+1.2	–5.0	+6.1
North West	–20.5	–12.0	–8.5	+3.8	–0.3	+0.5	–4.0
(b) TWO COUNTIES 1965–76							
Cleveland	–9.9	–15.4	–1.1	+2.8	–6.6	+10.0	+0.3
Leicestershire	–8.1	–15.4	–1.2	+5.5	+3.7	–2.5	+1.7

Notes: Figures represent percentage change from base-year level of manufacturing employment
Methods of estimation are described in Fothergill and Gudgin (1982) appendix C

The combined influence of the four factors accounts for most of the regional variation in manufacturing employment change, but does not sum exactly to the actual change in each region during these years. No doubt part of the reason is inaccuracy in estimating the employment change associated with each factor, and some of the residual variation reflects factors specific to individual regions (such as the troubles in Northern Ireland). But this is probably not the whole story because the residuals display a distinctive pattern: the southern and midland regions all fare a little better than we would expect, and the peripheral regions of the north and west a little worse. Moreover, the largest negative residual in Great Britain is found in the most peripheral region, Scotland. Over and above the four causes of uneven growth we have identified, there is therefore some evidence that peripheral regions grow more slowly.

The validity of our explanation of growth and decline is reinforced by a more testing comparison between two sharply contrasting counties, Cleveland and Leicestershire. Cleveland, on the north-east coast of England, is dominated by steel, chemicals and heavy engineering and by very large plants within each of these industries. In Leicestershire, in the heart of the Midlands, hosiery is the main employer, but a diversified light engineering sector has developed alongside this traditional industry and, unlike in Cleveland, there is a substantial heritage of smaller and medium-sized locally owned companies. The contrast between these areas in terms of industrial composition is reinforced by the different level of prosperity in each. Throughout the postwar period Cleveland has suffered from persistently high unemployment and has been designated a 'development area', while Leicestershire has remained prosperous and unassisted. The employment accounts in table 2.6b demonstrate that the same explanation of growth and decline can be applied to both areas, and also show why Cleveland, rather than Leicestershire, has become dependent on government aid.

Between 1965 and 1976 industrial structure did not differentiate between the two, showing that a concentration of 'heavy' industry, as in Cleveland, is not necessarily markedly unfavourable for employment change. Also the urban–rural shift benefited both counties. However, in Cleveland a large inflow of jobs attributable to regional policy was offset by a low rate of new firm formation (reflecting an unfavourable size structure) so despite government aid overall manufacturing employment change in Cleveland was no better than in Leicestershire. This is an important conclusion, and one which illustrates the usefulness of employment accounts, because it indicates that in the future, when regional policy is likely to be less effective due to the depressed state of the national economy, manufacturing employment change in Cleveland is likely to slip considerably below that in Leicestershire. Indeed, table 2.6b leaves little doubt that Leicestershire's high rate of new firm formation is probably at the root of its greater long-term prosperity and resilience.

Concluding remarks

It is our contention that four factors – industrial structure, urban structure, size structure and regional policy – form the basis for understanding the regional pattern of manufacturing growth and decline in contemporary Britain. The relative importance of these factors varies from place to place and from time to time, but collectively they account for the main disparities in employment change. In our view many existing ideas on regional growth which are still widely taught are therefore inappropriate. In some cases they should be abandoned; in others, including classical location theory, the strict limits on their applicability should be made clear.

Finally, the results of this study indicate what can be achieved by empirical rather than theoretical methods. It is inevitable that some theory is needed to guide applied work, but theory should be based on experience and facts, and should be used to guide one step at a time. Indeed, failure to follow this procedure in the past has meant that grand theoretical edifices have not only been unhelpful in the study of regional economic change: they have been positively misleading.

The components of change in metropolitan areas: events in their corporate context

P. E. Lloyd and P. Dicken

Introduction

Piecing together the complex processes of industrial change in metropolitan areas to produce an intelligible picture is a daunting task, particularly during times of rapid change. Although many of the individual pieces and even whole sections of the jigsaw puzzle can be identified, we are still some way from being able to complete the total picture. Indeed, we are coming to appreciate that the pieces of the metropolitan jigsaw are also parts of other, much larger-scale puzzles. In particular, we are becoming increasingly aware that the nature of the UK urban system has been undergoing dramatic change during the past two decades and that industry and employment have been closely involved in the nature of that change. At the same time, there has emerged an awareness of the changing nature of manufacturing industry itself, of the way it is organized, the changing balance of productive activities within it, the shifting hierarchy of decision-making and the increasing internationalization of its operations. Above all, of course, we in Britain have become confronted with the declining fortunes of manufacturing industry in the UK since the war and the ways in which shifting terms of trade, falling levels of investment and technical innovation, declining profits and market share have all worked their way into the fabric of the nation's manufacturing industry.

In attempting to complete the metropolitan industrial jigsaw, therefore, we need to take account of the impact of such general economic and organizational processes on the changing distribution of industry within metropolitan areas. But, as Keeble (1978) has pointed out, such 'fully interconnected' events have frequently been artificially separated and examined in isolation. In spatial studies of industrial change in particular, two dominant research approaches have tended to evolve: the 'components of change' approach and the 'geography of enterprise' approach (Wood, 1979). With a few isolated exceptions (e.g. Gudgin, 1978), these two approaches have remained as separate research strands. While the enterprise or corporate viewpoint has confronted the *decision matrix* through which events expressed 'on the ground' have been ordered, the components of change approach has begun with *events-on-the-ground*, categorizing them as births, deaths, transfers and so on and has subsequently sought to integrate upwards towards an understanding of the decisions that occasioned them. In approaching the problem from these two ends of the spectrum, but often failing to cross the 'middle ground', the essential connectivities of decision and action have often been lost. In what follows we make a partial attempt at bridging the gap by building on our earlier research in the two conurbations of Manchester and Merseyside.

Combining the components of change and enterprise approaches

In essence, our approach is to regard the metropolitan manufacturing economy as comprising overlapping sets of corporate groups – primarily single-plant firms and multi-plant firms of various types. These interact together (and, of course, with other 'interest groups' in the urban area: those who own land in it, manage its public services, and so on) in ways that characterize the functioning of the urban economy. Together these make up the major *actors* whose decisions condition significant events across the corporate interface (figure 3.1). The important point about such actors is that they behave and make decisions in the light of their own interests. Just because they appear within a particular metropolitan area does not imply that such interests coincide with those of other actors in that area. Each business enterprise, for example, is likely to be concerned first and foremost with its own 'economy' and in effect with its own 'balance of payments' with the rest of the world. Thus the causality of events in the metropolitan economy must be interpreted in this light. For business interests in particular, the degree to which the local urban economy itself figures in their effective environment will clearly vary. For small, locally based firms whose factor inputs and product markets lie within the same city it will clearly loom large. For branch and subsidiary operations of large multi-plant organizations on the other hand, conditions in a single metropolitan area may figure only lightly in the corporate balance-of-payments equation. Metropolitan economies, as a result, may be either more or less 'open'. For some areas, external events

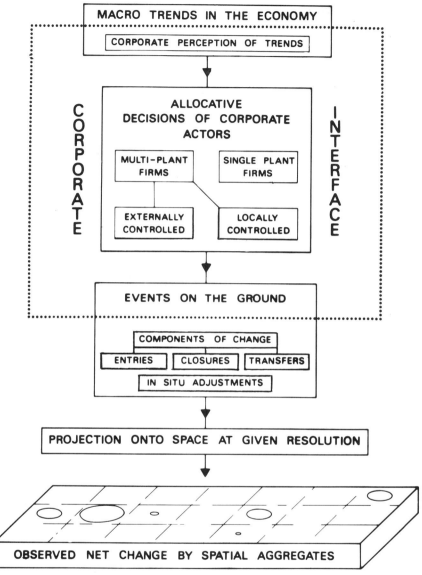

Figure 3.1 Events and decision paths: the corporate interface

may dominate the investment behaviour of their constituent firms in a direct sense while, for others, though external events are at one remove clearly important to their businesses, more local shifts in purchasing power, land values, planning policy and so on, may be more important.

As figure 3.2 suggests, the tangible events which occur 'on the ground' as industrial change within metropolitan – or any other – areas, are the outcome of a set of much broader macro-scale events at the level of the economy as a whole. As far as the organizational structure of manufacturing industry in the UK is concerned, recent developments at the national scale are now well-documented (see, for example, Prais, 1976; Hannah, 1976; Hannah and Kay, 1977). We need do little more here than note the salient characteristics of such trends. In common with all industrial societies in capitalist and mixed economies, manufacturing industry in Britain has become increasingly dominated by a small number of very large business enterprises. Indeed, Britain seems to have one of the highest levels of industrial concentration among the industrial economies. The relative importance of large enterprises has increased at the expense of smaller enterprises. For example, Prais (1976) estimates that in 1970 the 100 largest manufacturing firms in Britain accounted for 41 per cent of net output in manufacturing compared with only 16 per cent

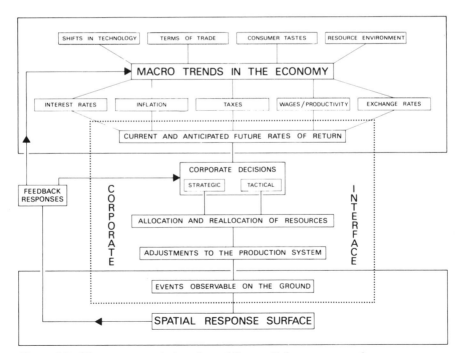

Figure 3.2 Macro-economic trends and the spatial response surface

in 1909. Expressed rather differently, he claims that, whereas in 1909 more than 2000 firms were needed to produce one-half of total manufacturing output in the UK, by 1970 a mere 140 firms were able to produce the same proportion. The corollary of such an increase in the relative importance of large firms is the decline in the importance of small firms, a decline which is only very inadequately documented.

Recent research suggests that the increase in firm concentration is only partly, if at all, explained by increases in plant size stimulated by developments in production technology. Prais (1976) in particular argues that the giant enterprises of the modern economy operate not a few massive plants but rather large numbers of plants. Though some of these may indeed be very large, most tend to be medium-sized or small. These comments refer to the 'giant' enterprises in the economy but it seems that in general there has been both an overall increase in average plant size together with a tendency for more and more firms to become multi-plant in their operations.

This is not the place to try to explain these developments; indeed, there is much debate about the primary variables underlying them. Clearly, they are the outcome of a number of complex interacting forces. However, one of these does merit our attention: the process of *acquisition and merger*. Disregarding *why* mergers occur, there is little doubt that it is one of the most important means by which business enterprises have grown. In aggregate terms, mergers tend to occur in a series of intensive waves or peaks separated by periods of relative quiescence. In Britain mergers were particularly prevalent in the periods 1919–20, 1926–9 and, more especially, in the middle and late 1960s (Hannah and Kay, 1977). During these periods very large numbers of firms 'disappeared' by merger. For example, between 1963 and 1968 more than 5000 firms in Britain were acquired by other firms. Although not all observers would agree, there are grounds for suggesting that the growth of at least the largest firms and, hence, the overall increase in business concentration has been produced very largely by merger activity. Certainly, this is the view stated recently by Hannah and Kay (1977) in the case of Britain, a view which would seem to be borne out by experience in the United States during the 1960s. The US Federal Trade Commission asserts that almost the entire relative growth of the very largest corporations in the United States was produced by merger. The commission estimates that, if they had *not* been engaged in mergers, the leading 200 corporations would have enlarged their share of total manufacturing assets from 42.4 per cent in 1947 to only 45.3 per cent in 1968. In fact, by very active merger activity they increased their share to 60.9 per cent.

Changes at the national level, then, form the broad context within which local changes need to be observed. At the local (i.e. metropolitan level), we view recent industrial change (and its components) through the lens of the enterprise. Using a classification scheme discussed more fully elsewhere (Dicken and Lloyd, 1978) we identify three major types of enterprise existing within the metropolitan economy: (a) single-plant firms, (b) locally headquartered multi-plant firms, and (c) externally headquartered multi-plant firms, which may be subdivided further into foreign and domestic firms.

Our basic assumption in employing such a typology is that plants in each category exhibit varying degrees of openness to events outside the metropolitan area in which they are located. In particular, their role within the enterprise may vary considerably. For example, it seems reasonable to assume that, as an interest group within a given metropolitan economy, multi-plant concerns may be expected to behave differently from their single-plant counterparts. Their interests are more diffuse (often both structurally and spatially) and, as a result, they may be expected to identify less readily with a particular place or community in which only a part of their operations is located. Events initiated by the multi-plant group may often generate overt conflicts between themselves and those other interest groups operating wholly *within* the metropolitan community. Their behaviour – rational in the context of their individual corporate economies – may appear unintelligible or even hostile when set in the community rather than the company frame of reference. Small wonder that newspapers today abound with complaints by community or other place-based interest groups faced with the apparently indefensible behaviour of multi-plant companies, parts of whose broader scale interests impinge upon them.

In particular, the growing geographical separation of production functions and control functions seems to be significant for an interpretation of industrial change in metropolitan areas and, more generally, for the variety and level of employment opportunities available. There is now very clear evidence that the increasingly high level of industrial concentration in Britain (see p. 54) is paralleled by an increasingly high degree of geographical concentration of corporate headquarters in London and the South East region (Evans, 1973; Goddard and Smith, 1978). As a result the geographical distribution of executive and decision-making functions is becoming highly skewed. Many local economies, therefore, are especially open to external influences transmitted through those of its plants which belong to multi-plant firms controlled from elsewhere. Among a set of regions, each housing distinct stages of the production process for a given company, the influence of an upturn or a slump in overall activity might well be experienced differently. While management functions might remain relatively stable (except, of course, in the event of acquisition by another company) fabrication and assembly-line production might respond sharply to cyclical or secular changes in output. In this way cyclical and secular tendencies within the economy at large might tend to be more or less exaggerated depending upon the way multiplier effects are transmitted among those regions or cities housing particular elements of the corporate production system.

Viewing the processes of industrial change on the ground – the openings of new plants and the closure of existing plants, the migration of some and the *in situ* expansion, contraction or stagnation of others – through the enterprise lens produces an extremely complex picture. Figure 3.3 outlines some of the ways in which the population of enterprises within a metropolitan economy may change over time. The organizational mix of an area, like its industry type and plant size mixes, therefore, is the result of a complex set of processes operating at both the plant and firm levels as the firms themselves expand or contract, takeover or merge with other firms, or are themselves taken over. At least some of the manufacturing employment change experienced by an area will be a reflection of *organizational* changes in its firm population, including change of ownership. Of course, these are not isolated processes. Some of the variation in a firm's performance will be related to the nature of the product market(s) in which it operates. Sectoral change and organizational change are closely related. But they are by no means synonymous. Some firms perform better (or worse) than others in the same economic sector whether that sector as a whole is growing, declining or stagnant. It may well mean, though, that some sectors are more prone to major organizational adjustments than others. Where an area is dominated by such economic sectors then sectoral change and organizational change may combine to produce particularly powerful change in the local economy.

Thus figure 3.3 represents a conceptual framework within which industrial change in an area can be examined in a way which sets changes at the plant level in their organizational perspective. Manufacturing plants, therefore, should be seen as being not only of a particular size or industry type but also of a particular organizational type. The framework has a general relevance to changes in any spatially defined area. The components of change approach is thus at its most powerful where events on the ground can be set not simply in terms of the size or type of industries for which they are observed but also in the context of those defined groups of corporate *actors* whose decisions promote them. Assigning ownership provides the essential interface across which events and causality may be linked. While many analyses by sector or even company may trace the chain of decisions to the events produced by them in terms of factory openings or closures, the components of change approach for all activities in a defined segment of space facilitates the evaluation of interactions between *all* those members of the set representing the business interests of a given local economy.

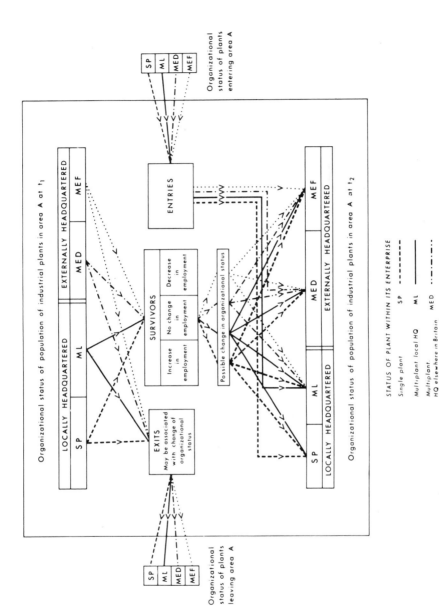

Figure 3.3 The organizational dimension of the components of industrial change

Industrial change in Greater Manchester and Merseyside 1966–75

The study areas used for this analysis are defined with respect to the coverage of the data which is comparable for 1966 and 1975. Thus 'Mersey-side' as employed here covers Wirral (including Ellesmere Port but excluding Chester) together with the old local authority areas of Liver-pool, Bootle, Litherland and Crosby. The bounds of 'Greater Manchester' correspond almost exactly with those of the original SELNEC conur-bation, but in the context of the post-reorganization county, Wigan and the districts of Ramsbottom, Littleborough, Saddleworth and Longden-dale are excluded.

Recent industrial change in Merseyside and Manchester has to be seen within the longer-term development of the two conurbations. Although both are essentially nineteenth-century industrial cities, both their industrial histories and their positions within the national policy environment are substantially different. Merseyside's industrial develop-ment reflects its historically important function as a major port. Until the early 1960s its manufacturing industry bore the strong imprint of port-related activities (for example, food processing). Its service sector also was strongly biased towards port activities. Manchester, in contrast, evolved as a textile and engineering complex having been the archetypal early industrial city. But it also developed a more substantial and more broadly based service sector, evolving an important role as the regional headquarters for a variety of public and private activities.

Such historical differences between the two conurbations have been reinforced during the last thirty years by fundamental differences in policy treatment by central government. Merseyside has enjoyed a high level of assisted area status since the late 1940s. Manchester received no regional assistance prior to 1972 when it was designated an intermediate area. Even then, however, the aid differential between the two conurbations was preserved because Merseyside was elevated to the status of a special development area. Government changes in regional policy announced in 1979 have removed intermediate area status from Manchester.

Comparisons between the two conurbations need also to be set against differences between them in their size as manufacturing concen-trations and in their internal geographical structure. In terms of manu-facturing employment, Manchester is very much larger than Merseyside. In 1975 total manual employment in manufacturing in the Manchester conurbation was 336,292; in Merseyside the figure was 168,121. Secondly, Manchester's internal structure is a good deal more complex than Mersey-side's. This is particularly obvious in the case of inner city definitions. On Merseyside it is possible, in industrial terms at least, to distinguish an 'inner' and 'outer' area. In Manchester, however, there exists not only the contiguous inner area core represented by the cities of Manchester and Salford but, in addition, a number of discrete 'inner areas' dominate the centres of outer ring towns, such as Bolton, Oldham, Rochdale and Stockport. The geographical distinction between inner and outer in Manchester is, therefore, far less clear than in Merseyside.

The combination of long-established historical differences and of more recent policy treatment goes a long way towards explaining the nature of manufacturing change in the two conurbations since the mid-1960s. In examining recent manufacturing change in the two cities from the perspective of enterprise-induced changes, we focus our attention upon the years between 1966 and 1975. During this time, Merseyside as a whole more or less broke even in terms of manufacturing employment while Manchester suffered massive decline. Since 1975, however, Merseyside has suffered a whole series of massive plant closures and contractions while Manchester's manufacturing fortunes have continued to decline, though in a less spectacular and therefore a less widely publicized way.

Table 3.1 summarizes the changes in manufacturing employment in the two conurbations between 1966 and 1975, broken down by major components of change. In total, the Manchester conurbation experienced massive decline in manufacturing employment, losing 111,314 manual jobs (one-quarter of its 1966 stock). Job loss occurred throughout the conurbation though the rate of loss was approximately twice as great in the inner area (−43.6 per cent) as in the outer area (−20.2 per cent). Over the same period, Merseyside experienced a very different pattern of employment change. Overall, the conurbation lost only 1489 jobs, a decline of a mere 0.9 per cent. Although, as in Manchester, there was substantial job loss in the inner area, its magnitude, even allowing for the scale differences between the two conurbations, was much smaller (−26.3 per cent compared with −43.6 per cent). The greatest difference between the two conurbations, however, occurred in the employment performance of their outer areas. Whereas outer Manchester lost one-fifth of its 1966 manufacturing employment, outer Merseyside *gained* almost 20 per cent. This increase of 18,515 jobs very nearly offset the inner area decline. In Manchester's case, outer area job loss magnified the inner area losses.

Table 3.1 also shows that these aggregate changes in the two conurbations were brought about by rather different combinations of components. In the case of Manchester, the pattern was extremely consistent. Though it has to be recognized that the database has an inevitable tendency to underestimate the scale of *in situ* change, it is clear that by far the most important force for change was the exit (closure) of plants. In total, 143,272 jobs were lost through closures as compared with a loss of

Table 3.1 Components of manufacturing employment change, Greater Manchester and Merseyside 1966–75

	Manual employment 1975	=	Manual employment 1966	+	Entries 1966–75	–	Exits 1966–75	+	(Balance of change in in situ survivors) 1966–75	Overall net change in employment (no.)	(%)
Greater Manchester											
Conurbation	336,292	=	447,606	+	51,192	–	143,272	+	(−19,234)	−111,314	−24.9
Inner Manchester	50,708	=	89,849	+	11,687	–	45,917	+	(−4,911)	−39,141	−43.6
Outer Manchester	285,584	=	357,757	+	39,505	–	97,355	+	(−14,323)	−72,173	−20.2
Merseyside											
Conurbation	168,121	=	169,610	+	26,696	–	30,280	+	(+2,095)	−1,489	−0.9
Inner Merseyside	56,083	=	76,087	+	6,257	–	17,094	+	(−9,167)	−20,004	−26.3
Outer Merseyside	112,038	=	93,523	+	20,439	–	13,186	+	(+11,262)	+18,515	+19.8

19,234 through the shrinkage *in situ* of surviving plants. As table 3.1 also shows, employment created by new entries was far too small to compensate for those massive declines brought about by closure and shrinkage. The loss of jobs through closure was almost three times greater than the jobs gained through new openings. On Merseyside the net decline of 1489 in the conurbation as a whole was produced by an excess of exits over both entries and *in situ* change. Almost 27,000 new jobs were created in new plants, a figure only 3584 short of cancelling out the 30,280 jobs lost in factory exits. However the behaviour of the individual components of change was very different between the inner and outer areas. Inner Merseyside, as we have seen, lost 20,000 jobs between 1966 and 1975. This net loss was made up of a little over 17,000 jobs lost through closure and a further 9000 net loss due to shrinkage of surviving plants. Only around 6000 compensatory new jobs were created in entries. The experience of outer Merseyside was, however, considerably different. Here, more than 20,000 new jobs were created in plant entries, a figure considerably in excess of the employment lost in plant exits (–13,186). Perhaps more striking was the 11,262 net gain of employment in plants which occupied the same location in outer Merseyside in both 1966 and 1975.

Both the increased employment in new entries and the net gain of employment in *in situ* plants in outer Merseyside reflect, primarily, policy-induced movement into the Merseyside special development area. The early 1960s was the most successful period for the impact of industrial incentives policy in Merseyside. Many large new branch plants opened in Speke, Kirkby, Ellesmere Port and the outer area in general. As these grew to maturity in the post-1966 years, they generated a substantial volume of *in situ* employment. As shown elsewhere (Lloyd and Mason, 1979) inter- and intra-regional industrial movement in the 1966–75 period reinforced these differences between Merseyside and Manchester on the one hand and between inner and outer Merseyside on the other.

More than half of all the new openings by firms from outside the North West region went to Merseyside; Manchester's share was less than one-quarter of Merseyside's. In terms of industrial movement within the North West region, Merseyside again stands out as the major recipient while Manchester was the major exporter of plants to Merseyside as well as to south Cheshire. 'Reverse flow', from Merseyside to Manchester, was negligible. An interesting feature of the movement of industry into Merseyside and its region from outside has been the extent to which it has been concentrated in the Runcorn and Skelmersdale new towns, both just outside the administrative county of Merseyside. There has also been a distinct tendency for new investment by mobile industry to seek out the conurbation periphery at such locations as Knowsley, Huyton and Ellesmere Port. However, since 1975, there is evidence that, among this same group of establishments, first opened in the 1960s, redundancies, closures and rationalization replaced what the earlier period reflected as a successful growth phase.

As suggested earlier (see figure 3.3), patterns of manufacturing change in an area over time occur within a particular structure of corporate organization. Table 3.2 summarizes the changing ownership profile of manufacturing industry in the two conurbations between 1966 and 1975. The most striking difference between Manchester and Merseyside as a whole in 1966 was the enormous difference in the extent of local, as opposed to external, control. For the Manchester conurbation as a whole, almost three-fifths of manufacturing employment was in locally head-quartered firms (both single and multi-plant). Although local control was substantially higher in the inner than in the outer area, Manchester's manufacturing population had a strong indigenous element. In stark contrast, Merseyside's ownership profile in 1966 was strongly dominated by externally controlled firms. More than three-quarters of the conurbation employment and almost 90 per cent of outer area employment was externally controlled. As in Manchester, the inner area had a larger local component than the outer. But, again, local control was only half as important in inner Merseyside than in inner Manchester. Within the externally controlled sector, foreign firms were of relatively little importance in Manchester but of very great importance in Merseyside (see Dicken and Lloyd, 1980).

By 1975, the degree of external control had increased somewhat in Manchester to 51.9 per cent overall, but this still meant that one in every two workers (one in two and a half in inner Manchester) was employed in locally headquartered firms. In Merseyside, the degree of external

Table 3.2 Ownership composition of manufacturing employment, Greater Manchester and Merseyside 1966–75

	Percentage of total manufacturing employment										
	Single-plant firms		Multi-plant firms						Local control		External control
			Local HQ		UK HQ		Foreign HQ				
	1966	1975	1966	1975	1966	1975	1966	1975	1966	1975	1966	1975
Greater Manchester												
Conurbation	26.0	19.6	31.4	28.5	38.7	42.8	3.9	9.1	57.4	48.1	42.6	51.9
Inner Manchester	43.9	34.5	30.1	26.3	24.3	33.5	1.7	5.7	74.0	60.8	26.0	39.2
Outer Manchester	21.6	16.9	31.7	28.9	42.3	44.5	4.4	9.7	53.3	45.8	46.7	54.2
Merseyside												
Conurbation	14.5	9.2	7.9	4.9	62.3	60.5	15.3	25.4	22.4	14.2	77.6	85.8
Inner Merseyside	23.4	18.0	13.1	10.3	62.6	65.6	0.9	6.1	36.5	28.3	63.5	71.7
Outer Merseyside	7.3	4.9	3.7	2.2	62.0	59.9	27.0	35.0	11.0	7.1	89.0	92.9

control increased even further: to 85.8 per cent for the conurbation as a whole and to 92.9 per cent for the outer area. Without any doubt, Merseyside had become almost totally a branch-plant economy. As suggested earlier, much of the employment growth in Merseyside between 1966 and 1975 could be attributed to the in-migration of plants. A large proportion of these were branch plants of very large UK and foreign firms.

The new jobs created by such plant openings under government sponsorship were almost exclusively to be found in the outer areas. As Lloyd and Mason (1979) show, over 60 per cent of the new openings of branch plants recorded by the Department of Industry between 1971 and 1976 found their way to Runcorn and Skelmersdale and the bulk of the remainder to peripheral industrial estates. Among the foreign group of firms, in particular, there was a clear tendency to choose sites at the suburban extremities and to avoid the inner area (Dicken and Lloyd, 1980). Since both the UK-controlled and foreign-controlled multi-plant concerns were by far the most successful in employment terms over the 1966–75 period, not only does this tendency underpin the growth of external control in the outer areas, but also it explains their favourable employment growth performance. Of course, this has served only to exaggerate the polarization of trends between the inner and outer areas further and to throw the industrial decline at the core of the conurbation into even sharper relief.

The large-scale losses of employment in Manchester between 1966 and 1975 were primarily in locally controlled firms. Much of this was due to the heavy losses experienced by the local single-plant sector which declined at roughly *double the rate* which might have been expected had it declined strictly in proportion to its share of 1966 employment. Losses of employment in the multi-plant group were also large in absolute terms, though some groups within it fared better than others. The local multi-plant group, for example, was in decline but at a rate more or less in proportion to its expected share. By contrast, the UK-controlled group lost fewer workers than anticipated and the foreign-controlled group expanded sharply (but from a base of small initial numbers). Ownership changes through acquisition and merger accompanied these differential rates of growth and decline. The inner area of Manchester suffered especially heavily from decline among single-plant firms. The demise of small plants in the inner area was a product both of conditions for small business in the general economy and of more localized influences such as the massive clearance programmes associated with redevelopment (Lloyd and Mason, 1978). Over half of the inner area's employment in single-plant firms was lost between 1966 and 1975, representing an important loss of local enterprise as well as jobs. Trends in the locally controlled multi-plant sector were parallel, with the heaviest net losses of these, generally larger, local enterprises also concentrated in the inner city.

These aggregate changes in the various ownership categories mask some important aspects of the dynamics of industrial change. As an illustration, we can examine the contribution of each of the ownership types to the more 'volatile' events in manufacturing change: the entry and the closure of establishments. In the last two or three years there has been an upsurge of interest – both academic and political – in the job-generating role of local firms as opposed to that of the large multi-plant corporation and its branch plants. Interest in this aspect of manufacturing change was much increased by the work of Birch (1979) who calculated that 'around 40 per cent of the birth-generated jobs and 60 per cent of the expansions' in the United States were produced by what he terms 'independent free-standing entrepreneurs'. In their East Midlands study, Fothergill and Gudgin (1979b) assert that job gains were widely spread among plants of different sizes and corporate status. They estimate that 15.1 per cent of all job gains between 1968 and 1975 were in newly formed independent single-plant firms and a further 18.5 per cent of all job gains were in existing single-plant firms which expanded. How were Manchester's and Merseyside's new jobs distributed among different types of firm between 1966 and 1975?

Table 3.3 shows crude entry and closure rates (in employment terms) for the two conurbations by locally and externally controlled categories of firm. For Merseyside, overall entry rates were highly variable, averaging around 1.6 per cent per annum but ranging from as high as 2.2 per cent per annum in the outer area to as low as 0.8 per cent in the inner area. Greater Manchester, by contrast, had relatively uniform overall entry rates across its inner and outer areas. Looking at these same data by way of the corporate control categories reveals a number of interesting additional points. Overall data for both conurbations reveal that entry rates primarily reflect the performance of the locally controlled group of firms and, in particular, the locally controlled single-plant firms. Similarly, within both metropolitan areas entry rates are considerably higher for locally controlled firms than for externally controlled firms. Looked at across the inner and outer sub-components of each conurbation, however, there is a clear difference between conditions in Manchester and those in Merseyside. Locally controlled single-plant entry rates are high both in the inner cities and in the outer areas of the two conurbations, but for outer Merseyside externally controlled establishments also achieve high entry rates.

For crude closure rates (table 3.3[b]) it is clear that here, too, the single-plant locally controlled sector figures prominently. In this respect it is important to emphasize that while many new jobs were indeed created by the first-time births of locally controlled single establishments, the death-rates among such establishments were also extremely high. In Manchester and Merseyside they were more than twice the levels for

Table 3.3   Crude entry and closure rates by corporate control groups, Greater Manchester and Merseyside 1966–75*

| | Average annual rates | | | | | |
| | Conurbation | | Inner city | | Outer area | |
	Greater Manchester	Merseyside	Greater Manchester	Merseyside	Greater Manchester	Merseyside
(a) ENTRY RATES						
Locally controlled multi-plant	0.75	1.33	0.97	1.42	0.70	1.07
Locally controlled single plant	1.95	2.86	1.73	2.12	2.06	4.77
Locally controlled total	1.29	2.32	1.42	1.87	1.25	3.53
Externally controlled total	0.94	1.36	0.95	0.22	0.94	2.02
Entry rate for all firms	1.14	1.57	1.30	0.82	1.10	2.19
(b) CLOSURE RATES						
Locally controlled multi-plant	2.87	2.01	4.76	2.49	2.42	0.64
Locally controlled single plant	4.72	4.87	5.85	4.70	4.14	5.32
Locally controlled total	3.71	3.86	5.40	3.91	3.12	3.75
Externally controlled total	2.51	1.18	4.27	1.29	2.27	1.12
Closure rate for all firms	3.20	1.79	5.10	2.25	2.72	1.41

Notes: * Crude Rates calculated as follows:

$$\text{Entry Rate} = \frac{\text{Manual Workers in New Openings, 1966–75}}{\text{Total Manual Workers in Base Year, 1966}} \times \frac{1}{100}$$

$$\text{Closure Rate} = \frac{\text{Manual Workers in Closures, 1966–75}}{\text{Total Manual Workers in Base Year, 1966}} \times \frac{1}{100}$$

The annual rate is not a 'true' rate. It is calculated simply by dividing the percentage of the 1966 job total lost or gained by the number of years between 1966 and 1975.

new births. While closure rates for locally controlled firms were relatively uniform across both conurbations, there was a significant difference in the closure rates of externally controlled establishments. For Merseyside, for example, closure rates among establishments headquartered outside the region were of the order of 1.2 per cent per annum. For Manchester, on the other hand, externally controlled firms had twice this rate of closure. This difference between the two conurbations was even further exaggerated in the case of the inner city. In fact, the closure rate of externally controlled firms in inner Manchester was in excess of three times that of inner Merseyside and even in the outer area of Greater Manchester closure rates among externally controlled firms were double those of the equivalent Merseyside area. While it is possible to extract much more from table 3.3, it seems appropriate simply to make the point that while the locally controlled single-plant sector did indeed generate a substantial proportion of new jobs created in entries, it was also responsible for vast job losses due to closures.

Table 3.4 summarizes the corporate composition of new jobs generated in new births and firms expanding *in situ* respectively. In the case of new births, locally controlled plants accounted for 41.4 per cent of Manchester's new births' job total compared with 25.9 per cent for Merseyside. Thus almost three-quarters of Merseyside's new birth employment

Table 3.4 Gross new job generation by component of change and by corporate control group, Greater Manchester and Merseyside 1966–75

	Greater Manchester		Merseyside	
	Jobs created	% Share	Jobs created	% Share
(1) *New births**				
Locally controlled plants	12,675	41.4	6,261	25.9
Externally controlled plants	17,913	58.6	17,879	74.1
	30,588	100.0	24,140	100.0
(2) *Firms expanding* in situ				
Locally controlled plants	18,438	40.7	2,980	11.7
Externally controlled plants	26,849	59.3	22,469	88.3
	45,287	100.0	25,449	100.0
Total gross job generation (1 + 2)				
Locally controlled plants	31,113	41.0	9,241	18.6
Externally controlled plants	44,762	59.0	40,348	81.4
	75,875	100.0	49,589	100.0

Note: * Internal relocatees have been extracted

was generated by firms controlled from outside the area. The local–external difference is even more striking in the case of the employment performance of *in situ* expanding firms. In Manchester the externally controlled sector accounted for 59.3 per cent of the new jobs in this category; in Merseyside the percentage was as high as 88 per cent.

It is clear, therefore, that in both conurbations, between 1966 and 1975 much of the growth in employment opportunities generated by expanding firms came from the externally controlled group. The same general picture emerges in the case of new births. In terms of the overall picture, Manchester derived 41 per cent of its job generation from the local sector (much of this came from locally controlled single-plant firms). The bulk, some 59 per cent, came from firms headquartered outside the Manchester area. For Merseyside, which had a much higher proportion of all its firms controlled from outside, the locally controlled sector generated only 18.6 per cent of all new jobs created while the externally controlled sector accounted for 81.4 per cent. While Manchester still retained a substantial body of local entrepreneurship and could still, despite the absence of government incentives, generate new jobs from home-based firms, Merseyside was much more heavily dependent upon the branch plants and externally controlled establishments brought in largely through the impact of regional policy.

It can be seen, therefore, that the patterns of manufacturing change were brought about by rather different groups of corporate actors in the two conurbations. By 1975 it was clear that Manchester was especially vulnerable to shifts in the business climate which created particular disadvantages for indigenous firms, since it did not have the policy status to attract the branch plants of large firms headquartered elsewhere. By contrast, Merseyside had gained a massive number of jobs in externally controlled branch plants because of its special development area status. Its vulnerability was less evident than Manchester's as long as such plants were adding to, or preserving, their employment. Thus, for a period in the 1960s, Merseyside had within its manufacturing population large branch plants in such industries as electrical engineering and motor vehicles which appeared to have better than average employment growth prospects. But the tide began to turn by the mid-1970s. In the general climate of manufacturing over-capacity and retrenchment, the real vulnerability of Merseyside's enterprise mix has become apparent.

Conclusion

In the introduction to this chapter, we proposed a conceptual viewpoint which sees the prime actors whose decisions condition industrial events over any segment of space as an overlapping set of corporate interest groups. Within this set each individual firm behaves and makes decisions in the light of its own interests and it is the multiplier effects of these that 'spin-off' on the local economy. While traditional components of change analysis focuses on the observable events which result from this behaviour, the enterprise viewpoint provides an interface associating such events with the decision-making agencies inspiring them. In the case studies of Manchester and Merseyside that followed we examined this interface, albeit in a largely exploratory manner. To do so we set up a simple taxonomy of industrial firms founded on the single-plant/multi-plant, local/external dimension of ownership. We did not begin, however, to attempt an analysis of the *causality* of decisions and events though we were able to shed light on some issues which, we believe, are important to an understanding of the nature of industrial change in UK metropolitan areas in recent years.

We showed, for example, the degree to which the composition of corporate interest groups may differ sharply between metropolitan areas, largely as a product of their industrial history. Merseyside is essentially an 'open' economy susceptible to extensive multiplier effects from external influences. Manchester, on the other hand, traditionally a headquarters centre and nineteenth-century leader of industrial change, retains some vestige of that role, despite the increasing centralization of corporate control of its enterprises in south-east England. From the viewpoint of the metropolitan community itself such contrasts in the identity of the business interests that control events within it mean that key decision-makers are more or less remote. While the pursuit of industrial success by the combined local interests of business, the scientific community and the body politic was an acknowledged factor in the nineteenth-century growth of cities like Birmingham, Manchester and Glasgow, modern conditions have made such concerted civic action considerably more difficult. For some urban areas, like Manchester, where a body of local industrial control remains, there is at least a limited foundation to build upon. For others, it has become a task devolved to central government and to a growing array of 'image-makers' in local industrial development offices. In this particular respect no greater contrast could be observed than that which exists between Manchester and Merseyside.

Analysis by broad enterprise groups also demonstrated that external control is increasing inexorably in provincial cities as a result of the growing concentration of enterprise in the country as a whole. The rise of the multi-plant, multi-product, multi-locational concern, increasingly well-documented at the scale of the nation as a whole, has a spatially distributed impact which has only recently received much attention. The inner cities, the heart of industrial enterprise in the nineteenth century, have, for example, become candidates for intensive care as the new generation of companies has withdrawn the life-support of new investment. For them, the success of a hundred years ago has come full circle leaving the hardened arteries of congestion, obsolescence and a worn-out infra-structure often made worse by the surgery of redevelopment. A trickle of new, independent enterprise remains but it is often short-lived. On the inventories of contemporary business the capital stock that is oldest and least efficient has a high propensity to be found geographically within the urban core. Decisions to restructure and create slimmer, more efficient concerns in a climate of uncertainty have, thus, contributed to an acceleration of inner area industrial decline.

The new cycle of investment which characterized the aggressively growing multi-plant concerns of the late 1960s also had its spatial referents in the urban context. New investment, often under the sponsor-ship of regional policy, sought out new towns and the suburbs of cities in development areas. While unassisted cities like Manchester continued to experience rapid industrial decline, spatially undifferentiated within the metropolitan area, assisted ones like Merseyside evolved a dual economy with a clear spatial expression. The inner areas, largely ignored by cor-porate location policy, retained the most marginal manufacturing con-cerns. These included both the small, short-lived, independent firm and the most vulnerable of the obsolete plants on the books of corporate business. Industrial closure was the dominant event here, preceded by redundancies and *in situ* shrinkage. For the outer areas, as we have shown, new openings, in-migration and the growth of a branch-plant economy testified to their favoured status as a new location for manu-facturing industry. But as the events of the late 1970s show only too clearly, such treatment did not produce a permanent recovery. Many of the shiny new branch plants injected in the 1960s to development areas such as outer Merseyside have begun to experience severe problems in the harsh circumstances of a turbulent world economy. The closing years of the 1970s have witnessed a whole series of large-scale plant closures or shrinkages on Merseyside, raising the critical question of where the sal-vation of such areas may be found. At present, government thinking favours the small firm – so long neglected by policy-makers – but such enthusiastic espousal of small business seems to be based upon very little real evidence that the marriage will be fruitful.

Note

The work on which this chapter is based was carried out during the period 1976–9 under the terms of SSRC Research Grant HR 4501.

4

Urban employment change

N. A. Spence and M. E. Frost

Introduction

The spatial pattern of employment change in Britain has two main components, as the previous two chapters have shown. The movement of people and jobs to the urban fringe and to the smaller towns beyond the green belts is by now a well-established trend. We also know that population and employment have been growing more rapidly in the southern regions of the country, but these regional processes seem to have affected various types of towns in different ways. In particular, a city's regional location together with its location relative to other city systems is important, and related to this is its size. As a generalization, the larger the urban area, the poorer the change performance for either population or employment.

The purpose of this chapter is to explore employment trends in urban Britain against the background of these two dimensions. It begins by looking at overall employment changes in the national urban system, distinguishing the performance of the three urban zones of cores, rings and outer rings and also differentiating between the experience of the seven largest cities and the rest of urban Britain. In the next section these overall trends are disaggregated by occupational and industrial group, using the same framework, but later in the chapter it is necessary to turn to the somewhat less satisfactory framework of economic planning region subdivisions (the so-called 'planning sub-regions') in order to examine the way in which urban and regional dimensions operate together to produce the patterns of employment change observed.

National employment trends

We begin by indicating some of the principal employment trends affecting urban Britain in aggregate from the early 1950s to the early 1970s.

Crucial for the achievement of such a perspective is a comprehensive and consistent areal base for urban Britain defined on the principles of the urban field or daily urban system linking places of work and residential areas. We use the framework of the 126 Standard Metropolitan Labour Areas (SMLAs) and Metropolitan Economic Labour Areas (MELAs) described earlier in the book (p. xx), embracing the threefold distinction of cores, rings and outer rings. Moreover, because national trends are dominated by events in the largest cities, some parts of the following analysis distinguish between the seven SMLAs with a 1971 population in excess of 1 million people (the so-called Million Cities of London, Birmingham, Manchester, Glasgow, Liverpool, Leeds and Newcastle) and the other 119 areas which make up the remainder of urban Britain.

Against this framework the main features of total employment change are shown in table 4.1. It can be seen that during the 1950s the cores, which contained 60.5 per cent of all employment, received the lion's share of employment growth. The rate of growth in the rings was similar to that of the cores, while employment in the outer rings declined absolutely. The 1960s, however, witnessed a dramatic divergence of core and ring, with the former moving into absolute decline and clearly dominating the overall national trend in employment.

Between the two halves of the 1960s the overall rate of employment growth fell markedly. This downturn was associated with a reduction in the rate of employment decentralization, with employment growth in

Table 4.1 Employment change by urban zone 1951–71

	1951–61		1961–6		1966–71	
	(000s)	*(%)*	*(000s)*	*(%)*	*(000s)*	*(%)*
Britain						
Cores	902	6.7	145	1.0	−591	−4.1
Rings	293	6.6	512	10.8	197	3.8
Outer rings	−14	−0.4	175	5.3	−39	−1.1
Million Cities						
Cores	231	3.1	−243	−3.2	−550	−7.4
Rings	164	8.9	276	13.8	71	3.1
Outer rings	15	2.6	41	6.8	6	1.0
Rest of Britain						
Cores	671	11.2	387	5.8	−41	−0.6
Rings	129	5.0	236	8.7	125	4.2
Outer rings	−29	−3.3	134	4.9	−45	−1.6

Note: The figures relate to the periods stated, so that the changes given for 1951–61 should be halved for direct comparison with the later periods

the rings fálling from 10.8 to 3.8 per cent and that in the outer rings from 5.3 to −1.1 per cent (table 4.1). The net effect of this lower growth on the structure of urban areas was, however, offset by a downward shift in the performance of the cores, which sustained massive job losses after 1966. These figures suggest that employment decentralization during the 1960s was dominated by new employment opportunities created in the metropolitan rings during the relatively buoyant years of the early 1960s and by job losses particularly affecting the cores of the urban system in the latter half of the decade.

Further examination of table 4.1 reveals that, although during 1961–6 employment growth continued to be registered in urban cores as a whole, this upward trend was solely due to growth outside the Million Cities offsetting already significant job losses in the cores of the Million Cities. Again in the later 1960s, not surprisingly, it was the cores of the Million Cities that experienced the most significant job losses. At the same time the Million Cities also saw much reduced rates of employment growth in their rings and outer rings.

A male–female split in employment trends gives some insight into the direct causes of these shifts in the urban system. Indeed, given that one of the most striking changes over this period was the increasing participation of women in the labour force, it would be surprising if this had not had a significant impact on the distribution of total employment between zones, particularly as women tend to work nearer their homes which in aggregate had been decentralizing rapidly. In fact, employment decentralization, especially during the 1960s, can be caricatured in terms of male employment losses in urban cores and the growth of new job opportunities for women in metropolitan rings. Between 1951 and 1961, female employment increased by 205,000 in metropolitan rings compared with only an 88,000 increase of male employment. In the next ten years 514,000 extra female jobs compared with 195,000 male jobs were recorded in metropolitan rings. Female employment was growing in the urban cores, but the increase of 266,000 between 1961 and 1971 was insufficient to offset a 705,000 loss in jobs for men.

The percentage rates of change for the 1950s and 1960s and shifts between the two decades can be seen in figure 4.1. The largest contrast between urban zones in rates of male and female employment change are found in the Million Cities. There are also marked differences between these and other cities in every zone. For example, during the 1950s, male employment was growing most rapidly in the cores of the rest of Britain (9.1 per cent) followed by the rings of the Million Cities (5.3 per cent). By the 1960s this pattern had changed considerably, with the highest rates of male employment growth occurring in the rings of the Million Cities while the cores of other cities began to experience a small loss of male jobs. By this decade, female employment was also declining in the cores

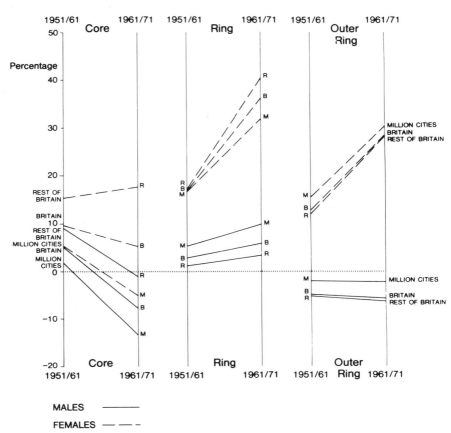

Figure 4.1　Male and female employment change by urban zone 1951–61 and 1961–71

of the Million Cities (–132,000), but growing dramatically in their inner and outer rings. However, in urban cores elsewhere there were significant increases in female employment opportunities (figure 4.1).

National occupational and industrial trends

The most significant feature of the postwar period has been the expansion of office jobs in the national economy – a development closely associated with the rapid growth of female employment in most parts of the urban system. Between 1966 and 1971, for instance, office employment in urban Britain increased by 11.4 per cent, whereas total employment declined by 1.8 per cent, and the proportion of total MELA employment accounted for by office occupation increased from 22.7 to 25.2 per cent. With clerical occupations comprising over three-fifths of all office employment and being dominated by women, it is not surprising that female employment increased rapidly over this period.

Before examining the trends in office jobs in more detail, two points should be noted. First, office employment is an occupation that can be found across all sectors of the economy including manufacturing industry, services and central and local government. Office employment is not just a feature of the financial and business services sector, although in these sectors it admittedly accounts for the majority of employment. As is well known, many of these sectors have different distributions within and between urban areas and have exhibited different patterns of locational change. Furthermore, employment data give no indication as to the organizational status of the workplace concerned; an office manager as recorded in the census may work in a detached city-centre head office of a manufacturing organization or at the production site itself, in a branch office or the headquarters of a building society and so on. The second point to note is that urban cores as defined for this study cover a much wider area than the central business district. In most large cities the urban core contains large inner industrial areas as well as the central business district. As a consequence contrasting trends for these two zones may be concealed.

In spite of these caveats, it is not surprising that office jobs are more important in the occupational structure of employment in the urban core than in all other zones. In 1966 they accounted for 26.5 per cent of all employment in cores; by 1971 this figure had risen to 29.1 per cent. This increase can largely be attributed to the decline in non-office employment in the urban cores. Table 4.2 shows that while total employment in urban cores fell by 4.1 per cent between 1966 and 1971, office employment increased by 4.9 per cent. This increase of office jobs was most pronounced in the urban cores in the rest of Britain *outside the Million Cities*. So in the Million Cities the loss of jobs in other types of employment was not compensated for by gains in the office sector. In fact clerical jobs declined absolutely in the cores of the Million Cities compared with significant increases in urban cores elsewhere. While there was a growth of managerial jobs in the cores of the Million Cities, the rate of increase was less than half that recorded in other urban cores.

Table 4.2 shows that office employment accounted for virtually all employment growth in metropolitan rings. Increases in clerical jobs were absolutely the most important component of this growth: however, in relative terms, the growth of managerial employment in metropolitan rings was more than 10 per cent higher than the growth of clerical employment. Broadly similar trends are apparent in the metropolitan rings of the Million Cities as compared with cities elsewhere, although the growth rates of both clerical and managerial employment were higher in the rings of smaller cities. Even in the outer metropolitan rings, office employment was growing while total employment declined.

Table 4.2   Office employment change by urban zone 1966–71

	Britain		Million Cities		Rest of Britain	
	(000s)	*(%)*	*(000s)*	*(%)*	*(000s)*	*(%)*
Cores						
Total employment	−591	−4.1	−550	−7.4	−41	−0.6
Total office	190	4.9	8	0.4	181	11.3
Clerical	25	1.0	−64	−4.5	89	8.9
Managerial	79	15.6	32	10.7	46	22.8
Other office	86	9.2	40	7.5	46	11.4
Rings						
Total employment	197	3.8	71	3.1	125	4.2
Total office	197	21.5	94	19.9	103	23.3
Clerical	95	18.0	47	16.7	48	19.4
Managerial	44	28.7	21	26.7	24	30.7
Other office	58	24.9	27	23.1	31	26.7
Outer rings						
Total employment	−39	−1.1	6	1.0	−45	−1.6
Total office	68	13.3	13	11.8	55	13.7
Clerical	33	10.5	9	14.6	23	9.5
Managerial	19	23.2	4	22.4	15	23.5
Other office	17	13.5	−0	−0.3	17	18.1

Clearly then, in a period of considerable decline in total employment, office jobs have been a very dynamic component of intra-urban change. Although office occupations have in aggregate contributed to offsetting the loss of other jobs in urban cores, this has been chiefly true of the smaller cities. In the Million Cities only managerial jobs have been increasing in urban cores but even then at a less rapid rate than elsewhere. Thus throughout urban Britain both clerical and managerial jobs have been decentralizing from urban cores to outer metropolitan rings.

Before turning to look at the composition of employment change by industrial sector, it is necessary to mention some limitations of this part of the analysis. First, it is concerned only with the total number of jobs, so the important implications of the differential growth of male and female jobs described previously have to be kept in mind. Problems were encountered as usual in making the industrial classifications compatible for both ends of the time period under analysis; specifically this meant making the 1968 standard industrial classification used in the 1971 Census comparable to the 1958 version used five years previously. This was necessary because it was only for the terminal date that the fine industrial detail was readily available. The result is then a comparable five-year change period 1966–71 based on the 1958 industrial classification at order level. It must be stressed that no account has been taken of the varying levels of unemployment at each census date in this and subsequent analyses. In June of the census years 1966 and 1971, the unemployment levels in Britain were 261,000 and 687,000 respectively. Regional variations in unemployment are likewise ignored.

The changes that took place in employment in British industries over this five-year period were remarkable. Out of the twenty-five orders of the standard industrial classification, only five managed to record growth in urban cores. The three most important were in the service sector, trends in financial, professional and administrative services mentioned before in the context of occupation change being substantiated. Some 375,000 new jobs were created in these three sectors with in addition individual sectors undergoing massive relative growth, for example, professional and scientific services by 15.4 per cent. Only one manufacturing activity, chemicals, grew in employment in core areas, and that only modestly.

In total, urban cores lost close on 600,000 jobs. It was two other service sectors, distributive trades and miscellaneous services, which made a principal contribution to this loss with a decline of around 300,000. Before considering the important underlying causes of this non-basic employment change some mention should be made here of the drift from primary activity, with really quite substantial absolute and relative decline occurring even in urban cores of the nation. In manufacturing almost all industries declined, making up around 450,000 jobs in all. In absolute terms the main components were engineering and electrical goods and textiles, with the latter individually managing to record the highest relative manufacturing decline. Related industries such as metals, metal goods and leather goods, clothing and footwear augmented this decline. Summarizing the dismal fortunes of the nation's central cities, a large decline also took place in the well-known sectoral indicator, construction.

The picture in the nation's metropolitan rings, although mirroring national industrial trends in general, is not by any means the same. As might be expected, much greater absolute decline in the primary sector took place due to its location characteristics. For manufacturing the situation, although not rosy, is not as gloomy. At least most manufacturing sectors grew in employment, with only refractory and leather products declining.

This growth is modest in absolute terms but for individual sectors it does represent a major increase in relative terms with, for example, timber products up by 16 per cent and paper and printing by 9 per cent. So at least some of the massive declines in the manufacturing sectors of the nation's core areas were finding their way into manufacturing growth in the rings. Probably the more important trend, though, was the switch to the service sector. All service sectors grew in the rings with the exception of utilities. Distributive trades of course are directly influenced by population change and even with the clear implications of changing technology and scale in the industry, this sector records growth in the rings. However, it is again the professional, administrative and financial sectors, joined to a lesser extent by the transport and communications group, which recorded the highest growth rates. In all of the first three sectors listed above the relative growth rates were higher than for the core areas. The absolute numbers involved are important too, with close on 200,000 new jobs being created in these sectors. The expected link with the growth in female activity rates in these areas can only be hinted at for the present, but clearly there is a link. The overall result of all of these trends was a growth of over 190,000 in the total employment in the metropolitan ring areas of Britain – a 3.6 per cent improvement to put alongside a 4 per cent deterioration in the nation's cores.

Although the outer ring areas of the country lost employment in total – some 38,000 or 1.1 per cent in fact – they lie intermediate between cores and rings in terms of their change composition. Again decline was heavily dominated by the primary sectors with well over 100,000 jobs lost which in relative terms must have had an important impact. The fortunes in manufacturing sectors were mixed; seven achieved growth and six declined. On balance it was the growing sectors which dominated at a rate of over two to one in terms of jobs. Interestingly it is the important engineering and electrical goods sector (as was the case in the metropolitan ring areas) which was achieving the best performance in absolute terms, making a 16.3 per cent growth. The fortunes of the service sectors were also mixed, three gained and four lost. The former, not unexpectedly, were the principal growth industries discussed previously with the 51,000 extra jobs in professional and scientific services being particularly noteworthy.

The Million Cities/rest of Britain split in the composition of these industrial trends is instructive. Consider the example of industries chosen in table 4.3. Here it can be seen that for engineering it is the performance of the Million Cities' cores which turns growth elsewhere in the cores into massive decline. Similar trends can be seen for the 'other manufacturing' sector with important absolute and relative declines apparent for the large cities although the rest of Britain in this case also did not manage to grow. With textiles the situation was not the same. Declines in the centres of small textile towns of northern England ensured important declines in the rest of Britain – to more than match those in the Million Cities. Distributive services, again a useful reflection of population change, were far more drastic in their declines from Million Cities' cores than elsewhere. On the other hand the two growth service sectors dealing in

Table 4.3 Selected employment change by urban zone 1966–71

	Million Cities		Rest of Britain	
	(000s)	*(%)*	*(000s)*	*(%)*
Cores				
Engineering and electrical goods	−112	−14.5	16	2.3
Textiles	−37	−30.1	−52	−20.4
Other manufacturing industries	−20	−17.3	−3	−3.4
Distributive trades	−163	−15.0	−56	−5.4
Insurance, banking and finance	28	8.5	23	13.3
Professional and scientific services	82	11.2	147	19.8
Rings				
Engineering and electrical goods	−9	−3.7	55	25.3
Textiles	−9	−14.4	−15	−12.9
Other manufacturing industries	3	7.9	11	29.9
Distributive trades	6	2.1	10	3.4
Insurance, banking and finance	10	20.7	8	22.9
Professional and scientific services	49	18.5	63	20.0
Outer Rings				
Engineering and electrical goods	4	7.8	33	18.7
Textiles	−4	−15.7	−12	−10.1
Other manufacturing industries	2	18.5	4	8.3
Distributive trades	−1	−1.8	−16	−4.8
Insurance, banking and finance	3	31.6	7	18.7
Professional and scientific services	12	18.3	38	14.0

activities traditionally thought of as Million City based achieved a much better performance in the other towns of Britain.

Much the same was true for financial and professional services in the metropolitan rings of the Million Cities and the rest of Britain. Distribution was, however, different. Here growth was occurring; what is more, it was faster in the rest of Britain than in the inner commuting hinterlands of the big cities. Similarly with the other manufacturing sector and even more significantly with engineering and electrical manufacturing sectors it was the ring areas of the rest of Britain which were providing the growth impetus. Textiles of course were ubiquitously in decline.

Textiles were also in decline in the outer rings, but interestingly neither engineering nor other manufactures recorded decline in this zone in either city set. At this outer ring scale some decline in distributive trades for cities in the rest of Britain was apparent, perhaps reflecting some centralization of employment consistent with increasing scale in this sector. The other service sectors, being nationally growing, performed well at this scale throughout Britain.

Urban and regional employment trends

In this section we will attempt to indicate some of the principal employment trends affecting the main urban regions of Britain, based on Frost
and Spence (1981). This analysis uses the spatial scale of the sixty-one
pre-1974 planning sub-regions of Britain, which although they do not
permit the same spatial detail as the MELA system, are a convenient unit
of analysis when dealing with disaggregated data. Although these areas
embody some elements of a functional division of space, especially
around the major conurbations, their boundaries do not follow any consistent definitional criteria of this kind. Inevitably then, figures for their
employment change require cautious interpretation. The method used to
illustrate the pattern of sub-regional employment change is the total shift
measurement taken from a shift-share analysis of sub-regional employment for both total employment and the disaggregation into male and
female employment. The results are presented in table 4.4.

The main spatial process that is apparent from the changes in total
employment is the decentralization of jobs from most of the large conurbations to the surrounding areas. The clearest case is, of course, the
decline in employment in Greater London (35) which is matched by a
relative increase in employment in all of the surrounding sub-regions of
the South East. It is arguable whether these jobs themselves were actually
decentralized to other sub-regions but for the purpose of this study it is
clear that Greater London is characterized by a massive reduction in the
number of jobs available within its labour market, whilst surrounding
areas show substantial expansion. The same process can be identified on
a smaller scale for some of the other conurbations, complicated only by
the awkwardness of sub-regional boundaries. Thus, in the North West,
the employment decline of Greater Manchester (15) is clear, but the
identification of the gaining area is more difficult. To the south of the conurbation, South Cheshire (13) shows clear and rapid expansion but the
situation to the north is much more confused with the only really clear
relative growth occurring in Furness (17). In the West Midlands the
pattern is slightly clearer with a marked decline of West Midlands: conurbation (27) matched by a sharp expansion of employment in West Midlands: Central (26). Apart from these changes the sub-regional boundaries
obscure most of the change in other conurbations. West Yorkshire (12),
for instance, has a widely drawn boundary encompassing the conurbation and some surrounding areas while Clydeside (54) is another large
sub-region. However, in spite of these problems it is fair to argue that
most of the major changes in the distribution of employment can be
interpreted as being related to the continuing processes of urban change
in Britain. This is true whether absolute or relative figures are taken, and
within this overall pattern by far the most substantial and widespread

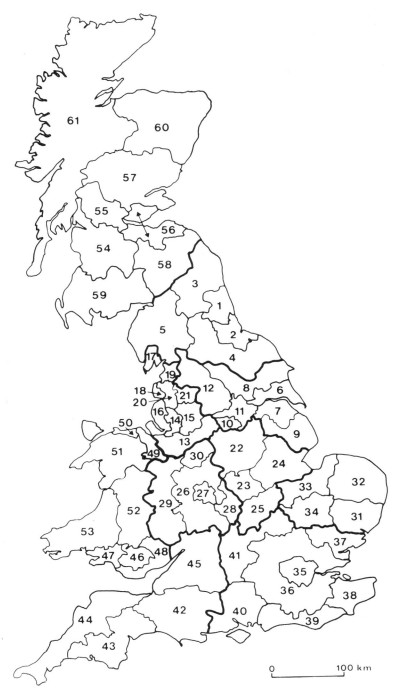

Figure 4.2 Great Britain: regional subdivisions

Note: See table 4.4 for key to numbers

Table 4.4   Sub-regional employment change 1966–71

Sub-Region	Total Shift	Male Shift	Female Shift
North			
1 Industrial North-East: North	−2.2	−3.7	1.5
2 Industrial North-East: South	1.5	−1.3	2.7
3 Rural North-East: North	−4.5	−5.3	0.8
4 Rural North-East: South	1.6	−0.4	2.1
5 Cumberland and Westmorland	0.1	−1.9	2.0
Yorks & Humb.			
6 North Humberside	−1.2	−3.5	2.3
7 South Humberside	4.4	2.5	1.9
8 Mid-Yorkshire	−0.3	−1.1	0.8
9 South Lindsey	3.4	0.9	2.5
10 South Yorkshire	−4.8	−4.2	−0.6
11 Yorkshire coalfield	−0.1	−3.6	3.5
12 West Yorkshire	−3.8	−2.6	−1.1
North West			
13 South Cheshire	4.0	0.8	3.2
14 South Lancashire	−1.2	−2.1	0.9
15 Manchester	−4.5	−3.0	−1.5
16 Merseyside	−1.6	−1.5	−0.1
17 Furness	4.6	2.3	2.3
18 Fylde	−2.5	−2.4	−0.1
19 Lancaster	−0.4	−1.2	0.7
20 Mid Lancashire	1.9	−0.4	2.3
21 North-East Lancashire	−5.2	−2.1	−3.1
East Midlands			
22 Nottingham/Derbyshire	−0.2	−1.7	1.5
23 Leicester	2.7	1.1	1.6
24 Eastern Lowlands	0.1	−2.2	2.3
25 Northampton	6.5	2.9	3.6
West Midlands			
26 West Midlands: Central	6.7	2.8	3.8
27 West Midlands: Conurbation	−3.2	−2.1	−1.1
28 Coventry Belt	−1.6	−2.1	0.5
29 West Midlands: Rural West	−1.5	−3.8	2.2
30 North Staffordshire	−0.3	−0.7	0.4
East Anglia			
31 East Anglia: South-East	4.6	1.4	3.2
32 East Anglia: North-East	4.4	0.9	3.4
33 East Anglia: North-West	6.5	2.6	3.9
34 East Anglia: South-West	10.8	5.2	5.6

Table 4.4—cont.

Sub-Region	Total Shift	Male Shift	Female Shift
South East			
35 Greater London	−4.0	−2.7	−1.4
36 Outer Metropolitan	6.3	2.7	3.5
37 Essex	9.7	4.8	5.0
38 Kent	0.9	−0.8	1.7
39 Sussex coast	4.5	2.2	2.3
40 Solent	8.6	4.4	4.2
41 Beds, Berks, Bucks and Oxon	8.5	4.1	4.4
South West			
42 South-West: Central	3.6	1.5	2.2
43 South-West: Southern	0.3	−0.4	0.7
44 South-West: Western	7.0	3.8	3.2
45 South-West: Northern	2.8	0.9	2.0
Wales			
46 Ind. South Wales: C. & E. valleys	−2.3	−4.2	2.0
47 Ind. South Wales: W. South Wales	2.9	0.2	2.7
48 Ind. South Wales: coastal belt	1.4	−1.0	2.4
49 North-East Wales	2.3	−0.7	3.0
50 NW Wales: North Coast	2.8	1.3	1.6
51 NW Wales: Remainder	−1.8	−4.6	2.8
52 Central Wales	0.7	−2.7	3.4
53 South-West Wales	−3.5	−4.7	1.1
Scotland			
54 Glasgow	−2.5	−2.9	0.4
55 Falkirk/Stirling	−3.6	−5.3	1.6
56 Edinburgh	1.0	−1.7	2.7
57 Tayside	−3.7	−2.7	−1.1
58 Borders	−7.0	−4.9	−2.2
59 Scotland: South-West	−0.8	−1.5	0.6
60 Scotland: North-East	1.8	−0.2	2.0
61 Highlands	3.8	0.6	3.2

Notes: All shifts are percentages of 1966 total (male plus female) employment.
See figure 4.2 for the location of sub-regions

changes are associated with the decline of Greater London and the expansion of the surrounding area.

The next question concerns the broader changes in regional balance. Having identified processes of change at the urban scale, is there any variation left which could be interpreted as a pattern of relative regional change? The key problem here hinges on the definition and use of the term 'regional', and the limits that are placed on what is regarded as the process of decentralization. Over a period of years there has been a tendency to equate the term 'regional' with processes identifiable at the spatial scale of standard regions. This is understandable in view of the quantity of work conducted at this scale. However, it must be done with the knowledge that very few of the standard regions have any functional basis in their areal definition. The Northern region is one of the few that can claim some functional significance in that it enjoys development area status over its entire area, and yet even here assistance to industry is varied by the inclusion of special development areas within its boundaries. Most other standard regions outside the South East, East Anglia and Midlands are more varied than this and with no urban functional basis for their definitions it is difficult to see why or how one might identify common tendencies for employment growth or decline operating over these areas. This problem is further complicated by the need to distinguish between urban in contrast to regional processes in order to respond to the question just posed. For example, in the case of Greater London it is clear from the results of the Department of Trade firm movement statistics that in the period between 1966 and 1971 many establishments moved from Greater London to all parts of the United Kingdom. Twenty-seven moved to the Northern region, thirty-five to the East Midlands and forty moved to Scotland. Which of these is exclusively attributable to processes of urban change and which to processes of regional equalization? In fact, within the East Midlands, over 60 per cent of the establishments moving from the South East (mainly Greater London) went to Northampton, a link that has much more to do with urban rather than regional processes. Of course there cannot be a clear answer to the question as it is posed above when the economic forces associated with the changes are inextricably mixed. However, the lack of an answer illustrates the problems of identifying, particularly in the area bordering the South East, any distinctly regional perspective in a set of figures dominated by processes of change at the urban level.

What is clear from table 4.4 is that there is considerable variation within each of the standard regions. Thus in the Northern region there is a clear tendency for the southern part of the area centred on Teesside (2), and the rural areas surrounding it (4), to show a small but significant employment growth, while the north of the region (1, 3) shows a much sharper tendency to overall employment decline. In Scotland, the North East (60) and the Highlands (61), together with the Edinburgh area (56), show significant growth in relative terms when all other areas are showing decline. In Yorkshire and Humberside the pattern of employment is a very complicated one with quite large gains in South Humberside (7) and South Lindsey (9) offset by substantial losses of employment in the larger centres of West Yorkshire and South Yorkshire (10, mainly Sheffield/Rotherham area). In fact within most of the standard regions, the patterns of change are fairly mixed with little support for any overall explanation of change. This largely confirms the results of Gudgin and Fothergill's (1979) work using Department of Employment information and does not conflict with Keeble's (1976) analysis of manufacturing employment. The results suggest little support, however, for summary explanation in terms of core–periphery, periphery–centre or alternative general models of employment change. Rather, there appears to be a dominant trend of urban decentralization apart from which growth and decline occurs on a very specific basis with considerable differences in experience between locationally proximate sub-regions.

Consider next the difference in performance between male and female employment. National female employment grew slightly between 1966 and 1971, whereas male employment showed a significant fall. This difference is also clear when the male and female components of the total shifts of employment for the sub-regions are considered in table 4.4. In practically all cases the change in female employment shows a greater gain or smaller loss than the corresponding male figure. The only exception to this is North-East Lancashire (21) where the textile industry is a case of a special localized industrial decline with a substantial effect on female employment. Apart from this one case, female employment is consistently more buoyant than male, but the margin of difference between male and female rates of change is something which shows considerable spatial variation. The main conclusion from this variation is a confirmation of the widely acknowledged but not particularly well-documented fact that it is female employment rather than male that provides what slight tendencies for growth are apparent in the development areas and other peripheral areas of the country between 1966 and 1971. In general the differences in growth arising from the two parts of total employment are not great in areas which appear to have benefited from the process of urban decentralization discussed above. Thus in the Outer Metropolitan Area (36) and most other areas of the outer south-east the differences in contribution are only a few percentage points, with the exception of Outer South-East: Kent (38) which behaves differently from the rest of the South East on practically every criterion associated with this study. This contrasts markedly with areas such as the Industrial North-East North (1), the Industrial North-East South (2), North Humberside (6) or Clydeside (54) where substantial differences exist between definite relative growths in female employment, which are more· than offset by considerable relative losses in the male section. This difference which is apparent in the sub-regions illustrates the division between the processes of urban decentralization and regional equalization probably more clearly than the changes in total employment do, showing the introduction of previously inactive females into the labour markets of local economies with only moderate overall growth in the assisted areas. This, of course, will be important in the interpretation of unemployment change in these areas but the division has to be treated with some caution since it is by no means totally clear, the figures revealing more of a continuum of difference between areas such as the South East and the North East rather than a sharp split.

The second main feature of the disaggregation in table 4.4 that merits some comment is the relative size of the male and female shifts. The figures in the table are a little deceptive since changes are expressed as a percentage of *total* employment in 1966 to facilitate the simple and comparable disaggregation of the total shift. This has the effect, however, of concealing the rate of change of female employment in comparison with males as it appears to underestimate the true buoyancy of female change. For example, in sub-region 34, if the two elements of the total shift are expressed as a percentage of the total male employment in 1966 and the total female employment in 1966 respectively, the relative balance of contribution changes dramatically. The male figure changes to 7.7 per cent from 5.2 per cent while the female increases from 5.6 per cent to 17.3 per cent. A similar change would occur in all sub-regions. Clearly if the figures were expressed in this fashion then their additive property would be lost, but this difference demonstrates a feature that runs throughout the figures. This is that, in terms of number of jobs, female employment change has contributed on a more or less similar scale to male in influencing a sub-region's tendency to grow or decline around the national rate of total employment change, with female increases always tending to offset male declines. However, this has been done on much smaller employment bases so that the tendency for greater female growth noted earlier has been transmitted to the sub-regions in the form of a greater propensity for employment change than that shown by male employment. When this is added to the fact that the distribution of female growth appears to be rather more uniform than the male, then it can be seen that female employment in shift terms has had a mild dampening effect on the variation shown by male employment alone. Thus the relative male performances show a greater range of experience from areas of relative decline to areas of relative expansion with female changes smoothing these out a little to produce the relative outcomes seen in the total shift figures.

Urban and regional industrial and occupational trends

The purpose of this section is to illustrate patterns of industrial and occupational change for the sixty-one sub-regions between the 1966 and 1971 censuses. The treatment is of necessity selective in this paper. The total, proportionality and differential shifts are presented in figure 4.3. These demonstrate some of the problems of employing this method to handle

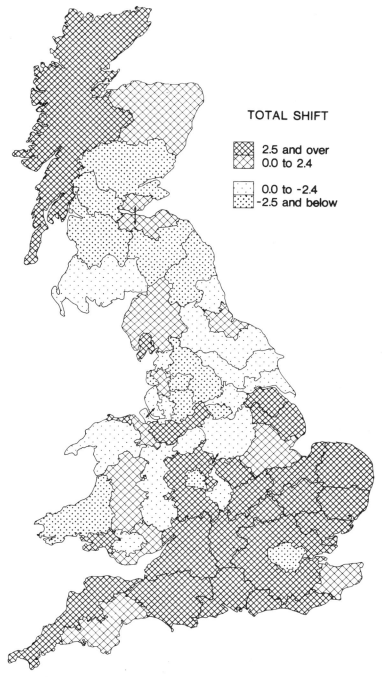

TOTAL SHIFT

⊠ 2.5 and over
⊠ 0.0 to 2.4

☐ 0.0 to -2.4
☐ -2.5 and below

Figure 4.3 Sub-regional employment change 1966–71: (a) total shift (b) proportional shift (c) differential shift

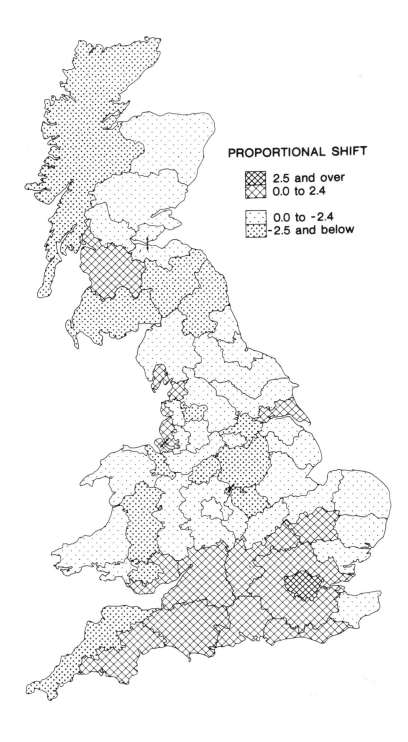

PROPORTIONAL SHIFT

2.5 and over
0.0 to 2.4

0.0 to -2.4
-2.5 and below

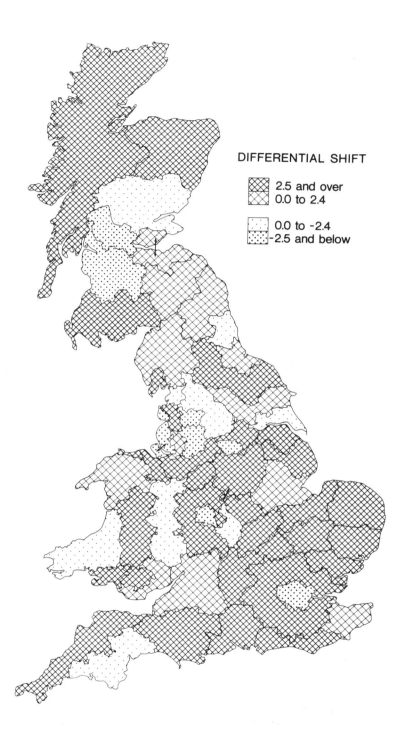

DIFFERENTIAL SHIFT

2.5 and over
0.0 to 2.4

0.0 to -2.4
-2.5 and below

this set of data over this particular time period. The division between the 'structural' and 'locational' effects is not over-useful and merely repeats in another form the evidence of processes of change presented earlier. Thus the dominant force in the differential shift figures is that of decentralization from the conurbations which produces positive shifts in areas like East Anglia, West Midlands Central and the Outer South-East. Clearly the process is occurring irrespective of the industrial structure of the receiving areas. The other main feature of note in the differential term is the effect of the unevenness of decline in the coal-mining industry. Thus the large positive terms of the Yorkshire coalfield (11) and Nottinghamshire/Derbyshire (22) are the result of decline in coal-mining employment, taking place at a much slower rate than the national rate, which was heavily influenced by the considerable reductions in employment in the coalfields of north-east England, Scotland and Wales. Other features of interest are essentially individual occurrences illustrating again the varied and particular experiences of the sub-regions. The relative growth in South Humberside is almost wholly due to the expansion of the steel industry at Scunthorpe, while the relative growth of South Lindsey is largely the result of nearly 11,000 extra armed service personnel being brought in to a predominantly rural area. The experience of South-West Western (44) is also interesting. Here, the substantial apparent growth represented by the differential term is in part the result of the fact that Cornwall is one of the few areas of the country where employment in mining actually increased in this period, in an industrial order totally dominated by coal-mining decline. The lesson of this, of course, is that it is difficult and dangerous to generalize overmuch on the basis of these differential elements.

The proportionality shift figures are much simpler to interpret. In a negative sense they reflect expectations based on the joint decline of mining and agriculture, selecting areas of specialization in these industries. On the positive side they show the dominance of Greater London in employment associated with financial and professional services, this being the only sub-region with a substantial positive 'structural' element.

A more detailed appreciation of sub-regional employment trends requires a disaggregation into primary, manufacturing and service sectors in order to establish in general terms the industrial nature of the total relative employment changes which have already been discussed. From this analysis two dominant and more or less ubiquitous effects on employment structure can be identified. A consistent relative decline of male employment in primary activities is matched against an equally consistent relative increase in female service employment. Between these two extremes are found the more varied performances of male and female manufacturing together with male service employment. Female primary employment is generally too small to be of much interest.

However, manufacturing employment change deserves some more detailed consideration, if only because this aspect of economic change has been more extensively analysed elsewhere with results and conclusions that lie at the roots of this study. In these studies (Moore and Rhodes, 1973) of manufacturing employment change, set in the context of government regional policies, relatively rapid growth was identified in the assisted areas of the country in the second half of the 1960s. This relative change, which was attributed largely to the effects of the government policies, was however identified at the level of standard regions or larger groupings. It is thus worth considering how this change is represented at sub-regional level. Figure 4.4 presents the broad patterns.

First note that comparison with studies at a larger scale is made rather difficult by the movement of jobs away from the larger conurbations mentioned earlier. The clear effect of this change can once again be detected in the sub-regions of the South East and East Anglia together with other 'reception' sub-regions, all of which show marked tendencies to relative growth in manufacturing employment, particularly in male employment. Some caution has to be used here, though, in interpreting a large set of consistent positive shifts since all the changes are percentages of initial total employment in the sub-regions in order to control for differing size. Thus, in the South East region as a whole, Greater London's apparently small drop of 2 per cent is in fact a relative loss of 85,251 jobs, whereas all of the positive changes made by the rest of the region only amount to a relative gain of 77,584 jobs, in spite of some impressive-looking percentage levels. Notwithstanding this, it is still clear that these figures represent major changes in the distribution of manufacturing employment. However, allowing for such changes which are the result of essentially urban change and evolution, rather more remains of interest in these results than was the case with the comparable results for total employment considered previously. This is particularly so if attention is focused on male employment performance (figure 4.4). Here the process of movement towards the peripheral areas of the country, which is identified and discussed at some length by Keeble (1976), is much more apparent. In northern England, Scotland, Wales and south-west England practically all of the signs for relative change are positive with some substantial percentage increases, which are significant even if the bases on which they are calculated are rather small. This process supplements the tendencies to urban decentralization. It leads to a very simple pattern of manufacturing change where all of the significant relative declines in employment take place in the large conurbations or centres of industrial activity with some relative growth occurring everywhere else. Thus only thirteen sub-regions show negative relative performance in male manufacturing employment, and of these the most significant (> 1 per cent) are South Yorkshire (Sheffield/Rotherham), West Yorkshire, Manchester,

PER CENT SHIFT

▨ 3.00 and over
▧ 1.50 to 2.99
▢ 0.00 to 1.49

▢ 0.00 to −1.49
▦ −1.50 to −2.99
▉ −3.00 and below

0   100 km

MALE

FEMALE

Figure 4.4   The contribution of male and female manufacturing employment to total empl-
ment shift, by sub-region 1966–71

Note: All shifts are per cent of 1966 total employment

North-East Lancashire, West Midlands Conurbation, Greater London and Glasgow/Clydeside. Given the nature of sub-regional boundaries this is as clear a pattern as could be expected.

One interesting feature is that the pattern of change is not quite as clear for female employment as it is for male. It must be stressed that female employment in manufacturing is much smaller than male so that the relative changes in distribution are likely to be of far less total importance to the pattern of change than those of males. This is reflected by the generally lower rates indicated by figure 4.4, with exceptions for those sub-regions where concentrated decline in particular female-dominated industries has occurred. The obvious examples of these are in West Yorkshire in wool textiles and tailoring, in the Lancashire cotton textile area and in the woollens area of the Scottish borders. The interest in these figures, however, relates to an earlier finding, that in total employment terms, it was female employment which had provided substantial support to what expansion there was in the assisted areas of the country. The results here show clearly that it is not female employment in manufacturing industry that lies at the foundation of this conclusion but the substantial increases in service employment that have had an impact on the total economies of their areas.

Next, male service employment can be considered to be of critical importance for, although the other changes in male employment yielded interesting and interpretable results, they were dealing with changing shares in a predominantly declining set of industries, in employment terms at least. In contrast, the service sector contains the most rapidly growing activities albeit mixed with service industries showing rapid decline. This heterogeneous collection of activities is reflected in a complicated set of results for relative changes in male service employment. These range from the relative loss by Merseyside (16) which reflects, in part at least, an absolute loss of over 38,000 port-related workers, to rapid growth in Beds, Berks, Bucks and Oxon (41), which seems to have been caused by an influx of 45,700 members of the armed services. Thus these figures are really rather too mixed and unspecific to allow sensible interpretation.

Occupational change of course occurs within the context of industrial change, the two being so closely interrelated (especially in the census classifications) that some consideration must be devoted to both facets of what are fundamentally the same economic changes. Certain orders of the occupational classification do permit the identification of skill or status out of a particular industrial setting. The consideration of whether an industry in a particular area specializes in the employment of skilled, professional or unskilled workers is likely to be of much importance to its pattern of behaviour over time.

Census information on the national structure of industrial employment classified by industry in 1971 and 1966 allows the measurement of the proportion of workers in any particular industry that fall into a specific occupational category for each date. From this it may be calculated how many professional workers, for example, would be expected from the industrial structure of a particular area in either 1966 or 1971 if that area's industries employed professional workers in the same proportion as the industries did at a national level. This, in effect, permits a measure of an area's over- or under-skilling in the occupations employed by its industries. The degree of changing over-endowment or under-endowment of the occupational groups may be calculated as being the change expected in the number within occupational groups which would result from industries in an area behaving in a fashion similar to their national counterparts with respect to their occupational composition. This in effect permits a measure of an area's deskilling or reskilling in the occupations employed by its industries. In essence these figures measure occupational specialization and changes in specialization in the industrial structure of the sub-regions.

Only one category has been selected for illustrative purposes here, with table 4.5 listing the sub-regions where deskilling and upskilling were greatest in absolute terms. The table shows the differential shift components for professional male employment in each area taken from a standard shift-share analysis, together with the deviation between actual change and expected change based on attributing national rates of occupational change to the industrial structures of each area. The surplus/deficit of employment in comparison with national shares applied to each area's industrial structure for 1966 and 1971 is also given.

When considering the pattern of specialization in professional employment the dominance of Greater London is apparent. This is particularly the case in male employment where, in 1966, this sub-region has 65,710 more professional employees than its industrial structure would have suggested. No other area possessed a concentration of this sort, and even the apparent concentration in sub-region 45 (mainly Bristol and surrounding areas) represented only 4,370 extra jobs. Clearly London was dominant in 1966 and the change between the two censuses showed only a slight modification in this position. In 1971 its percentage surplus can be seen to have slipped a little but it is still by far the dominant centre of the country. It is useful here to compare this differential shift component with the deviation controlling for industrial change. The large negative differential effect indicates a poor overall performance in employment terms which is, of course, caused by the processes of movement away from the conurbation discussed earlier. The much smaller deviation expression, however, shows that the poor performance overall has had little effect on the degree of specialization within the industrial structure since the large-scale decline of employment in the capital is absorbed in the change in industrial employment which is excluded from

Table 4.5 Extremes in sub-regional industrial change and occupational structure 1966–71 for Occupational Order 25 Professional (Male)

Sub-region	Differential shift absolute	Actual change minus change expected from industrial change absolute	Actual minus expected from industrial structure			
			1966 absolute	%	1971 absolute	%
Absolute deskilling						
16 Merseyside	−1,723	−3,090	−3,160	−7.6	−6,250	−13.6
15 Manchester	−6,770	−3,140	1,620	2.2	−1,520	−2.0
35 Greater London	−20,459	−2,900	65,710	19.6	62,810	17.4
12 West Yorkshire	−3,841	−1,810	−5,150	−11.1	−6,960	−14.2
27 West Midlands: Conurbation	−5,335	−1,770	−1,980	−2.8	−3,750	−4.9
1 Industrial North-East: North	−885	−1,660	−2,680	−7.2	−4,340	−10.5
6 North Humberside	−1,788	−1,440	−860	−8.0	−2,300	−22.1
Absolute upskilling						
36 Outer Metropolitan	11,427	7,930	7,380	4.9	15,310	8.3
40 Solent	8,953	4,660	−1,620	−4.1	3,040	5.6
54 Glasgow	1,984	3,510	−6,480	−11.5	−2,970	−4.5
45 South-West: Northern	3,201	2,320	4,370	8.5	6,690	10.8
22 Nottingham/Derbyshire	−3	500	−380	−0.9	120	0.3
56 Edinburgh	3,286	1,020	−590	−2.3	430	1.3

the figures in the second column of table 4.5. In the same way it can also be seen that the relative growth of professional employment in the Outer Metropolitan Area (36) is achieved mainly from a great increase in specialization within the industries of the area, and only to a lesser extent by a relative overall growth of those industries.

The full results of this analysis of professional employment shifts have been described by Frost and Spence (1981). They show that, relative to the national rate of change for this occupational order, gains have been recorded by East Anglia, the South East outside Greater London, most of the South West, and individual areas in the East and West Midlands. Significant growth for this occupational group can also be seen in Glasgow/Clydeside, Edinburgh and Tayside (57) but the other striking feature is the uniformity of relatively poor performance in much of northern England, South Wales and even parts of the Midlands. For example, the whole of the northern region shows relative decline whilst only one sub-region from the Yorkshire and Humberside region shows any relative growth. As with the service industry results discussed earlier, these figures suggest a process of concentration rather more than the dispersion found in the change of manufacturing employment.

However the results of this analysis of differentials around the national average do not all follow this simple pattern. For instance, the main centres of employment in Manchester, Leeds, Birmingham, Liverpool and London all show substantial relative losses which must be due, in part, to the general process of decentralization. The degree to which simple expansion or contraction of industry has created the nature and size of the shift elements can be assessed by comparing these with the deviations in the second column of table 4.5. This shows that in many of the large northern cities, together with Birmingham, the poor performance of professional employment was not wholly the result of an overall decline of their industrial bases but also resulted from a clear tendency for what industries they had to have a lower than average expansion of professional employment. Thus the Industrial North-East North: West Yorkshire, Manchester, Liverpool/Merseyside and the West Midlands Conurbation (27) all show significantly poor performances even after the effect of their industrial changes have been taken into account. All except Manchester start the period with a deficit of professional employees and all of them are worse off in 1971. This negative picture contrasts markedly with the performance of those areas which have benefited from the process of decentralization. The full results of this analysis (Frost and Spence, 1981) show that, in areas like South Cheshire, West Midlands Central: Northampton (25) and most of the South East and most of East Anglia, a positive differential component is complemented by positive industrial deviations.

From these industrial and occupational observations, a general view of spatial economic change can be formed. All areas of the country are characterized by a decline in primary employment upon which is superimposed a powerful trend for manufacturing and also clerical employment to move away from the main conurbations, mainly to the surrounding area but also with a longer distance component to the peripheral areas of the country. However, this trend is partially offset by a tendency for the concentration of the more functionally central service employees to be concentrated closer to the main centres but generally not in the conurbation centres themselves. Thus the areas receiving gains from decentralization processes gain both from manufacturing growth, and within and alongside it, the relative growth of high-level service activity. Conversely the urban centres tend to lose on both counts, being supported more by their female performance rather than the male.

The reasons why

There seems to be no one reason why the older metropolitan areas typical of Britain's industrial heartland are in decline while elsewhere some, usually smaller urban systems, are proceeding apace. The process of urban change is clearly multifaceted. Similar observations have been made for the USA, where Berry (1975) has shown that growth has adopted a dual form, focusing on the amenity-rich locations of the western and southern 'rimland' at national scale and at and beyond the outer edges of metropolitan areas on a regional scale. It is therefore instinctive to relate the analysis of the American experience to the position in Britain.

Sternlieb and Hughes (1975) have outlined six components underlying these changes in the USA. First is the 'decline of European immigration'. This is a point specific to the United States and concerns the supply of labour fuelling the commercial and manufacturing functions of the central city. If anything Britain's central cities have received an increased flow of foreign immigrants during the process of decline. Although certain immigrant groups do seem to be responsible for small-scale entrepreneurial activities, for the most part these and other labour skills seem to be lacking from such groups. Second is 'the overspecialization of structures'. This concerns the nature of production infrastructure especially its age, its maintenance, its obsolescence and its efficiency. On all counts the major metropolitan areas score badly, an important explanatory feature of both nations (Goddard and Spence, 1976). Third is 'the stiffening of the arteries of the older areas'. This relates to the inflexibility of the older metropolitan areas to change either in terms of changing land uses or changing industrial labour practices. Also associated with this are the higher levels of welfare dependency, for a variety of reasons, of the population and higher levels of unemployment. Fourth is 'the new automation and rationalization of processes in hitherto labour intensive industries'. Although the overall effect of technological change on employment and unemployment is not fully understood it is clear that certain labour-intensive activities have been replaced by machines with consequent loss of jobs. In addition new employment opportunities generated by the new technologies may not be complementary to existing labour supplies either in terms of skill levels or location. Fifth is 'spatial and labour homogenization'. This notion elaborates on the idea that new areas of production have become highly competitive with the traditional old industrial metropolitan centres. The new productive capabilities are both domestic and international. New technology, especially as it is related to transport, is often the key factor together with wage rates in helping to transform the zones of spatial competition. Lastly is 'the critical mass phenomenon' which relates to markets. In the past the large metropolitan centres benefited so much in this respect, but with the processes of suburbanization and communication improvements of various sorts, specialist services are becoming more dispersed.

So, all in all and to varying degrees, each of the last five points can be applied to the British scene with profitable results in terms of interpretation. The only feature which is rather different on this side of the Atlantic, save for the simple spatial scale of things, is the nature of urban systems regulation through planning. The true impact of the variety of urban and regional planning process in Britain together with the various national planning initiatives having different spatial consequences is not known. But it is difficult to escape the observation that the trends in the two nations, although evolving under much different degrees of intervention, are remarkably similar.

The changing distribution of service employment*

J. Marquand

Introduction

The service sector, however defined, has never attracted the attention of analysts or policy-makers to the same extent as the primary (extractive) sector or the secondary (industrial) sector. It has tended to be assumed that it is capable of looking after itself, or alternatively, that its economic contribution is such that it should not be encouraged, or indeed that it would not be responsive to encouragement. Almost unnoticed, the service sector has grown to the point where service sector *industries* accounted for 57 per cent of the employed labour force in 1977. Already in 1971, an even higher proportion – 61 per cent of those who worked – were employed in service *occupations*. Who are these people? What do they do? What determines where they do it? Does it matter what they do and where they do it? In what ways have their activities and the location of their activities been changing? Do the changes resemble those for manufacturing employment or are the service trends different, reflecting a different set of influences?

In this chapter we examine how far recent work allows us to begin to answer these questions. We look first at the nature of service employment and at its recent behaviour in national terms, before considering some of the main spatial concepts relevant to service location. We examine the light thrown by existing work on the behaviour of consumer services (final services to households) and producer services (intermediate services to firms) in relation to these concepts, in relation to the main trends in the location of manufacturing activity, and in relation to

* Note that the views expressed in this chapter are those of the author and do not necessarily represent those of the Department of Industry or the Manpower Services Commission.

issues of current analytical or policy concern. We conclude, as we have started, with a series of questions. Unlike the questions in this introduction, the questions in the conclusions are related to specific concepts and rooted in empirical work. We know more about the service sector than we tend to think.

What is the service sector?

For practical purposes, the service sector is usually taken to comprise the industries in SIC Orders XXII–XXVII (1968 classification):

XXII   Transport and communication
XXIII   Distributive trades
XXIV   Insurance, banking and financial services
XXV   Professional and scientific services
XXVI   Miscellaneous personal services
XXVII   Public administration.

Similarly, for practical purposes the service occupations are regarded as consisting of the predominantly white-collar occupational orders from the 1966 and 1971 censuses of population:

XIX   Transport communications workers
XX   Warehousemen/storekeepers/packers/bottlers
XXI   Clerical workers
XXII   Sales workers
XXIII   Service, sport and recreation workers
XXIV   Administrators and managers
XXV   Professional and technical workers, artists.

These industrial and occupational classifications evidently overlap, but equally clearly there are some workers in service industries who are not in service occupations and some who are in service occupations who do not work in service industries. In particular, 14.2 per cent of the UK's whole workforce in 1971 were in service occupations within manufacturing industry, while nearly 11 per cent of UK workers held manual jobs in service sector industries. Put another way, just over one-third of those working in manufacturing industries were in service occupations and nearly one-fifth of those employed in service industries held manual jobs. There are even some who are in service occupations on the census definition but are not on an alternative occupational definition used by the Department of Employment for some of its statistics.

Amid this welter of classifications and cross-classifications there is no evident consistent strand. Why is a typist classified as a non-manual worker in a service occupation whilst a typesetter is classified as a manual worker in an industrial occupation? Why is the typist in the marketing department of a firm which makes biscuits – or cars – classified to the industrial sector, whilst the typist in the advertising agency which handles the account of that same manufacturing firm is classified to the service sector? Attempts to provide economic logic for the industrial classification of some industries as service industries have all foundered. (For discussion see Fuchs, 1968; Gershuny, 1978). It is sometimes argued that goods are tangible while services are not, or that services are transitory whilst goods have a longer life. Neither of these distinctions can be sustained; what is less tangible about the repair service provided to the good once it has been sold, than about the final checking of the good before it leaves the factory? And the music written by a composer, the contract drawn by a solicitor, or the ruling made by a judge may all have lives much longer than that of so-called durable goods.

Moreover, the relevant distinction when considering employment is not the distinction between goods and services themselves, but the distinction between the activities involved in the production of goods and the activities involved in the production of services. The example of the typist, or the manager, or the office or factory cleaner, show that many activities are common to the production both of goods and services. Yet there is little more logic to occupational classifications of service activities than there is to industrial classifications of the output of services. It appears indeed that we act as though we think we know a manufacturing or an extractive process when we see one, and hence that we can recognize whether an establishment is predominantly engaged in manufacturing or extractive processes, or construction or provision of public utilities, and classify it to the appropriate industrial sector. Then everything not so specified is in the service sector. We can of course subdivide the service sector itself into those workers concerned with transfer of goods from one place to another or from one owner to another, those concerned with the provision of (non-informational) services to persons, and those concerned with the generation, transmission, transformation and interpretation of information. The last category includes decision-takers of most kinds – although logically of course the chemical worker who relies on information on a control panel to adjust the process also uses information to take decisions about the production of goods and is a decision-taker within this definition too, as indeed is any worker who has any discretion in the performance of his tasks. But, as with the manufacturing process, we are all alleged to recognize the decision-taker when we see one.

Given that service industries are those which are not extractive industries and are those which are not included in the Index of Industrial Production, and that service occupations are those which are predominantly found in service industries thus described, plus office and laboratory occupations wherever found, we can consider various distinctions which may be relevant to the distribution of employment within these industries or occupations.

Two closely linked distinctions which are often drawn are the distinction between publicly and privately provided services; and the distinction between non-market and market services. Whether nationalized industries should be classified to the public sector depends on the purpose of the classification. Wherever they are classified, they belong in the sector providing market services. These apart, with only a few self-financing exceptions the public sector provides non-market services, whilst the private sector, except charities, provides market services. (Bacon and Eltis (1976) have ignored the market/non-market distinction, and written about all services as though they were outside the market. In practice, about two-thirds of services employment is in market services (see Central Statistical Office, 1977)). The location of market services will be related closely to the needs of the market; the location of non-market services may be determined by other considerations. Where non-market services are intended to provide a direct service to persons, social costs and social benefits rather than private costs and private benefits may enter into the locational decision-taking process. Where non-market services have other, institutional, clients a whole range of political and administrative factors may enter into decision-taking about their location.

The clearest examples of administered decisions about location in the non-market sector lie of course in decisions about the location of the armed forces, and in decisions about the dispersal of certain functions of central government departments. We shall see that the distribution of these service activities, unlike that of almost all others, exhibits no simple spatial regularity.

Within the market sector, a common distinction is that between 'basic' and 'induced' activities. It is sometimes held that activities which strengthen the balance of payments position of an area in respect of other areas are the 'basic' activities which are a prerequisite for that area to move towards self-sustaining growth at acceptable levels of income and employment. If an area is well supplied with basic activities, as local expenditures rise so other activities will be induced within the area; there is no need to make explicit policy provision to encourage them. Although it is a gross oversimplification to identify manufacturing with basic activities and services with induced activities, it is an identification which has often been made, or used as a justification for policy discrimination against services.

It is in practice difficult to identify whether a given service firm is a potential contributor to the net export position of an area. Thus, although the concept is one which merits serious examination, an alternative distinction discussed by Greenfield (1966) and Smith (1972), that between firms which provide (intermediate) services to other firms, and firms which provide (final) services direct to consumers, is in fact easier to use in examining trends in service location. It is probable that firms which sell their services to other firms can potentially contribute, directly or indirectly, to the net export position of the area where they are located *vis-à-vis* all other areas. It is less clear that firms which sell services to local consumers can contribute in this way. Whether sufficient of them are always 'induced' into a particular area and whether they perform any economic role beyond that of satisfying the local market are questions which we shall pursue.

The course of service sector employment

The growth of service sector employment, whether classified by industry or occupation, has been rapid during the past two decades. Employment in service sector industries overtook that in production industries (SIC Orders II–XXI) in 1965 and was over a third as much again by 1977, when the former accounted for 13 million of the UK's workers compared with 9.3 million in production. Only in the service industries has employment been growing, up by 28 per cent between 1960 and 1977 in contrast to declines by 47 per cent and 16 per cent in agriculture and industrial production respectively. Female employment has contributed very strongly to the growth in the service sector, rising by 48 per cent during 1960–77 compared to an 11 per cent increase in male employment and causing the number of men employed in service industries to be overtaken by the number of women in the early 1970s. Much the same picture is presented by the growth of employment in service occupations. No data are available later than the 1971 Census, but the growth over 1961–71, at 13 per cent, is identical with the 13 per cent growth in employment in service sector industries over 1960–70.

Table 5.1 looks more closely at the growth of employment in service industries between 1960 and 1973. An attempt is made to distinguish between consumer service industries (marked C), intermediate services supplied to producers (marked I) and mixed producer and consumer services (marked M). Predominantly public sector services (marked P) are also shown. It can be seen that employment growth was concentrated overwhelmingly in producer (intermediate) services: forty-six industries (Minimum List Headings) were examined; the fastest growing quartile and the slowest growing or fastest declining quartile are shown. Seven of the eleven fastest growing industries comprise six out of the seven industries included in the insurance, banking, financial and business services SIC Order. The declining services are mainly a collection of consumer and mixed services, overtaken by technological change which either reduces the demand for their product (repair of boots and shoes, laundries,

Table 5.1 Fastest and slowest growing industries 1960–73 and 1973–6

Bank position	1960–73 (UK)	Employment 1973 as % of 1960	1973–6 (GB)	Employment 1976 as % of 1973
15 fastest growing services				
	(Note: 3% leads to 147 over 13 years)		(Note: 3% leads to 109.3 over 3 years)	
1	*I Other business services	270.1	C Other miscellaneous services	125.9
2	I Central offices	214.7	C Sport and other recreations	120.9
3	M Air transport	200.0	I Research and development	114.4
4	C Other miscellaneous services	180.3	C,P Medical and dental services	113.3
5	C,P Education	177.6	C,P Education	113.2
6	I Other financial institutions	170.8	I Banking and bill discounting	112.7
7	I Advertising and market research	168.4	I Central offices	111.8
8	I Miscellaneous transport and storage	167.1	I Miscellaneous transport and storage	111.0
9	C Betting and gambling	166.1	C Clubs	110.7
10	I Property owning and managing	157.1	I Accounting	110.1
11	I Banking and bill discounting	155.7	C/M Catering contractors	110.0
12	I Research and development	150.8	C Public houses	108.8
13	C,P Medical and dental services	146.8	C Hotels and residential establishments	107.2
14	C Public houses	146.3	I Dealing in other industrial materials	107.1
15	I Other professional and scientific	145.7	P National government service	106.8
15 slowest growing/fastest declining services				
46	C Repair of boots and shoes	35.3	C Repair of boots and shoes	78.3
45	I/M Port and inland water transport	53.7	I Wholesale distrib. of petroleum etc.	80.0
44	M Railways	54.2	C Laundries	83.0
43	C Laundries	55.2	I Road haulage contracting	86.3
42	C Dry cleaning, dyeing etc.	57.7	C Dry cleaning, dyeing etc.	89.3

41	M	Sea transport	66.4
40	C	Retail: food and drink	78.8
39	C	Road passenger transport	79.9
38	I	Dealing in coal/oil/builders materials	80.1
37	C	Cinemas, theatres, radio	85.7
36	C	Religious organizations	97.0
35	I	Wholesale distribution of food/drink	100.4
34	C	Hairdressing	101.0
33	C	Hotels and residential establishments	104.6
32	C/M	Catering contractors	107.0

M	Sea transport	89.3
I/M	Port and inland water transport	91.0
C/M	Motor repairers, garages etc.	94.5
I	Other financial institutions	94.9
I	Advertising and market research	95.3
C/M	Restaurants, cafes, snack bars	96.5
C	Retail: food and drink	96.6
M	Postal services & telecommunications	96.7
C	Religious organisations	96.8
I	Dealing in coal/oil/builders supplies	96.9

* *Note:* C – Consumer service industries
I – Intermediate services supplied to producers
M – Mixed producer and consumer services
(See page 103 for explanation.)

dry cleaning) or by technological change in processes, reducing the labour required for a given output (port and inland water transport, railways, retail sales of food and drink).

The corresponding occupational changes over the period 1966–71 show fastest growth among administrators and managers (Occupational Order XXIV) and professional and technical workers (Occupational Order XXV), with their employment up by 20.7 per cent and 15.8 per cent respectively, a long way ahead of the next Order (XXI: clerical workers) at 4.6 per cent. Within the two most dynamic occupational orders, the occupation with the greatest growth, both in numbers and proportionately, was the residual category 'Scientific and engineering workers not elsewhere classified', which includes systems analysts, computer programmers, safety officers and time-and-motion-and-methods officers. These, along with other rapidly growing groups such as mechanical engineers and managers of most kinds, will largely be employed within the secondary Index of Industrial Production industries sector. Together with the growth of employment in the insurance, banking, financial and business services industries, this pattern of growth in employment suggests a picture of an economy adapting the processes and upgrading the level of expertise used in production both of goods and producer services, creating significant numbers of jobs in new occupations between one census and the next.

In the period since 1973, it would seem that this has changed. Table 5.1 shows that employment was growing fastest in a collection of consumer services and in the public-sector provision of health and education. Employment in research and development, central offices, and banking and bill discounting was still growing by 3–4 per cent each year. The earlier boom in the growth of central offices has, however, slackened to reach only this rate, and the rate of growth of the various other business services, which were among the fastest growing industries in the period to 1971, has slackened still further.

No information is available for the period since 1976 to judge whether this change in trend has continued, but casual observation suggests that it probably has. There are two contributory factors, but we do not know how much weight to attach to each. First, there is the general slackening of growth in the economy as a whole, which implies a slower rate of growth in the industries which provide the customers for producer services. Secondly, there is the impact of technological change upon service employees, particularly office employees. The less skilled clerical workers are increasingly being replaced by various forms of automated data processing. In the most recent period, the need for typists, previously immune to major technological change, is being reduced by the introduction of word processors, and almost every office occupation is likely to be affected sooner or later by the microchip revolution.

Thus in future we may see an increase in the hard-to-measure output of office services and producer services generally, both to the limited extent that overall economic growth takes place and because the nature of that growth is likely to entail increased reliance on the input of higher level services whether within the manufacturing firm or outside it. But we cannot predict that this growth in output will be associated with any corresponding growth in employment. Employment in the most highly skilled occupations is likely to increase, or at least not to diminish. Employment in the less skilled producer service occupations is likely to grow significantly only if we are slow to adapt to technological change.

Because aggregate statistical data is scanty and out of date, and because technological possibilities are changing rapidly, formal forecasting techniques tell us little about likely future employment trends. But there are numerous studies of the likely consequences of the effect of microprocessors and other major innovations, particularly in telecommunications, which affect office work. These studies include, for example, reports by Acard (1978), the Department of Employment (Sleigh *et al.*, 1981) on microprocessors, and work on the impact of telecommunications (Clark, 1979; Goddard and Pye, 1977; Goddard, James, Marshall and Waters, 1980). They all provide further details to support the same general picture.

The outlook for consumer services is equally unpredictable. A first response to table 5.1 would be to argue that consumer services will expand in employment to take up some of the slack left as employment in manufacturing and perhaps even in producer services starts to decline. This would be too facile an interpretation. Let us leave aside public sector employment, growing rapidly till 1976 but less rapidly since then, since the rate at which such employment grows depends in the first instance on decisions about the rate of growth of public expenditure, and only in the second instance and more indirectly upon measures of need for the services provided. For consumer services in the private sector, the rate of growth of employment depends mainly on the rate of growth of demand for the services in question. In the short term, this depends largely on the rate of growth of the incomes of consumers. Cross-section studies (Marquand, 1979, ch. 2) show the marginal propensity to consume most kinds of services rising as incomes rise. In a period of little growth in real incomes, there will be little increase in the demand for consumer services. Moreover, if such growth as is achieved arises from much higher productivity of those who are employed, unless major social changes take place to spread employment more widely through the population, the dichotomy between the high incomes of those in increasingly productive employment and the lower incomes of those unemployed may widen. To the extent that the production of consumer services does not share in the technological advances likely to take place in the production of goods and producer services, the relative price of consumer services will rise, leading to a lower rise in employment there than the general increase in incomes might lead one to expect.

In the longer term, the outlook is more problematic still. Gershuny (1977) has argued that we are witnessing the growth not of the service economy but of the self-service economy. Consumer demand for services over periods of decades rather than years does not rise relative to demand for goods. Instead the pattern of change, over the postwar period at least, has been that the relative price of consumer goods which provide services for their owners has fallen, demand for them has risen and demand for the services which they replace has fallen. The washing machine has replaced the laundry; the car has replaced the bus and the train. The television set has replaced the cinema and the cassette recorder the concert. In addition, as housing standards have risen, so that the home could become the subject of increased attention, and as the relative price of formally provided labour-intensive goods and services has risen, we have seen the growth of the informal economy and the black economy. The exact nature of these trends, the structure of suppliers' preferences as between formal work, informal work and leisure, the way in which the same people viewed as consumers like to spend their time, all need the deeper examination which Dr Gershuny is giving them. But the general lesson is clear: we cannot take for granted the continued expansion of employment in consumer services as projected by the extrapolation of past trends, even when variations in conventional variables such as the growth and distribution of real incomes are taken into account.

Forecasting is a high-risk activity. When information is scanty, as with the service sector, it is particularly hazardous. The lack of information by occupation, the arbitrary (or managerially determined) division between producer services organized within the larger firm and producer services bought into it from separate producer service establishments, and the uncertain impact of known changes in technology, all combine to make forecasting of producer service employment particularly difficult. Consumer service employment is scarcely easier to forecast. Here the complicating factors are the shifting dividing lines between buying in goods which yield services and buying the services directly, and the changing consumer preferences between formal work, informal work and leisure, as well as the usual uncertainties about the likely growth of real incomes. (Some discussion of the hazards is found in Gershuny, 1978; Marquand, 1979a. Some careful forecasts are found in Robertson, 1980.) This shifting background suggests that it may be equally hazardous to attempt to analyse changes in the spatial distribution of services. In practice, we shall see that the spatial trends are more clearly explicable and perhaps more predictable than the trends in the overall growth of service activity.

Table 5.2 Concentration ratios[1] – comparison of 1971 with 1966 using Hannah–Kay indices, 126 MELAs

		exponent (α)			Comment: 1971 in comparison with 1966
		1.001	1.50	2.00	
Population	1971	58.2	33.9	21.2	More dispersed
	1966	56.1	32.0	19.9	
Employment	1971	52.1	28.3	17.1	More dispersed
	1966	50.6	27.3	16.6	
Industries					
Transport &	1971	35.7	16.1	9.5	More concentrated
Communication	1966	36.6	17.0	10.1	
Distributive Trades	1971	50.3	26.8	16.2	More dispersed
	1966	47.3	24.9	15.1	
Insurance, banking &	1971	23.3	9.1	5.4	More dispersed
financial services*	1966	22.1	8.6	5.3	
Professional services	1971	50.6	26.9	16.1	More dispersed
	1966	48.6	25.2	14.9	
Miscellaneous services*	1971	45.8	22.1	12.6	More dispersed
	1966	43.6	20.5	11.7	
Public Administration	1971	49.6	25.6	14.8	More dispersed viewed from lower end but more concentrated viewed from top end of distribution
	1966	49.2	25.6	14.9	
Office occupations					
All office occupations	1971	36.1	16.4	9.5	Much more dispersed
	1966	33.7	14.9	8.8	
Clerical workers	1971	37.1	16.8	9.8	Much more dispersed
	1966	33.6	15.0	8.9	
Administrators &	1971	36.6	16.4	9.6	Much more dispersed
managers	1966	33.9	14.9	8.8	
Remainder (mainly	1971	33.3	15.3	8.8	More dispersed
professional workers)	1966	33.3	14.6	8.5	

Notes: * On 1966 definition.

[1] Concentration ratios of the form $n(\alpha) = \left(\sum_i s_i^{\alpha}\right)^{\frac{1}{1-\alpha}} \alpha > 0, \alpha \neq 1$ where n is the number of MELAs, s_i is the share of MELA i in total population or total employment in the relevant industry or occupation, and where α takes a range of value from (in this case) 0.75 to 2.25, were estimated. An increase in $n(\alpha)$, the 'numbers equivalent' ratio, between two dates indicates a decrease in concentration. If there is an increase for every value of α, the decrease is unambiguous whether the larger or the smaller MELAs are given a heavy weighting in the calculation of the concentration ratios. In particular, where $\alpha \rightarrow 1$, the ratio becomes the Theil entropy index of concentration $n(1) = \sum_i s_i \log s_i$, where the smaller MELAs carry more weight. When $\alpha = 2$, the ratio becomes the Herfindahl index of concentration $n(2) = \dfrac{1}{\sum_i s_i^2}$ where most weight is given to the largest MELAs.

Changes in the distribution of services

We can start by looking at an analysis of the concentration of services between the 126 Metropolitan Economic Labour Areas (MELAs) in 1966 and 1971. A powerful method of estimating concentration ratios, which allows us to determine unambiguously whether one set of observations is more concentrated than another, or whether concentration of a given activity has increased or decreased over time, whatever the weighting attached to the different portions of the distribution, is that developed by Hannah and Kay (1977). Table 5.2 uses Hannah–Kay indices to show the comparison of concentration of employment in service SIC Orders and in service occupational orders across the 126 MELAs between 1966 and 1971. With the exception of transport and communication (also the only Order where overall employment fell between the two dates), increased dispersion was apparent in all the other categories examined. Admittedly, for public administration, there was movement both to disperse activity towards the smallest MELAs – perhaps a consequence of changes in the location of local government services – and to concentrate it in the largest – presumably the effect of the growth of national government employment. For all the other categories, the increase in dispersion was unequivocal, whatever weighting is given to the MELAs at either end of the distribution. The wider dispersion in 1971 by comparison with 1966 is particularly marked for office occupations, especially clerical workers, and administrators and managers.

How are we to interpret this widening dispersion? Is it a consequence of movement of service activity out of London and the larger conurbations into the less heavily urbanized areas? Is it a consequence of relatively greater growth of new or already established service activities in the less heavily urbanized areas? Is it a consequence of policy, or does it in effect run contrary to the directions which policy has been trying to impose? Has it continued beyond 1966–71? This is after all only a short period which ended over ten years ago. The evidence for more recent years is scantier, but none the less we can attempt to set it in context and to examine it in relation to some of these issues.

In the 1970s the previous pattern was maintained. Between 1971 and 1977 service sector employment grew by nearly 12 per cent, while employment in the production industries declined by more than 8 per cent. One characteristic which became more marked in the 1970s was the growth of part-time employment among women, with almost two-thirds of the 1.2 million increase in service sector jobs between 1971 and 1976 being provided by this source (Harris and Taylor, 1978). None the less, even when full-time equivalents are used, growth is found to have been recorded by all sectors except transport and communications and by male as well as female employment (table 5.3).

Table 5.3 Change in full-time-equivalent employees in the service sector, UK 1971–6

	Males		Females	
	absolute change (000s)	% change	absolute change (000s)	% change
Transport and communication	−91.7	−7.1%	−8.0	−3.3%
Distributive trades	11.0	1.0%	0.2	0.0
Insurance, finance and banking	59.2	12.7%	47.0	10.8%
Professional and scientific	158.9	17.0%	334.5	21.4%
Miscellaneous services	63.4	7.7%	139.0	17.2%
Public administration	22.8	2.3%	83.9	18.7%
Total	223.6	4.0%	596.6	12.9%

Source: Robertson (1982) table 28

We know something about the spatial distribution of this overall growth, both inter- and intra-regional. Analysis by MELAs after 1971 is not possible, but Damesick (1979) has examined sub-regional changes in service employment for 1971–6. He finds that the South East took a declining share of national employment in services in 1971–6, entirely because of loss of jobs in Greater London, which was not fully offset by the gains in the rest of the region. All other regions except the North West recorded increased shares of national employment in services. This pattern suggests that the movement out of the large conurbations, already observable in the 1966–71 comparison, may lie at the root of the observed changes in regional patterns.

However, until data for functional areas become available, we cannot judge with confidence how far changes in the service location generally match the pattern observed in chapter 2 by Fothergill and Gudgin for manufacturing industry, involving greatest relative decline in the conurbations and with proportionate increases in employment becoming greater the more rural the area examined. Because many service activities, especially office activities, tend to take place in or near the centres of cities, it is unlikely that any such effect would be as marked as it is for manufacturing. Some examination of the question is possible for the period from 1971 to 1977, using county changes in employment by SIC Order.

Figure 5.1 shows percentage change in total service employment by county (England and Wales) and region (Scotland). The areas with below-average increases included five of the eight main conurbations – Greater London, West Midlands, Manchester, Merseyside and Strathclyde – but the other areas with low growth are a very diverse collection. Apart from

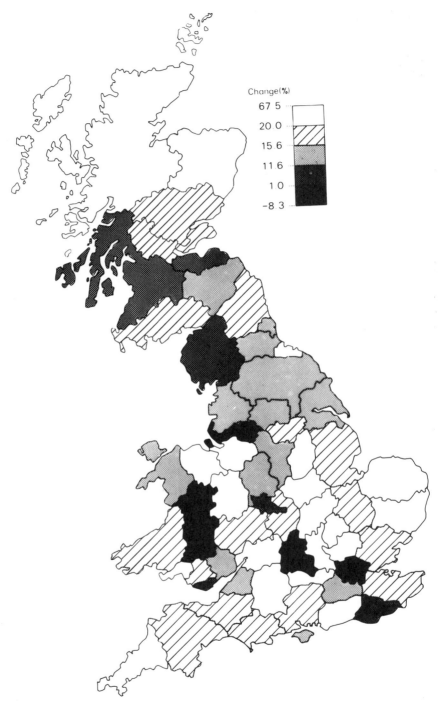

Figure 5.1 Change in total service employment by county 1971–7

the areas directly associated with North Sea oil, the main area of growth has lain in a belt on the north of London, stretching from Berkshire in the south to Nottinghamshire in the north and to Essex and Suffolk in the east.

The pattern of greatest growth for individual service sectors varies slightly. For the crucial insurance, banking, financial and business service sector, shown in figure 5.2, the belt of greatest growth stretches from Hereford and Avon in the west, south to Dorset and east to Essex, Suffolk and Cambridgeshire. The only conurbations with below-average growth are Greater London, Greater Manchester and Merseyside. The growth of miscellaneous services, for example, is much more dispersed than this, with the fastest growth in Orkney, Shetland and Grampian, followed by Northumberland, Clwyd and Oxfordshire. But the dominant pattern for most service sectors is the same, with the greatest growth taking place within about 100 miles of London (although not in London itself) and also in the areas directly associated with North Sea oil. Whilst some of the conurbations, above all Merseyside, London and Manchester, but to a lesser extent Strathclyde and the West Midlands, are consistently among the counties with low growth, there is not nearly such a striking urban–rural distinction as found for manufacturing employment trends over similar periods by Fothergill and Gudgin in chapter 2 or by Keeble (1980). Instead, we have a strong bias in new service activity broadly towards the non-assisted areas of the country, if the boundaries prior to July 1979 are taken, with the glaring exception of London. Yet we know (Goddard and Pye, 1977; Marquand, 1979a) that the observed cost advantages to such a location, mainly communication cost advantages, are very small.

Beyond this brief account of gross service employment changes, we know almost nothing of recent trends in service sector behaviour. Whereas for manufacturing industry there are numerous studies of the components of employment change for particular areas or conurbations, for the service sector no major databanks have been compiled and only a handful of such studies exist. For office employment, we have Damesick's (1979a) floor-space analysis by sub-regions, which extends to 1974. He finds that inequality in the distribution of office floor-space in England and Wales declined significantly during this period (by 5.4 per cent using a Theil entropy index), but that this reduction arose almost entirely from reductions in the inequality of the distribution within regions rather than any inter-regional change, except for a small decline in the share of floor-space in the South East arising from the substantial decline in the proportion of floor-space in Greater London. This proportionate decline none the less represented an increase of office floor-space of 28 per cent compared with a national average increase of 38 per cent. The greatest increase, 60 per cent, was found in the rest of the South East.

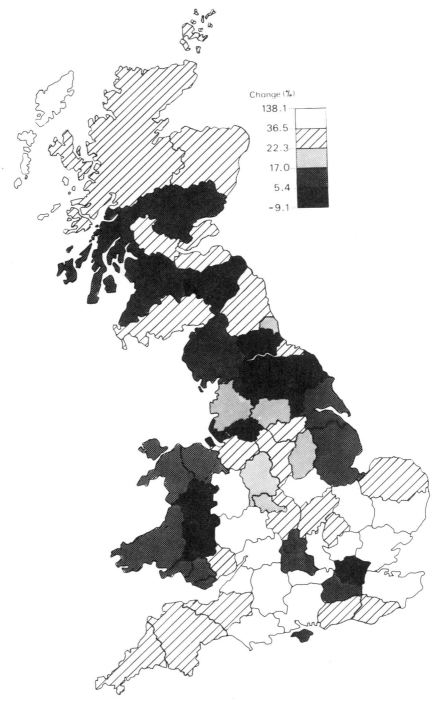

Change (%)

138.1

36.5

22.3

17.0

5.4

-9.1

Figure 5.2 Change in employment in insurance, banking, financial and business services by county 1971–7

Although 'within region' inequality in the distribution of office floor-space declined on balance during 1967–74, the trend was not the same in all regions.

> The most notable reductions in intra-regional concentration were recorded in the South-East, West Midlands and North-West. In the first two of these regions the trend towards dispersal was accounted for by straightforward relative decline of the London and Birmingham conurbations respectively; in the North-West, however, the reduced geographical concentration was due to the relative decline of Merseyside, with the second largest floorspace stock in the region, while the Manchester conurbation actually increased its proportion of the regional total. In the Northern Region, Yorkshire and Humberside, Wales and the South-West the level of 'within region' inequality increased from 1967–74, indicating a relative concentration of floorspace growth in and around the major urban centres in these regions. (Damesick, 1979a, 163–4)

Finally, Damesick finds that

> the expansion of office floorspace 1967–74 in relation to total subregional employment in 1971 . . . showed a significant tendency to be greatest in areas with an occupational bias towards managerial and professional workers and of high urban centrality; these attributes also characterised the most important areas of office development in absolute terms in this period to a high degree. (Damesick, 1979a, p. 194)

In a detailed examination of office location in the Manchester conurbation, he shows however that the increase in office employment took place not in central Manchester (where office employment declined from 1966–75) but in outer parts of the conurbation; the overall increase in office floor-space was not matched by a corresponding increase in office employment, but rather by a change in its location.

For services in particular areas, the most substantial databank is that compiled by Hughes and Price (1977), covering service industries in Glasgow. Only a limited amount of analysis has been undertaken; it shows net natural growth in all parts of the city, but with lowest birthrates of establishments in the core and lowest death-rates in the outermost ring. The majority of moves of establishments took place within Glasgow itself.

Other components of change studies of service cited by Lever *et al.* (1979) cover only parts of cities. They comprise Gripaios's work (1976, 1977) on parts of South East London, Damesick's work (1979a, 1979b) on offices in Manchester, and Blake's work (1978) on relocation in Liverpool. On this limited evidence, Lever *et al.* (1979, 35–6) comment:

> The patterns of change bear striking similarities to those for manufacturing although with a few notable differences. The services sector, for example, has been growing nationally, unlike manufacturing, so that the number of establishments and employment has generally increased even in the inner city. The higher birth rate in other parts of the conurbations, however, has produced the same net effect as that for manufacturing, namely relative decentralisation. Again, as with manufacturing, movement of establishments plays a relatively minor role and is less important than *in situ* change. Overall, however, the extent of decentralisation of service activities is less marked than in manufacturing with many sectors showing a continuing affinity for central locations.

We have seen from figure 5.1 that the London, Manchester, Merseyside and Glasgow conurbations are among the counties of slowest growth in service activity in the country. Thus it cannot be taken for granted that their pattern of decentralization from central districts to outer districts, recurring more because of differential birth- and death-rates of establishments than because of relocation by existing establishments, and with most relocation taking place over only short distances, will hold true for areas other than these major conurbations. But that most moves are over only short distances holds for manufacturing too, whether within or outside conurbations (Howard, 1968; Nunn, 1980; Pounce, 1981). Moreover, wide differences between birth-rates and death-rates in particular conurbations and areas larger than conurbations, together with other *in situ* change when employment rather than number of establishments is considered, appear to be a more important influence on manufacturing employment change than is movement (Marquand, 1980a).

In respect of employment change and change in the number of establishments within the region, it would appear then likely that service industry follows much the same patterns of change as manufacturing, albeit with employment still growing on balance rather than declining. It is the broad inter-regional patterns of employment change which differ. Some of the possible explanations can be eliminated quickly. None of the many studies of the effect of the substantial regional incentives for manufacturing industry suggest that these have sufficient influence to account for this difference in pattern (Marquand, 1980a and, especially for directly relevant analysis, Keeble, 1980), while the service industry grant scheme is many times smaller, with total cumulative payments of £7.9 million by March 1979, compared with £192 million in payments of grants of other regional selective assistance to manufacturing industry over the same period and £1870 million for regional development grants.

Admittedly Office Development Permit policy was in active operation throughout the period, more active than IDC policy in terms of refusals, but even so these ran at an average rate of only about thirty each year after 1970, and it would appear that more than half those refused subsequently obtained permission to locate in the controlled areas (Wettmann *et al.* 1979). Thus neither the carrot nor the stick was strong. Since directly observable costs associated with more distant locations are not high (Rhodes and Kan, 1971; Goddard and Pye, 1977; Marquand, 1979a), unless these marginal differences have an apparently disproportionate effect, much of the explanation must lie elsewhere.

There are two main candidates for this explanation, which are not incompatible. Their relative importance cannot begin to be resolved without more knowledge of the organizational structure of service industry. We do not know what proportion of service industry in general, or of new service industry, comprises branch plants of multi-site firms, and what proportion is independent single-plant establishments. Probably, as with manufacturing, there is a dual economy, with single-plant establishments closely linked to the area where they are found, whilst multi-plant establishments have a much wider choice of location. Possibly it is the latter which are growing fastest in the area relatively near to London. Possibly, especially for them, but also for plants where higher level services are particularly important, the weight placed on ease of maintaining communication links is much greater than is suggested by the attempts objectively to measure the costs involved. Possibly or even probably, the rapid growth of service activity relatively near London is associated with the growing concentration of headquarters in the South East, with merger reducing the level of decision-taking at more distant plants (Goddard and Smith, 1978). Possibly the rapid growth of some higher level service activity is associated with the relative ease of communication from the South East to the main European Golden Triangle and elsewhere (Dunning, 1979; Erlandsson, 1979; Marquand, 1980b).

But all these possible explanations remain little more than speculation until we know much more about the nature of the service activities which are growing; their occupational, locational and organizational structure, their perceived reasons for locating where they do and the disadvantages they perceive to locating elsewhere. Only when we know more about these matters can we begin usefully to consider whether policy should or could be used to encourage services, especially higher level services, to locate more widely throughout the country.

Whilst there is no data to allow more detailed analysis over time, we can gain some further understanding of the determinants of service behaviour by looking closely at characteristics of the distribution of services in 1971, as indicated by population census data. We start with some hypotheses.

Spatial analysis of services: the relevance of functional areas

There are two main strands of theory concerning the location of service activities; information diffusion theories and hypotheses loosely derived from central place theory. The former strand (see Pred, 1971) and works cited there) argues that the ready availability of relevant information is the crucial determinant of the location of service activity, service activity within the secondary sector as much as service industry itself. The more important the part that information linkages play in the day-to-day life of the firm, the more important ease of contact becomes as a determinant of its location. Higher level managerial and professional activities in particular are heavily dependent on receiving and often emitting a rich mix of information. Such activities will tend to cluster at points where communication with the sources and recipients of information is easy. Thus the theory predicts clustering in major centres of such activities, which will be predominantly some producer services and the higher level service occupations within the secondary sector. A relevant factor in determining clustering in one centre rather than another will be ease of transport and communication between the centre and its hinterland and between the centre and other major centres. More generally, the theory predicts increased clustering of the relevant services, the richer a centre becomes in the relevant contacts. As a first approximation, we might indicate this by the amount of employment in the centre in question. More refined indicators might be restricted to particularly relevant types of employment, but such indicators have not been developed and used in the work reported here.

The second approach does not take special account of producer services; indeed it is usually taken, whether explicitly or by default, to apply only to consumer services. It is derived loosely from central place theory, based on the work of Christaller (1966) and Losch (1967). The essential underlying hypothesis is that there is a minimum necessary size of market for each service sector activity. Activities for which this market is small will be very widely dispersed; as markets become increasingly specialized, so the appropriate services are provided from fewer centres. Thus a hierarchy of cities is generated, each step in the hierarchy containing progressively more specialized service activities in addition to the activities found in cities of lower order. This account is of course oversimple; it has been shown (for example, see Berry, 1967a; Beavan, 1977) that simply ordered hierarchies rarely exist; different clusters of services may be represented in different cities of similar order in the hierarchy. The account begs the question of whether it is necessary for a service to be located near its customers, and assumes implicitly that there is a minimum effective unit of provision for each type of service. Both of these assumptions may hold more closely for some services than for others. Whether they hold can be tested empirically.

Both these approaches, if they are to be tested, presuppose that we can draw boundaries to city areas which will distinguish the area dependent on one metropolitan centre appropriately from the area dependent on the next. We must not assume that the standard economic planning regions are appropriate spatial units for the analysis of service sector location. Likewise, it cannot be taken for granted that smaller administrative areas comprise appropriate units. When we examine the spatial distribution of service sector activities, we are concerned with the spatial distribution of places where people work. Thus travel-to-work areas, indicating the boundaries of labour supply, would appear to be of some relevance to the provision of services.

Travel-to-work areas are of course relevant to the distribution of secondary activities as much as of services. But the converse, which may loosely be regarded as the travel-to-shop area, is peculiar to consumer services, a subset of all service sector activities. As a first approximation, we shall assume that functional areas based on travel-to-work flows can appropriately be regarded as travel-to-shop areas too.

Whether analysis can be pursued at this particular level of disaggregation depends on the availability of appropriate data. For the United Kingdom, 1971 (and 1966) Census data are available on the basis of Metropolitan Economic Labour Areas. The 126 MELAs cover less than 65 per cent of the area of Great Britain, but include some 96 per cent of the total population. Subject to the qualification that each MELA is allocated to that economic planning region where its core is found, the MELAs can be aggregated to economic planning regions.

The validity of conclusions drawn on the basis of areas delimited according to a particular set of criteria depends, perhaps crucially, upon the relevance and logical consistency of the criteria applied. Those adopted in producing MELAs have been subjected to critical scrutiny, first by Kennett (1978a) and more recently, as part of a major exercise in designing functional areas on a logically consistent basis by Coombes, Dixon and Openshaw (1979). In compiling their new classification, this team started from a critique of the 1971 MELA system. Thus their observations, based on a consistent computerized analysis, can be used to illumine the detailed results of analysis of 1966 and 1971 service location using the 1971 MELA classification as a basis.

The location of service activity in 1971

We can start by examining the 1971 distribution of service activity in some detail, before considering how this distribution has been changing over time. We start by examining the extent of concentration of different activities.

Table 5.4 Concentration ratios (Hannah–Kay indices) – industrial groupings 1971, 126 MELAs

Industrial groupings	*MLH*	*Exponent (α)*		
		1.001	1.50	2.00
Producer and Mixed Services, in order of concentration viewed from the top end (α = 2.00)				
Business services	864, 865, 866	14.4	5.6	3.7
Business and personal services, of which:	860, 861, 862, 863, 709	22.6	8.8	5.3
Banking	861	22.2	8.4	5.1
Insurance	860	23.7	9.7	5.9
Professional services	871, 873, 879	27.6	11.2	6.6
Communications	708	32.1	13.7	8.0
Transport (producer services)	703, 704, 705, 706, 707	33.9	16.3	9.9
Wholesalers and dealers	810, 811, 812, 831, 832	39.9	19.9	12.1
Transport (mixed)	701, 702	42.9	21.6	12.8
Public services (footloose)	901	43.8	22.9	13.7
Research	876	30.6	20.3	15.1
Consumer Services, mainly in order of concentration viewed from the top end (α = 2.00)				
Public service (non-footloose)	872, 874, 906	53.6	29.7	18.1
Retail trade	820, 821	53.9	29.8	18.1
Various consumer services	875, 881, 882, 883, 886	45.4	21.7	12.4
+	888, 891, 893, 895, 899			
Various mixed services, of which:	884, 885, 887, 892, 894	56.4	31.7	19.1
Cinemas, etc.	881	16.0	6.2	3.9
Laundries etc.	892, 893	42.7	21.2	12.4
Restaurant	885	47.0	23.6	13.8
Religious organizations	875	49.6	25.1	14.5
Hairdressing	889	56.9	31.8	19.2
Hotels	884	53.0	31.2	19.5
Pubs and clubs	886, 887	55.4	32.8	21.0
Sport and betting	882, 883	55.8	32.9	21.0
Motor repairers, etc.	894	60.3	35.8	22.3
For comparison:				
Employment		52.1	28.3	17.1
Population		58.2	33.9	21.2

Notes: 'Numbers equivalents' – higher values indicate wider dispersion
      The lower the value of *α*, the more weight is given to the smaller MELAs
      See table 5.2 for details of concentration ratios

In table 5.4, Hannah–Kay concentration ratios for a range of different service industries in 1971 are shown for a range of producer and consumer services. A clear distinction in locational behaviour emerges between producer and consumer service industries. No producer service (except research, 'numbers equivalent' 15 when $\alpha = 2.0$) has a 'numbers equivalent' greater than 14 when $\alpha = 2.0$ or greater than 44 when $\alpha = 1.0$. No consumer service (except cinemas, theatres, etc.) has a 'numbers equivalent' less than 12 when $\alpha = 2.0$ or less than 43 when $\alpha = 1.0$. Several consumer services (public services including education, health, local government; retail trade; hairdressing; hotels; public houses and clubs; sport and betting; and motor repairers and garages) are more evenly distributed than employment itself, and one (motor repairers and garages) is more evenly distributed between MELAs than is population. The distinction between producer services in general, concentrated especially in the larger MELAs, and the much more widely dispersed consumer services, is unmistakeable.

In table 5.5 the concentration ratios for a selection of occupational groups are shown. All the highly qualified occupational groups concerned with providing services to industry, or indeed found within industry, or contributing actively to the dissemination of industrially relevant information, are highly concentrated in the largest MELAs, with concentrations comparable to those of the producer services in table 5.2, except university teachers and miscellaneous professionals, who are indeed more widely dispersed than employment itself. The dispersion of clerical workers closely resembles that of managers; the dispersion of scientific and technical support workers closely resembles that of the scientists and engineers whom they support.

By contrast, the dispersion of mainly public sector workers serving the local population is much wider (table 5.5). Social workers are an exception. They are clustered in the larger urban areas to about the same extent as the group of ten consumer service industries taken together which is shown in table 5.4. Other public sector workers, in education, in fire and police services, and above all in the health service, are very widely dispersed indeed between urban areas of different sizes – although less widely dispersed than some consumer services, than employment itself or than population. Support is provided for the prediction of information diffusion theory that it is information-rich activities in particular which will be found to cluster in the larger urban agglomerations.

Regression analysis can illumine the locational pattern further, and allow analysis of the concentration of particular industries in particular MELAs. Regression analysis postulating an exponential relationship between the amount of employment in a particular service occupation or industry, and total employment or population in a particular MELA, is to

Table 5.5   Concentration ratios (Hannah–Kay indices) – Occupational Groupings 1971, 126 MELAs

	Exponent (α)		
	1.001	1.50	2.00
Various occupational groups relevant to 'contract-richness' in order of concentration viewed from the top end (α = 2.00)			
Authors, journalists, actors, etc. (206, 207, 208)	18.7	6.9	4.3
Trade and professional associations	17.9	7.8	4.9
Accountants	24.1	9.6	5.8
Managers (public admin.) (173, 174)	26.4	10.1	5.9
Legal services	25.7	10.4	6.2
Surveyors, etc.	31.8	13.7	8.0
Company secretaries	33.3	14.3	8.4
Managers (private sector)	37.7	17.3	10.2
Scientists and engineers	44.2	23.4	13.3
University teachers and misc. prof.	53.8	29.1	17.4
Supporting services:			
Clerical workers	36.7	16.6	9.7
Scientific and technical support workers	45.4	23.3	13.7
Mainly public sector groups:			
Social workers	43.1	21.2	12.5
Fireman and police	48.9	27.8	15.5
Health	52.6	28.7	17.3
Education	48.5	27.6	17.5
For comparison:			
Employment	52.1	28.3	17.1
Population	58.2	33.9	21.2

Notes: 'Numbers equivalents' – higher values indicate wider dispersion
The lower the value of α, the more weight is given to the smaller MELAs
See table 5.2 for details of concentration ratios

be preferred to regression analysis postulating a linear relationship, which will emerge as a special case from the exponential relationship if it is indeed appropriate.

Residuals from the regression analysis enable us to determine the extent to which individual MELAs are 'over' or 'under' endowed with particular services by comparison with the overall national relationship. The exponential regressions in practice produce a balanced scatter of residuals which allows the concept of relative over- or under-servicing to be applied to MELAs outside London, whilst the linear regressions

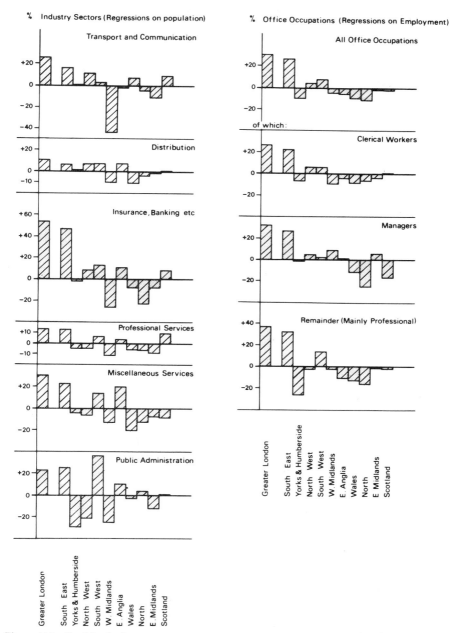

Figure 5.3 Residuals from exponential regressions as a proportion of actuals, by region and industry

equivalent to the estimation of location quotients make the whole of the country outside London appear to be an under-serviced desert (Marquand, 1979b).

Figure 5.3 shows the patterns of residuals from the exponential regressions for the industrial and occupational orders, with MELAs aggregated into the standard economic planning regions. London, and indeed the South East as a whole, appears to be extremely well-endowed with services. So, to a lesser extent, are the South West, East Anglia and Scotland. The West Midlands above all, and to a lesser extent the northern region, Wales, the East Midlands and Yorkshire and Humberside are poorly endowed with services of almost all kinds. The North West presents a mixed picture.

Looked at sector by sector, a different story emerges (figure 5.3). The South East is unduly well-endowed with every kind of service activity, but the selection of other regions which is well endowed varies from one industry to another. For transport and communications, it is the North West, Scotland and Wales. For the distributive trades, it is the North West, the South West and East Anglia. For the important insurance, banking, financial and business service order, it is the South West and East Anglia, followed by the North West and Scotland. For miscellaneous services, it is East Anglia and the South West. Professional services are dominated in quantitative terms by the public sector health and education services; they are found disproportionately in Scotland, the South West and East Anglia. Public administration, located by administrative decision as far as central government is concerned, is found disproportionately in the South West especially, but also in East Anglia and the northern region.

Office employment in general, and employment of clerical workers, is high only in the South West and the North West. But managerial employment presents a different pattern, perhaps partly reflecting the location of industry rather than services, with over-representation in the West Midlands, the East Midlands and the North West. Outside the South East, other (mainly professional) office workers abound only in the South West.

Crum and Gudgin (1977) have analysed the distribution of non-production activities in UK manufacturing industry in 1971. Whilst many workers in 'non-production' activities are office workers, Crum and Gudgin's work goes wider, to include all workers in tertiary occupations in manufacturing industry. Table 5.6, derived from table 3.1 in their study, shows that, when allowance is made for the effects of industrial structure, the South East is overwhelmingly the region with more than its share of non-production workers in manufacturing. The East Midlands and the South West have slightly more such workers than expected on the basis of their industrial structures. In crude quantitative terms the

Table 5.6 Regional disparities in non-production employment 1971

Region	Actual employment (000s)	Residual employment (000s)	Structural effect (000s)	Differential effect (000s)	Differential effect as % of actual employment
North	137.6	−40.9	7.0	−47.9	−34.8
Yorks & Humb.	246.8	−27.2	−21.0	−6.2	−2.5
East Midlands	184.5	−16.0	−22.9	6.9	3.7
East Anglia	68.1	−6.6	3.9	−10.5	−15.4
South East	981.6	+242.0	41.0	201.0	20.5
South West	149.9	+4.1	1.8	2.3	1.5
North West	387.4	−54.8	7.1	−61.9	−16.0
West Midlands	354.9	−28.7	−20.2	−8.5	−2.4
Wales	97.5	−27.7	−2.1	−25.6	−26.3
Scotland	215.5	−44.2	5.5	−49.7	−23.1
Great Britain	2823.8				

Source: Derived from Crum and Gudgin (1977) table 3.1

Note: The residual employment is the difference between actual employment and expected employment if regions had national proportions of non-productive workers in each industry, divided into a structural effect because their industrial structure differs from the national one, and a differential effect

deficiencies elsewhere are greatest in the North West, Scotland and the North. Expressed as a proportion of manufacturing non-production employment, the deficiencies are greatest in the North, Wales and Scotland. Either way, the general pattern resembles that for services as a whole except that the relative position of Scotland appears worse. Although these regional patterns of endowment with services conceal wide variations in employment in the individual MELAs within a region, none the less they provide a picture of where the strengths of the service sector as an employer lie. Scotland and the North West emerge as important subsidiary centres of service employment, with the main centre comprising the area to the south and east of the Severn–Wash line. Within each of these areas, we shall see below that service activity tends to be concentrated within the larger urban agglomerations, producer service activity more than consumer services.

Much of the regional variation in endowment with producer services, particularly office services, arises from variations in organizational structure. Crum and Gudgin (1977) show that if regions are standardized for the proportion of plants belonging to multi-regional companies, much of the disparity in levels of office employment disappears. In particular, the North West and the northern regional disparities are largely explained in this way. However, as James (1978) points out, this is not the

whole explanation; branch plants in the northern region still have proportionately fewer office workers than branch plants in the nation as a
whole. This may be a function of technology; branch plants in the
northern region are typically rather large, and it may be that careful
standardization for industrial structure would remove the anomaly.
Alternatively, the explanation may lie in a relatively low degree of managerial autonomy, with a greater lack of representation of some of the
range of managerial functions than in other regions.

By contrast, the over-representation of non-production workers in
manufacturing in the South East, in addition to over-representation of all
the service industries themselves, is associated with the great and growing concentration of headquarters of multi-regional and multinational
companies in that region (Goddard and Smith, 1978). Functions such as
general management, marketing, research and development, public relations, legal services and sales tend to be concentrated at or near to head
offices and hence in the South East. Together with the concentration of
such functions at or near headquarters, there is the tendency for branch
plants to make use of such headquarters functions rather than go to local
business service firms. It is the headquarters rather than the branches
which draw on such specialized services. Thus Burrows and Town (1971)
found that 90 per cent of head offices and independents used outside
business services directly, compared with only 60 per cent of branch
plants. Similarly, Marshall (1979c) found that it was mainly independent
firms in the northern region which made use of services in the area. With
the concentration of headquarters in the South East, we should not be
surprised to find a corresponding concentration of business services in
the same region.

We can use 1971 Census data to examine the location of producer
services in more detail, and in particular to attempt to relate it to the
urban structure rather than simply examining broad regional differences.
Already, in the sixteenth century, Vasari could comment that 'it is
Nature's custom, when she creates a man who really excels in some
profession, often not to create him by himself, but to produce another at
the same time and in a neighbouring place to compete with him' (quoted
in Burke, 1972). The same comment holds good today. Information-rich
producer services and the industries which depend on them will, if these
information links are indeed important, tend to be clustered together in
areas within which the exchange of information is relatively easy. To test
this, some sweeping simplifications have to be made to identify approximately the information-rich industries and occupations. We have to
ignore some important questions, concerning for example the impact of
modern communications, communication costs, and the nature of business travel (Goddard and Morris, 1976; Goddard and Pye, 1977; Marshall, 1977; Goddard, James, Marshall and Waters, 1980). The heroic

assumption that contact richness is proportionate to employment could be modified, but has none the less been made in the work reported. And we have to assume that the areas taken for the analysis are appropriately defined. This last assumption is discussed in the section after next, when consumer service location is examined.

Given all these simplifications and assumptions, one would expect that producer services in general, and information-rich activities in particular, would be located more in relation to employment than in relation to population, and that the concentration of such services will be disproportionately greater in the larger functional areas. A correlation analysis of the relationships between employment in a range of (producer and consumer) service industries and activities and employment and population by MELAs produced good fits except in two cases, namely research and public administration (central government). Apart from these two exceptions, the coefficients of determination (R^2) exceed 0.70 (for 126 observations). This extreme goodness of fit is by no means a consequence of the form of the relationship fitted; similar regressions fitted for employment in all other (non-service) SIC Orders produced no correlations as great as this. Although most of the correlations are in fact significant at the 1 per cent level for non-service industries as well as for service industries, such a result is indeed to be expected from the form of the relationship; what is worthy of remark is the uniformity with which the service industry employment relationships with total employment were closer than those for the non-service industries.

A close relationship of service employment with local levels of employment or population (themselves closely related) is indeed the peculiar characteristic of services. The correlation analysis also showed that the distribution of producer services and occupations is more closely related to employment than to population. The difference in fit is only small, but it is consistently in the direction predicted, for all service industries and occupations which can confidently be regarded as predominantly producer service activities.

The slope of the regressions indicates significant clustering in the larger MELAs for some producer service industries and several producer service occupations. Employment in transport services to firms, in wholesaling and dealing, and in business services, is significantly clustered (at the 5 per cent level of significance). Similarly, clerical workers, accountants, surveyors, architects and town planners, and legal services are found predominantly in the largest MELAs. There is some presumption, although only a weak one, that the same may be true of certain other occupations, such as managers, scientists and engineers and their support staffs, authors, journalists and actors, etc, and trade and professional associations. The only 'information-rich' occupation perversely distributed in relation to size of MELAs is that of university teachers (combined with miscellaneous professionals). This undoubtedly reflects the policy decision to disperse universities widely, often to small towns rather than major cities.

The relationship of service employment with size of MELA is certainly compatible with the broader regional description of the distribution of service employment. However, it also shows that it is essentially only the South East that is well-endowed, and that there are few individual MELAs outside the South East and the South West, and to a lesser extent the East Midlands and the North West, which are abundantly endowed with workers in higher level service occupations. The distribution certainly remains compatible with predictions based on theory.

Why the distribution of producer services matters

We have noted the variations in the pattern of endowment with producer services, but we have not asked whether it matters that the distribution of these activities is uneven. In an age of rapid technological change, what is particularly important about certain producer service activities are that these provide the source and the mediators of that change. Various managerial and technical activities within firms, whether in the secondary or the tertiary sector, and various producer services which the firm may purchase in one way or another, such as research and development, business services of various kinds, and management and technical training, are the means whereby technological development and improvements in managerial methods are incorporated in the activities of firms up and down the country. Of course, not all producer services are of this kind, loosely and inadequately grouped together sometimes as 'quaternary services' (to do with information) or as 'higher managerial and professional services' (which include various other activities too). For the purposes of this argument, we are scarcely concerned with such producer services as transport of goods, wholesaling, and provision of cleaning services to firms.

Any discussion of the role of producer services in growth has to start from the growing body of evidence that the comparative advantage of the developed world lies increasingly in products which are human-capital intensive rather than physical capital intensive (Steinherr *et al.*, 1977; Freeman, 1979). Comparative advantage lies not only in being ahead of the game, but also in keeping ahead of the game. Ability to see new opportunities and to seize them rapidly is the most valuable ability to have. And nearly all the occupations relevant to development and rapid adoption of technical and managerial change are service occupations, with the relevant activities organized sometimes within the manufacturing firm, and sometimes in separate service sector organizations.

For innovation in particular, the links in the chain are becoming reasonably well-documented. That there are links between innovative activity and competitiveness in international trade has been recognized for nearly two decades (Vernon, 1970). More recently, Pavitt (1979, 1980) shows an association not only between national shares of world innovative activity (measured by US patents) in eleven OECD countries and national shares of manufacturing exports, but also between per capita innovative activities and per capita exports. He shows moreover that there is a close relationship between the growth of innovative activity and the growth of national manufacturing productivity, which cannot be explained by the greater or lesser success of national policies to produce growth.

It sounds plausible that what holds for the relative rate of innovation between countries may also hold for the relative rate of innovation between regions. The argument where technology is concerned has been set out by Thwaites (1978), and fuller accounts of possible regional factors in influencing the rate of technological change are found in Ewers and Wettmann (1979) and Goddard *et al.* (1979). Empirical evidence is provided by Oakey, Thwaites and Nash (1980) who have analysed the regional distribution of innovative manufacturing establishments in Britain. It was already known that R and D activity was heavily concentrated in and near the South East (Buswell and Lewis, 1970); Oakey, Thwaites and Nash show that the same is true of significant product innovations over 1975–8, which tended both to be produced in the factory where they were first specified. The distribution of production between the South East, other mainly non-development area regions and the three main development area regions of the North, Scotland and Wales was in the approximate proportion 2:3:1. Manufacturing employment is distributed between the same areas in the proportion $1\frac{1}{2}$:3:1, thus suggesting some over-representation of the South East where first introduction of innovations is concerned.

When Oakey, Thwaites and Nash (1980) related the regional structure of the adoption of innovations to the regional proportion of non-production workers per industry as given by Crum and Gudgin (1977), they concluded (p. 247) that

While great caution should be maintained in interpreting these results there appears to be a very close relationship between the expected levels of innovation based on the regional structure of non-production employment and the actual levels of innovation discovered in the research study. . . . The possession of a very advantageous structure of non-production employment in the South East which may produce a high level of innovation could be the result of the increasing concentration of control of British manufacturing industry in this same region in recent years (Goddard and Smith, 1978). As a result the higher order functions associated with decision-making and inventive activity have been centralised in and around London (see also Buswell and Lewis, 1970; Leigh and North, 1978).

If there is some presumption that higher level non-production activity within the firm is crucial to the production of innovations, and perhaps (though this is still to be investigated) to the rate of diffusion of new technologies, then it is of crucial importance to establish what is required for the growth of such activities within the regions. We can distinguish between multi-plant firms, where the problem is to persuade them to locate technically advanced activities in their various regional branches, and indigenous one-plant establishments, where the problem is to determine what is needed to encourage or enable them to respond rapidly to new technological developments and new market opportunities. Ready access to appropriate information and to supplies of appropriate expertise would appear likely to be part of the answer; how big a part we do not yet know.

Finally, we need to consider the clustering of higher level information-rich resources on a broader level than the regional or even the national one. Many such resources are internationally mobile; we should look at higher level service activity at least on a European basis. The clustering round primate cities and a few other special service centres is an EEC-wide phenomenon (Marquand, 1980b, 1980c); to it we can relate the clustering of multinational headquarters in the so-called Golden Triangle, stretching from London, Paris and the Randstad to Munich and perhaps Milan (Hamilton, 1976). The whole phenomenon of clustering of higher level activities, and the question of how far the dynamism of each cluster can stretch, raises a major question for EEC as well as national regional policies (Wettmann *et al.*, 1979; Marquand, 1980b, 1980c).

The distribution of consumer services – a perfect market?

There are two main questions to ask concerning the spatial distribution of consumer services. First, are the more specialized services clustered in the larger functional areas, as central place theory would predict? Secondly, given whatever clustering is observed, are consumer services evenly spread in relation to population, without gross deficiencies or excessive abundance? In other words, are they induced by the market, as export base theory alleges?

Theory predicts that consumer service distribution will be related more to population than to employment, and that consumer services will be increasingly concentrated in the larger MELAs. The more specialized the market for the service, the greater the clustering in the larger MELAs. When multivariate analysis was used to test these hypotheses, it was found that employment in consumer services is indeed more closely related to population than to employment in each MELA. The fit of the regressions was excellent except for hotels, whose location is obviously determined by factors other than the presence of a market among the local population. Secondly, there were indeed signs of significant clustering in larger MELAs for various service industries serving both industry and the consumer: road and rail transport; communications; business and personal services such as banking and insurance; professional services (largely dominated by education and health services); and local government. In more detail, cinemas and theatres, employment in sport and betting, restaurants, pubs and clubs, and laundries all showed a significant degree of clustering in the larger MELAs. Thus there is some support for the predictions of central place theory at the level of MELAs when considering the distribution of the more specialized consumer services.

Yet when we came to examine the residuals from the regressions for individual MELAs, despite the good fit of many of the regressions and the consistent story which emerges for consumer services as it did for producer services, we found that the pattern of residuals is far from random. The pattern was not, however, the same as for office services or for producer service occupations. First, MELAs which are deficient in one consumer service tend to be deficient in all, to a greater extent than was found for producer services. This suggests that it is sensible to seek some explanation of the distribution of consumer services collectively, rather than attempting to draw distinctions between them.

Second, the MELAs of gross deficiency in consumer services are scattered throughout the country. Even in the South East, Basildon, Basingstoke, Chatham, Harlow, Hemel Hempstead, Luton, Stevenage and Thurrock, stand out as MELAs with widespread deficiencies. There appears in general to be a fairly close match, although it has not been systematically tested, between MELAs which are heavily endowed with industry and MELAs which are deficient in consumer services. This may arise purely for definitional reasons; if a high proportion of the population is employed in industry, only a low proportion remains to be employed in services. Thus careful testing is needed to see if the apparent relationship is any more than a reflection of this. But none the less, in the West Midlands it is only Shrewsbury, Worcester and Hereford; in the East Midlands only Lincoln and Nottingham; in the northern region only Carlisle, and nowhere in Wales that appears among the MELAs relatively generously endowed with consumer services in general.

One way to indicate which MELAs are deficient in consumer services is to list those which have deficiencies (negative residuals) of more than 10 per cent for both distribution (SIC Order XXII) and miscellaneous

Table 5.7   MELAs with deficiencies in consumer services 1971

Region	MELA	Deficient in:	
		Distribution	Miscellaneous services
South East	Basildon (*)	00	000
	Chatham	0	00
	Harlow (*)	0	00
	Luton	0	0
	Stevenage	0	0
	Thurrock (*)	0	00
	Walton & Weybridge (*)	0	0
Yorks & Humb.	Doncaster	0	0
	Huddersfield	0	0
	Scunthorpe	0	0
North West	Bolton		00
	Bury		00
	Leigh	0	00
	Rochdale		00
	St Helens		00
	Warrington	0	0
	Wigan		000
Wales	Newport	0	0
	Port Talbot	0	00
	Rhondda (*)	00	00000
North	Darlington	0	0
	Hartlepool	00	000
	Sunderland	0	0
East Midlands	Corby	0	0
	Derby	0	0
	Mansfield	0	00
West Midlands	Birmingham	0	0
	Coventry	0	0
Scotland	Falkirk	0	0
	Greenock	0	000
	Kilmarnock	0	00
	Motherwell	00	0

Notes: * MELAs omitted from analysis because of boundary definition problems (see text)
Deficiency levels: blank = 10 per cent or less; 0 = 11–30 per cent; 00 = 31–50 per cent;
000 = 51–70 per cent; 0000 = 71–90 per cent; 00000 = over 90 per cent
All MELAs are listed which are deficient by more than 10 per cent in both *distribution* and
miscellaneous services, or deficient by more than 30 per cent in one of these. *All* MELAs listed
under this criterion are also deficient in insurance, banking and financial services by at least
10 per cent, except Basildon and Walton and Weybridge (both in South East)

services (SIC XXIV), or deficiencies of more than 30 per cent in one of these. This is done in table 5.7, where deficiencies in professional services for these MELAs are also shown.

Before attempting any explanation of the deficiencies in terms of the economic or social composition of the areas, it is necessary to see whether apparent deficiencies may arise simply because of quirks in the boundaries of the MELAs used in the analysis. A critical examination of the characteristics of the 1971 MELA boundaries by Coombes (1979) classifies all MELAs as to the characteristics of their boundaries according to consistent definitional criteria based on daily urban systems. His classification casts doubt on the boundaries of some of the MELAs listed in table 5.7. In particular, Basildon, Harlow, Thurrock, Walton and Weybridge, and Rhondda are more plausibly regarded only as component parts of larger labour market areas. If we posit, in accordance with the regression results, that consumer services, to the extent that they are not evenly distributed, are concentrated in the relatively central portions of the larger labour market areas, then areas which are appropriately regarded as (non-central) portions of larger areas will tend to appear deficient in services. By contrast, areas which are underbounded, where the appropriately defined area is more extensive than that used in the regressions, will tend to appear over-serviced. Thus the fact that Luton, Birmingham, Coventry and Greenock appear to be too narrowly defined in the MELAs only serves to increase the probable extent of their under-servicing, indicated in table 5.7 by the size of their regression residuals. These MELA boundary problems make it appropriate to omit Basildon, Harlow, Thurrock, Walton and Weybridge, and Rhondda from our analysis. Amongst the remaining MELAs listed in table 5.7, it is noticeable that most are old or relatively old industrial towns, with dependence even recently on steel, shipbuilding, textiles or coal. Even in the South East, Chatham, one of the three remaining MELAs with deficiencies, can be regarded as an old industrial area, and Luton, whilst not old, is certainly industrial.

Systematic investigation of the location of the deficiencies in relation to industrial structure and in relation to social structure, where socio-economic groupings are taken to reflect both occupational structure and, less precisely, relative income levels, has yet to be undertaken. But the presumption must be that the areas of deficiency are older industrial areas in need of adaptation, or newer industrial areas where policies to develop industry have not brought a corresponding market response in the development of consumer services. There is probably a tendency for areas deficient in consumer services to be areas where the socio-economic composition is weak in managerial and professional groups at the upper end of the scale, but although such a composition might turn out to be a necessary adjunct of gross deficiency, it is by no means apparent that it is likely to be a sufficient condition for it to happen. It is likely that determined planning policies and other local authority initiatives, for example, can have a significant influence. It appears over-simplified to suggest that consumer services necessarily arise wherever there is a market, but it also appears that areas where they are deficient may have identifiable characteristics in common, some of which may indeed be associated with aspects of the nature of the local market.

Conclusions

Services are much more important than is often thought, both as a source of employment (although their role here is beginning to be widely appreciated) and as contributors to the well-being of the economy. However, data concerning their role and location are still relatively scanty, so that analysis of their behaviour lags behind analysis of manufacturing.

The straightforward classification of data by service industries is not particularly helpful in functional terms. More emphasis on occupational data, on the distinction between higher level service activities and the rest, on the distinction between producer and consumer services, and on the distinction between multi-branch and single-unit organizations are all needed. Equally important is the facility to analyse by functional area; clear patterns of service behaviour emerge on this basis which are masked when data is available only by broad administrative areas of one kind or another.

This said, we need to know more about the role of services in the job generation process. Are service firms volatile, or do they provide long-lasting jobs? Are disparities in provision of consumer services related to incomes and tastes as indicated by socio-economic groupings, or are they the consequences of unimaginative planning policies? How far is the standard of provision of consumer services important in attracting activity to an area? Most important of all, we need to know more about the role of higher level services in promoting growth and technical change. Does the great and growing regional disparity in their distribution have the grave implications for regional economic development which are suggested by some tantalizing incomplete pieces of evidence?

For what we must remember above all about service activities are that they are growing; that although they are increasingly dispersed within regions, their growth is increasingly concentrated in areas within about 100 miles of London but excluding London itself; and that in this respect especially, and in the close relationship of their distribution to functional areas, their behaviour is unlike that of manufacturing.

Social class change in British cities

S. Pinch and A. Williams

Introduction

It is now becoming apparent that in the 1960s there were considerable changes in the way in which people were distributed within the British class system. Although the notion of social class embodies a wide range of attributes and attitudes, it is widely recognized that occupation is a key element. It is thus in the changing characteristics of the occupational structure that we must seek an explanation of these social class changes. These occupational changes have in turn been determined by two inter-related, but conceptually distinct, processes. The first process is technological innovation leading to changes in the skills required *within* particular industries (sometimes termed an 'occupation effect'). Thus, within industries there has been a considerable growth of non-manual occupations of a managerial, technical and clerical character, and a decline in manual work of both a skilled and unskilled character. This development in the 1960s was the continuation of a process which has been in operation throughout most of the twentieth century (Routh, 1965). In contrast, the second process, changes in the *relative sizes* of industries (sometimes termed an 'industry effect'), is much more recent in origin. This is essentially the growth of the 'post-industrial society' involving the relative decline of manufacturing employment and the growth of the service sector. Between 1931 and 1961 the size of the service sector as a proportion of the British economy remained remarkably stable (changing from 50.3 per cent to 48.7 per cent) but in the 1960s the service sector began to develop rapidly so that it reached 52.8 per cent by 1971 (Department of Employment, 1975). This expansion of services, mostly within the public sector, has also led to a considerable growth of professional, managerial and other intermediate forms of non-manual employment which, with the exception of the increase in unskilled manual service employment, has reinforced the occupational effects within industries. The net effect of these changes, combined with increased educational opportunities, has been a general increase in the volume of upward social mobility.

These aggregate societal changes have been accompanied by two important spatial processes. The first is the comparatively recent, but by now well-known, process of population and employment decentralization from the inner areas of British cities into either their surrounding commuter hinterlands or else beyond into smaller settlements in the urban hierarchy. The second process is the traditional pattern of population migration from 'northern' to 'southern' regions of Britain. Despite our knowledge of both the geographical movements and the aggregate social class changes, there is a striking lack of information on the inter-relationships *between* these social and spatial processes. The causal connections are certainly likely to be complex. The changing character and location of employment will be an important determinant of the occupation and class structure of an area but the location of the workforce *by residence* is also affected by changing commuting patterns (which are in turn affected by occupational changes). Social and geographical mobility are frequently synonymous, and the increased living standards associated with upward social mobility have led to decentralization and increased journey-to-work distances. At the same time the relocation of new employment into commuting hinterlands of cities has been affected by the changing distribution of population.

Many questions therefore remain to be answered: has there been a tendency for social classes to decentralize from inner city areas at different rates? What are the regional dimensions of class change and how do these relate to intra-urban patterns of change? What are the effects of this social and geographical mobility upon the class structure of inner cities and their commuter belts, and what is the evidence for a process of 'social polarization' whereby the relatively affluent middle-class non-manual and skilled manual workers have moved out of inner cities leaving behind a growing proportion of relatively deprived low-status semi-and unskilled manual workers? Although a number of studies have examined these issues in particular cities (e.g. Davidson, 1976; Dugmore, 1975; Hamnett, 1976; Harris and Lyons, 1971; Pinch, 1981), they have ignored the full ramifications of these changes throughout the urban system as a whole. This chapter attempts to make good the deficiency by examining social-class changes within the functional urban areas pioneered in this country by Hall *et al.* (1973) and redefined by the Urban Change Project at the London School of Economics (Department of Environment, 1976a).

Definitions and their limitations

The concept of social class is both complex and contentious. A full under-standing of class structures must therefore involve study of many factors including the various dimensions of inequality associated with class, the relationships between classes, the perceptions of these inequalities and relationships by various individuals within the social system, together with changes in all these factors over time. The aims of this study are inevitably less comprehensive. We are not concerned with 'explaining' social class or elaborating its many social implications but instead wish to draw attention to the ways in which the broad outlines of the class struc-ture have changed within the British urban system. This requires the use of an efficient indicator to encapsulate the various dimensions of class. Of the many indicators available, occupation is widely recognized as the most useful. Thus, given a person's occupation, there is a strong chance we can make a reasonable estimate of their income, housing tenure, educational attainment, political affiliations and life style.

The most widely available and commonly used information on occupational groupings are the seventeen socio-economic groups derived by the Registrar General. This classification aims to group 'people whose social, cultural and recreational standards of behaviour are similar' (Office of Population Censuses and Surveys, 1970, 10). For the sake of providing a manageable number of groups it was necessary in this analysis to aggregate the original seventeen socio-economic groups into broader categories. Within the constraints of maintaining a reasonable degree of within-group homogeneity, the main concern of the aggregation was to isolate the extremes of the social class hierarchy, and to differen-tiate the broad middle along manual and non-manual lines. Four classes were chosen. Social class A, termed here 'professional and managerial', comprises socio-economic groups 1, 2, 3, 4 and 13 and is constituted by employers in industry, commerce, etc., professional workers and farmers (employers and managers). Socio-economic groups 5 and 6, consisting of non-manual foremen and supervisors and junior non-manual workers, form social class B, termed 'intermediate non-manual'. Social class C, or 'skilled manual', is made up of socio-economic groups 8, 9, 12 and 14, namely manual foremen and supervisors, skilled manual workers, own-account workers (other than professional) and own-account farmers. Social class D, 'semi- and unskilled manual', containing groups 7, 10, 11 and 15, consists of personal service workers, semi- and unskilled manual workers and agricultural workers. This fourfold classification excludes groups 16 (members of the armed forces) and 17 (inadequately described occupations).

The limitations of such a relatively simple and arbitrary division into social groups for statistical purposes are numerous (see Goldthorpe and Hope, 1974). The groups might be interpreted as 'upper-middle-class', 'lower-middle-class', 'skilled working class' and 'unskilled working class' but these divisions may be very different from the complex class and status distinctions recognized by persons at various levels in the social hierarchy. Furthermore, the divisions tend to conceal the extremes of poverty and wealth which in Britain, as in other capitalist societies, are derived primarily from inequalities in the ownership of private property (Westergaard and Resler, 1975). Clearly, both these perceptions and economic aspects of social class require a different type of research design to that attempted here. It should also be recognized that the groupings may obscure similarities in income, life style and attitude as, for example, between low-status non-manual clerical workers and skilled manual workers. Nevertheless, we have avoided lumping together both intermediate non-manual workers and skilled manual workers into a 'new middle-class'. Although some commentators claim to have perceived either the 'embourgeoisement' of skilled manual workers through rising incomes, or else the 'proletarianization' of white-collar workers through increased trade union affiliation and 'militancy' in the labour market, the bulk of evidence indicates that there are substantial and persistent differences in material rewards, status and life styles between manual and non-manual workers (Roberts *et al.*, 1977; Westergaard and Resler, 1975). We have, nevertheless, avoided the mistake of creating a blanket non-manual category by distinguishing the professional workers from the intermediate clerical strata.

Given the aims of the analysis two further and potentially more serious limitations derive from the fact that the socio-economic groupings used in this chapter are based upon the number of *economically active males*. First, this ignores the impact of differential rates of unemployment at the two census dates. In 1961 unemployment totalled 266,000 but by 1971 this figure had risen to 724,000. Since low-status manual occupation groups, and particularly those in the less prosperous regions, are more likely to become unemployed during a recession, this will have an effect upon the observed patterns of change. The most likely consequence is that the decline of manual employment will be exaggerated, but the precise effect of this factor cannot be known. A second limitation is that, since the analysis concentrates upon employed *males*, this ignores the socio-economic groupings of employed females. (Analysis of changes in the numbers of economically active females was not possible because of a lack of information for 1961.) Between 1961 and 1971 female participation in the workforce increased by 14.3 per cent while during the same period male employment declined by 6.4 per cent. Much of this increased participation of women in the workforce involved clerical work and our analysis of males will therefore not reflect the true expansion of intermediate non-manual occupations in the 1960s. Nevertheless, the occupations of males can be assumed to be the best indicator of the overall status and life style of a household.

Finally, on the subject of definitions, the analysis in this chapter uses the 126 functional urban areas described on p. xx, recognizing the distinction between the Standard Metropolitan Labour Areas made up in cores and rings and the Metropolitan Economic Labour Areas which also include the outer rings. Further details of these spatial and occupational definitions are given in Spence *et al.* (1982).

National patterns of socio-economic change between 1961 and 1971

The considerable extent of the upward shift in the social class structure of Britain between 1961 and 1971 is revealed by table 6.1. This has resulted from the fact that both the absolute and percentage changes have been of greatest magnitude at the two extremes of the occupational hierarchy. The largest absolute and percentage *increases* were in the high-status professional and managerial occupations, while the largest absolute and percentage decreases occurred in the low-status semi- and unskilled manual occupations. There were smaller absolute and percentage increases in the intermediate non-manual occupations, and smaller absolute and percentage declines in skilled manual occupations. Even taking into account the greater probability of unemployment in low-status occupations, due to the cyclical economic downturn in the early 1970s, which is likely to have exaggerated the true decline of manual employment, the extent of the changes are such that differential unemployment by itself cannot be regarded as a complete explanation.

Table 6.1 Changes in socio-economic groups in Great Britain 1961–71

Socio-economic group	Numbers (000s)		Changes between 1961–71		Proportion of total	
	1961	1971	Absolute (000s)	%	1961	1971
Professional and managerial	2,288	2,757	469	20.5	14.1	17.3
Intermediate non-manual	2,661	2,785	124	4.7	16.4	17.5
Skilled manual	6,398	6,182	−217	−3.3	39.4	38.8
Semi- and unskilled manual	4,311	3,661	−649	−15.1	26.6	23.0
Armed forces and inadequately described	574	533	−41	−7.1	3.5	3.4
Total	16,232	15,918	−314	−1.9	100.0	100.0

The effects of these changes upon the occupational structure were an increase in the proportion employed in professional and managerial occupations, and a decrease in the proportion employed in semi- and unskilled manual occupations. The proportions employed in intermediate non-manual and skilled manual occupations remained largely unchanged. Overall, there was an increase in the proportion of the workforce employed in manual occupations from 30.5 per cent to 34.8 per cent, and a decrease in the proportion employed in non-manual occupations from 66 per cent to 61.8 per cent. Although these data are based upon economically active males and thus ignore the considerable increase in part-time clerical work undertaken by women, they do nevertheless serve to emphasize the considerable shifts in the occupational structure that have accompanied the growth of the post-industrial society in Britain.

Intra-zonal patterns of socio-economic change between 1961 and 1971

Table 6.2 shows the extent of these aggregate national changes are manifest in the three main types of zone which form the constituent parts of the British urban system. Once again there is a certain symmetrical character to the pattern of absolute changes. The high-status professional and managerial groups increased in all zones with the largest increase of 305,000 in the metropolitan rings, while the semi- and unskilled groups decreased in all zones, with the largest decrease of 353,000 in the urban cores. The intermediate non-manual and skilled manual occupations decreased in cores and increased in both the rings and outer rings.

Table 6.2 Changes in socio-economic groups in cores, rings and outer rings in Great Britain 1961–71.

	Cores			Rings			Outer rings		
	(a)	(b)	(c)	(a)	(b)	(c)	(a)	(b)	(c)
Professional and managerial	89	8.7	−12.9	305	38.1	16.6	74	21.3	−0.3
Intermediate non-manual	−99	−6.6	−11.4	161	20.8	16.1	60	20.1	15.3
Skilled manual	−457	−13.2	−9.4	152	9.0	12.7	75	7.6	11.4
Semi- and unskilled manual	−353	−15.6	−0.5	−125	−11.6	3.5	−143	−18.6	−3.5
	−820								
Total	−806	−9.5	−7.2	479	10.6	11.3	30	1.2	4.1

Notes: (a) Absolute changes (000s)
(b) Percentage changes
(c) Percentage shifts
Total also includes armed forces and inadequately described

The percentage changes, also shown in table 6.2, help to clarify the extent of decentralization displayed by the various socio-economic groups. In percentage terms the increase in professional and managerial groups was largest in the metropolitan rings, and at 38.1 per cent was far above both the national percentage increase in this group, and the percentage increase for all occupation groups in metropolitan rings. Conversely, the rate of decline in the semi- and unskilled manual groups was smallest in the metropolitan rings. These two groups at the extremes of the occupational hierarchy were therefore both decentralizing in relative terms. The pattern of change for the intermediate non-manual and skilled manual occupations is a more simple one of absolute decentralization with decreases in the cores and increases in the rings and outer rings. In this context it is worth noting that there is little difference in respective percentage increases of these intermediate occupation groups in the two types of ring. This contrasts with the professional and managerial and semi- and unskilled manual workers which both displayed a tendency towards relative concentration in the rings.

Although these patterns of change are clear, it is somewhat difficult to interpret the relative differences in the growth rates of the various zone types because of the considerable national changes in the different socio-economic groups. Shift-share analysis which attempts to extract the influence of national change is of obvious use in this context. A positive shift indicates that a socio-economic group in a zone type either has increased more than the national average increase in the socio-economic group, or else has decreased less than the national average decrease in the particular socio-economic group. Conversely a negative shift indicates that the decrease in a zone is greater than the overall national decrease for the particular socio-economic group, or else the increase is less than the overall national increase in the group. In the following analysis these shifts are presented in percentage terms (formed by dividing the absolute shift of an occupation group by the size of the occupation group in 1961) so that the relative change of the groups can be more easily discerned.

The percentage shifts in table 6.2 confirm that, after national changes are taken into account, *all* the occupational groupings were decentralizing, with negative shifts in the urban cores and positive shifts in the rings. However, the magnitude of the percentage shifts are very different within the various socio-economic groups. The rapidly growing professional and managerial occupations have the largest negative percentage shifts in the cores and the largest positive percentage shifts in the rings. In contrast, the rapidly declining semi- and unskilled manual occupations have the smallest negative percentage shift in the cores and the smallest positive percentage shift in the rings. The intermediate non-manual and skilled manual groups both had shifts which are of a magnitude similar to the professional and managerial occupations, but unlike the latter (which had a small negative shift in the outer rings) both have positive shifts of almost equal size between the rings and outer rings.

INTRA-ZONAL PATTERNS: THE MILLION CITIES AND THE REST OF BRITAIN COMPARED

Previous examinations of change within the British urban system have indicated that the large conurbations may be changing in a manner which is rather different from urban centres in the rest of the country (Department of Environment, 1976a). It is therefore instructive to divide the previous data set and to compare the patterns of intra-zonal change within MELAs of over 1 million population size (London, Birmingham, Manchester, Glasgow, Liverpool, Leeds and Newcastle) with all the remaining MELAs in the rest of Great Britain.

Table 6.3 shows that of a total population loss of 806,000 in urban cores between 1961 and 1971, no less than 663,000 or 82.3 per cent occurred in the cores of the Million Cities. In contrast, of the total population growth of 479,000 in the rings, no less than 339,000 or 70.8 per cent occurred in the rings of the MELAs in the rest of Britain outside the Million Cities. Clearly, then, the vast majority of the decline in skilled manual and semi- and unskilled manual occupations in the 1960s took place in the cores of the large cities, while the bulk of the growth in occupations in non-manual work took place in the rings of the rest of Britain. All the occupation groups had either larger decreases or smaller increases in the cores of the Million Cities, while, with the exception of the semi- and unskilled manual occupations, all socio-economic groups had larger increases in the rings outside the Million Cities. The semi- and unskilled manual occupations are unusual in that they have larger declines in the rings and outer rings of the rest of Britain than in the Million Cities. The extent of this decline is such in the outer rings of the non-Million Cities that overall there is a small net decline in occupations in this zone.

The percentage changes in table 6.3 serve to emphasize the differences in the relative growth rates of urban zones in the Million Cities and the rest of Britain. There is a much larger percentage decline of total occupations in the cores of the Million Cities and a much larger percentage increase in total occupations in the rings of the rest of Britain. Both the non-manual occupation groupings have larger percentage increases in the metropolitan rings of the cities below 1 million in size while both the manual occupation groupings have much larger percentage declines in the cores of the Million Cities. It is also worthy of note that, with the exception of the semi- and unskilled manual grouping, the relative growth of occupations is greatest in the outer metropolitan rings of the Million Cities while, in the rest of Britain, the relative growth rates are highest in the rings. The semi- and unskilled manual occupations have relatively large percentage decreases in all zones of both Million Cities and the rest of Britain.

Table 6.3 Changes in socio-economic groups in cores, rings and outer rings in the Million Cities and the Rest of Britain 1961–71

	Million Cities			Rest of Britain		
	Cores	Rings	Outer rings	Cores	Rings	Outer rings
Absolute change (000s)						
Professional and managerial	8	117	24	80	188	50
Intermediate non-manual	−112	32	16	13	129	44
Skilled manual	−354	29	14	−111	123	60
Semi- and unskilled manual	−228	−38	−21	−125	−87	−122
Total	−686	140	33	−143	353	32
Percentage change						
Professional and managerial	1.6	28.2	36.4	15.9	48.7	17.7
Intermediate non-manual	−14.0	7.7	26.4	1.9	36.2	18.4
Skilled manual	−20.0	4.0	8.0	−6.4	12.6	7.5
Semi- and unskilled manual	−19.8	−9.3	−16.0	−11.3	−13.0	−19.5
Total	−15.4	7.1	7.2	−3.4	13.5	−0.1
Percentage shift						
Professional and managerial	−18.9	7.8	15.9	−4.5	28.2	−2.8
Intermediate non-manual	−18.6	3.0	22.1	−2.8	31.6	13.7
Skilled manual	−16.7	7.4	11.4	−3.0	16.0	−14.0
Semi- and unskilled manual	−4.8	5.8	−0.9	3.8	2.1	−4.1
Total	−13.5	9.0	9.1	−1.5	15.4	1.78

Note: Total also includes armed forces and inadequately described

The pattern of percentage shifts in table 6.3 reveals the extent of decentralization by the various occupational groupings with the greatest clarity. As might be expected from the previous information, all occupational groupings have larger negative percentage shifts in the cores of the Million Cities and larger positive percentage shifts in the rings of MELAs in the rest of Britain. The direction of the shifts are somewhat different in the case of the semi- and unskilled manual occupations but, in contrast to all the other groups, there are relatively little differences in the magnitude of the shifts in this low-status group in the various types of urban zone in either large or small cities. The percentage shifts also confirm the way in which the relative growth of occupation groups is concentrated in the outer rings of the Million Cities and the rings of the rest of Britain.

INTRA-ZONAL PATTERNS: SUMMARY AND DISCUSSION

Drawing together the information presented in tables 6.2 and 6.3 a number of generalizations can be made. First, there is evidence of a positive relationship between the overall growth rate of an occupational grouping and its extent of decentralization. The fastest growing group, the professional and managerial occupations, had the largest negative percentage shift in the urban cores and the largest positive percentage shift in the rings. Conversely, the occupational grouping which declined at the fastest rate, the semi- and unskilled manual occupations, had the smallest negative shift in the cores and the smallest positive shift in the rings. Second, there is evidence of a negative relationship between city size and occupational growth. Most of the absolute increase in the rapidly growing manual occupations has been in the rings of MELAs below 1 million in population size while most of the absolute decrease in the rapidly declining manual occupations has been within the cores of the Million Cities. Third, there is some evidence of a positive relationship between city size and the extent of relative decentralization. In the Million Cities the largest percentage increases and positive percentage shifts occurred in the outer rings while, in the remaining cities, there were in most cases negative shifts in the outer rings and the largest positive percentage shifts in the rings.

These occupational changes can to a large degree be explained by the changing patterns of employment within the constituent zones of the British urban system. The Department of Environment (1976a) has shown that, of the twenty-five orders within the standard industrial classification, only five managed to record growth in urban cores between 1966 and 1971. The fact that the most important increases were in professional and scientific services, public administration and defence, and insurance, banking and finance helps to account for the growth of professional and managerial occupations in urban cores. Furthermore, the increase in office jobs was concentrated in the cores in the rest of Britain outside the Million Cities, helping to explain the growth of both the professional and managerial occupations and the intermediate non-manual occupations in these zones. The much larger absolute and percentage increases in the high-status non-manual occupations in the rings in cities of all sizes can be explained by two factors. First, many professionals, managers and other non-manual office workers employed in cores are resident in the rings and outer rings, and second, since offices and services have also been decentralizing, many professional and managerial groups now live and work in the rings. Of the total growth in occupational groups in rings, 75.4 per cent has therefore been in the non-manual category. Given the large scale of both population and employment decentralization away from the Million Cities into smaller surrounding urban areas, the large absolute and percentage growth of non-manual occupations in both the cores and rings of the non-Million Cities is likely to reflect both the decentralization of offices and services out of the large cities, together with longer commuting journeys made by those who are resident in either the cores or rings of the smaller MELAs but still employed in the larger Million Cities.

In sharp contrast to offices and services, almost all manufacturing industries declined in urban cores between 1966 and 1971, with losses being particularly large in the fields of engineering, electrical goods and textiles (Department of Environment, 1976a). This helps to account for the large declines in both skilled manual and semi-skilled and unskilled manual occupations which constitute the vast majority of the total decline in occupations in cores between 1961 and 1971. Most types of manufacturing grew in the rings but this growth has been concentrated in fields involving skilled manual labour, since semi- and unskilled manual occupations declined in all zones. The close relationship between manufacturing change and skilled manual occupations is emphasized by the fact that both experienced the largest absolute declines in the cores of the Million Cities and the largest absolute increases in the rings in the rest of Britain. Together with shifts in the location of employment, the decentralization of skilled manual workers is again likely to have been determined by changing patterns of residence. Rising living standards have meant that many of the more prosperous manual workers have been able to gain access to owner-occupied housing in commuter hinterlands or, alternatively, have been forced by constraints within the housing market to purchase new dwellings near the urban periphery.

In sharp contrast, the access of the unskilled workers to owner-occupation is greatly restricted. This has no doubt contributed to their decline in all types of zone and their lack of relative decentralization in comparison with other groups. The main reason for the decline of this low-status group would thus seem to be changes in the economic structure of areas rather than migration patterns.

Regional patterns of socio-economic change between 1961 and 1971

THE STANDARD REGION LEVEL

The existence of regional differences in the distributions of social class groups is well-known and documented (Hall and Smith, 1968; Coates and Rawstron, 1971) but the ways in which these distributions have changed in recent years is less certain. Considerable variations in the shift from manual to non-manual occupations might be expected in the regions for a variety of reasons. Not the least of these reasons is the fact that economic changes and regional policy have led to a differentiation of regional performances in the 1960s. This has been highlighted by a number of shift-share analyses which have shown that in the early 1960s manufacturing in the peripheral regions of Britain was growing less rapidly than would be expected given these regions' industrial structures. In the latter part of the decade, when there were changes in the spatial division of labour (Massey, 1979) and regional policy was far stronger (Keeble, 1976; Moore and Rhodes, 1976) this position was reversed. This reversal was one of the main findings of Buck and Atkins (1978). Comparing regional and national change rates in manual occupations, they showed that between 1961 and 1966 assisted areas had less than national average growth, but that between 1966 and 1971 it was the unassisted areas which had less than national average growth. It is therefore of interest to note how these changes have been reflected in the economic planning regions for the entire period between 1961 and 1971 and for the two groups of manual occupations, the skilled and the semi- and unskilled.

In contrast to the manual groups, non-manual occupations were far less affected by regional policy. Office location policy after 1965 did contribute to some decentralization of jobs from London, but most of these jobs moved only short distances, often within the South East and rarely as far as the assisted areas (Goddard, 1975). Even in manufacturing, non-manual jobs tended to be far more concentrated in the South East than manual jobs (Goddard, 1978a). However, non-manual occupations were not a uniform group. Evidence in both office and manufacturing employment suggests that professional and managerial occupations were far more likely than intermediate non-manual occupations to be concentrated in the larger cities and the South East.

This section analyses the changes which occurred between 1961 and 1971 for manual and non-manual occupations, and for the individual social class groups, for MELAs aggregated to the level of regional economic planning regions. The main emphasis is on relative changes, but where relevant, reference is also made to the absolute changes. The effects of these changes on the social class composition of the regions are also considered.

The relative changes are shown in table 6.4. The manual and non-manual occupations exhibit a clear regional dichotomy. All the regions with increases in non-manual jobs exceeding 14 per cent are in the South or Midlands, whereas the peripheral regions have increases of less than 11 per cent. In absolute terms, the most important change was the increase of 278,990 non-manual jobs in the South East, almost a half of the total increase in this sector of 593,230.

The same dichotomy is observed for manual occupations, with the greatest decreases being in the periphery and especially in Scotland. These relative changes represent absolute decreases in the numbers of manual jobs in the peripheral regions of between 46,400 (in Wales) and

Table 6.4 Percentage changes in socio-economic groups in MELAs in Great Britain 1961–71, at economic planning region level

Region	Non-manual			Manual		
	Professional and managerial	Intermediate	All non-manual	Skilled	Semi- and unskilled	All manual
Scotland	18.5	−4.0	5.5	−10.3	−15.3	−12.4
North	13.9	8.7	11.0	−4.3	−23.0	−7.2
North West	15.8	−0.5	6.7	−6.2	−14.2	−9.5
Yorks & Humb.	12.2	5.4	8.6	−3.3	−18.7	−9.4
East Midlands	24.9	11.8	17.9	+0.8	−15.5	−5.2
West Midlands	22.7	9.6	15.9	−2.7	−8.4	−4.8
Wales	11.1	3.8	7.1	−1.4	−23.7	−11.0
East Anglia	22.7	16.2	19.6	10.2	−9.8	+0.9
South East	26.3	4.6	14.4	−4.4	−14.7	−8.5
South West	26.4	10.4	17.9	1.9	−11.8	−3.7
Great Britain	20.5	4.7	12.0	−3.7	−15.1	−8.1

139,660 (in the North West). The smallest losses, and in the case of East Anglia actually an increase, occurred in the South. The exception is the South East, which experienced a relative loss of 8.5 per cent, that is, at a rate greater than the national decline. In absolute terms this represents a loss of 257,710 manual occupations out of a national loss of 865,850.

The changes in the individual groups exhibit a more complex pattern. The professional and managerial occupations grew at above the national rate for this group in the South and Midlands, as expected. This suggests that the highest status occupations remained concentrated in the South East and indeed this region had 229,940 out of a total national increase of 468,920. Where decentralization occurred, it was probably over relatively short distances to adjacent regions. This simple pattern was repeated for intermediate non-manual occupations, with one significant exception. In the South East the rate of increase was below the national average (although still accounting for 49,050 out of a total increase of 124,310). It is not an unreasonable assumption that the lower growth rate in the South East was the result of decentralization of office functions to the adjacent regions with high growth rates, especially East Anglia.

Interpreting the patterns for skilled manual occupations is more complex. At the extremes, the increases in the South West and East Anglia and the large declines in Scotland and the North West do conform to the simple regional dichotomy. However, the rates of decline in the North, Yorkshire/Humberside, Wales, West Midlands and South East are all broadly similar. Two factors may explain this. First, regional policies and changes in the requirements of manufacturing industry may have ameliorated the decline of manufacturing employment in some peripheral regions and, second, industrial decline is spreading to previously high-growth, prosperous regions (Keeble, 1979; Hudson, 1978).

Finally, the semi- and unskilled manual occupations reveal broad conformity with the simple regional pattern. All regions were affected by the national decline, but the greatest losses were in the peripheral regions, especially the North and Wales (possibly a result of the decline in coal-mining). The rates of decline were least in the more prosperous regions, especially East Anglia and the West Midlands. The absolute changes were dominated by the South East which experienced a loss of 176,000 jobs out of a total national loss of 649,310 jobs.

The overall social changes in Britain can therefore be seen to have affected the regions in different ways. For manual and non-manual occupations, and for the individual social classes, a regional dichotomy existed. The South and Midlands had the greatest increases in non-manual occupations and the smallest decreases in the manual group, while the inverse changes occurred in the peripheral regions. There were two main modifications to this pattern. In the South East there were very high growth rates in professional and managerial occupations but smaller increases in the more routine non-manual occupations. In skilled manual jobs there was some distortion of the simple regional dichotomy, especially in the South East and the West Midlands.

The changes observed are not likely to have greatly affected the social class profiles of the regions, the South having the largest proportions of non-manual occupations and the peripheral regions having the largest proportions of manual occupations. If anything, the changes can be expected to have increased these differences. The socio-economic profiles of the regions in 1971 (table 6.5) reveal that a regional dichotomy does continue to exist in the distribution of manual and non-manual occupations. In all the regions in the South and Midlands more than 30 per cent of employment was non-manual, with the South East being outstanding with 42.6 per cent. This is by far the greatest proportion and of the other regions, only the South West has more than 33 per cent in non-manual employment. Manual occupations reveal the inverse pattern, with the South East, East Anglia and South West all having less than 60 per cent compared to rates exceeding 68 per cent in Wales and the North. Between these extremes the pattern is not so clear.

Examination of the individual socio-economic groups allows the analysis to be refined. At the two social extremes the pattern is clear. The largest proportions in professional and managerial work are in the South, especially the South East, and the smallest proportions are in the peripheral regions, especially the North and Wales. The reverse is observed for

Table 6.5 Socio-economic profiles of MELAs in Great Britain in 1971, at economic planning region level

Region	Non-manual			Manual		
	Professional and managerial	Intermediate	All non-manual	Skilled	Semi- and unskilled	All manual
Scotland	14.9	16.6	31.5	39.7	25.9	65.6
North	12.9	15.3	28.2	43.8	25.2	69.0
North West	15.7	16.7	32.4	39.9	25.4	65.3
Yorks & Humb.	14.4	14.9	29.3	43.9	24.4	68.3
East Midlands	15.2	15.8	31.0	44.3	21.7	66.0
West Midlands	15.6	14.8	30.4	43.4	23.9	67.3
Wales	13.1	15.2	28.3	43.5	25.4	68.9
East Anglia	17.0	14.9	31.9	36.4	25.6	62.0
South East	21.3	21.3	42.6	33.7	19.8	53.5
South West	17.9	17.7	35.6	37.0	21.8	58.8
GB average	17.3	17.7	35.0	38.8	22.9	61.7

Note: The row totals do not add up to 100 per cent as the armed forces and inadequately described socio-economic groups have been omitted

semi- and unskilled manual work. For the other two class groups the position is less distinct, although a general division between the South East, and the periphery does exist. There are two main exceptions. First, the Midlands have large proportions in skilled manual occupations, further emphasizing the importance of skilled manufacturing employment in these regions. Secondly, Scotland and the North West have relatively large proportions in the intermediate non-manual group. Therefore, it is this group rather than the professional and managerial which contributes to the high levels of non-manual jobs in these two regions.

It is possible here to perceive the links between the change rates and the social profiles. It is largely the regions with the highest proportions of the non-manual groups which have experienced the highest growth rates in these groups, and it is the regions with the largest proportions in manual employment which have experienced the largest decreases in these groups. There is no evidence of a decline in the dominance of the South in the higher-status groups as a result of social changes between 1961 and 1971. It is important to note that this is true in particular of the South East, even though the changes in this region were not always in conformity with the remainder of the South and Midlands.

REGIONAL PATTERNS: THE SMLA LEVEL

The aim of this section is to refine the aggregate patterns described previously. It is important to know whether aggregate changes reflect trends prevalent throughout a region, or whether there are conflicting trends in different parts of the region or in cities of different sizes. Figure 6.1 shows the socio-economic changes in the individual SMLAs. The maps reveal three main features: first, at this scale there is broad conformity with the aggregate regional patterns; second, in the South East there is marked intra-regional redistribution; and third, the largest SMLAs have had very different experiences to the rest of the urban system. Each of these points is considered in turn.

Within most of the regions, relatively uniform trends may be observed. The SMLAs in the peripheral regions tend to have the smallest increases in the non-manual groups and the largest decreases in the manual groups. This can be illustrated with some examples. In the professional and managerial group all SMLAs in the Northern region, except Teesside, have relatively small increases of less than 20 per cent. In the intermediate non-manual group, all SMLAs in the South West have increases of 10–20 per cent. In the skilled manual group all cities in Scotland have decreases, and in the semi- and unskilled group all SMLAs in East Anglia, excepting Peterborough, have decreases of less than 20 per cent. Although these are some of the more notable examples, broad conformity is observed in the other regions for all the groups (figure 6.1).

There is, however, one major exception to this pattern and this is the South East. Within this region there is a great contrast between the experience of London and of its surrounding SMLAs for all the social classes. For professional and managerial occupations, while London had only a modest increase of 11.7 per cent (but an absolute increase of 61,230) the surrounding SMLAs had some of the highest rates of increase in Britain; for example, 104 per cent in Basildon, 98 per cent in High Wycombe and 84 per cent in Crawley. There was an even more distinctive pattern for the intermediate non-manual occupational grouping. In London there was a decrease of 8.4 per cent but other SMLAs in the South East were experiencing very high rates of increase; for example, Harlow 80 per cent, Maidstone 57 per cent and Aylesbury 54 per cent. In skilled manual occupations, while most of the country was experiencing decreases, the South East with the exception of London was experiencing increases. Thus, Basingstoke, Harlow and Basildon had increases of more than 30 per cent, in a period when London had a relative decrease of 15 per cent (representing an absolute decline of 166,820 jobs). In the semi- and unskilled group, London had one of the largest decreases in the country of 21 per cent, while most of the region had moderate declines or even, in a

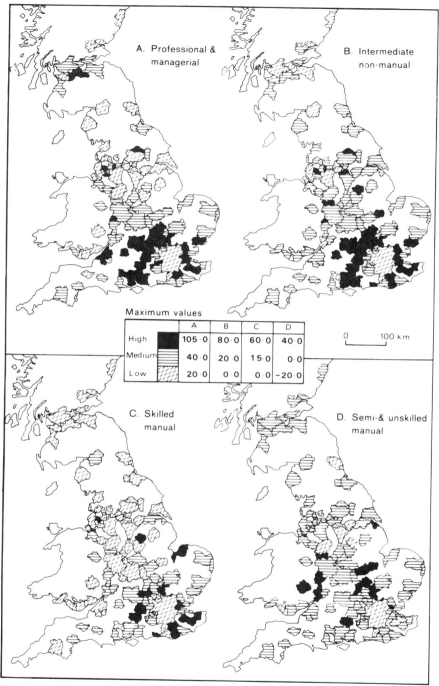

A. Professional & managerial

B. Intermediate non-manual

Maximum values

		A	B	C	D
High		105·0	80·0	60·0	40·0
Medium		40·0	20·0	15·0	0·0
Low		20·0	0·0	0·0	−20·0

0   100 km

C. Skilled manual

D. Semi-& unskilled manual

Figure 6.1   Percentage changes in the socio-economic groups in SMLAs in Great Britain 1961–71

few cases, small increases; for example, Crawley 31 per cent, Harlow 29 per cent, Milton Keynes 23 per cent.

This intra-regional pattern in the South East has considerable significance. This of course reflects decentralization from London to the surrounding SMLAs, a trend which has been noted by a number of observers (Lock, 1976; Stone, 1978). However, this analysis confirms that the decentralization occurred for *all* groups. Decentralization was only relative for professional and managerial occupations, illustrating London's continued strength in this field, but there was absolute decentralization of the other social classes. Other analyses have noted the trend for decentralization at smaller scales. For example, with respect to office employment, it has been observed that within the GLC professional and executive jobs in 'inner' London were increasing, while routine office functions were decentralizing in absolute terms from 'inner' to 'outer' London (Daniels, 1977). This analysis has shown that similar changes for the non-manual group, as a whole, were occurring at the scale of the SMLAs.

The intra-regional analysis also helps to explain the relatively low growth rates in all the groups in the South East. The aggregate regional patterns reflect not so much a diminishing of growth in the South East as in London. Omitting London, it is observed that the rest of the South East is still the main focus of growth for all social classes in Britain.

Finally, considering the third aspect of the changes in the SMLAs, it is observed that the largest cities have experienced changes which are different to the urban system as a whole. The changes in the seven Million Cities are shown in table 6.6. In the professional and managerial group, although all the largest cities have increases, notably Birmingham (22.4 per cent) and Glasgow (23.1 per cent), they are all at rates which are less than those experienced in the rest of Britain. In the intermediate non-manual group three cities had increases and four had decreases, but none of the increases exceeded 6 per cent compared to a growth rate of 14.5 per cent in the rest of Britain. The most significant change, however, occurred in the skilled manual group. National change rates had revealed a decrease in this group. It can now be seen that a major contributor to that decline was the largest cities. While decreases of 6–17 per cent were recorded in all these cities, the rest of Britain had an increase of 2 per cent. The changes in the semi- and unskilled are more complex than in the other groups.

REGIONAL PATTERNS: SUMMARY AND DISCUSSION

It is now possible to state some conclusions with respect to the changing spatial distribution of social classes in Britain. First, it is clear from both the aggregate regional patterns and the inter-urban changes that there are

Table 6.6   Percentage changes in socio-economic groups in the Million Cities of Great Britain 1961–71

	Professional and managerial	Intermediate non-manual	Skilled manual	Semi-unskilled manual	Population 1971
London	14.0	−6.6	−14.1	−20.3	8,836,847
Birmingham	22.4	5.4	−6.4	−6.4	2,836,631
Manchester	13.1	−8.8	−11.6	−16.3	2,088,591
Glasgow	23.1	−12.0	−16.5	−15.8	1,681,338
Liverpool	6.1	−7.1	−9.9	−15.9	1,485,889
Leeds	15.8	2.5	−6.8	−11.6	1,206,524
Newcastle	11.9	5.3	−8.2	−26.0	1,047,032
Rest of British urban system	27.2	14.5	2.0	−13.8	

still considerable differences in the social class profiles of the regions. The largest proportions of non-manual jobs are in the South and Midlands and the largest proportions of manual jobs are in the periphery. This is par- ticularly true of the South East which, despite relatively disadvantageous changes 1961–71, still had by far the largest proportion of non-manual jobs, especially those of a professional and managerial character. Second, changes in the manual and non-manual groups had a simple pattern. It was the regions with the largest proportions of non-manual jobs which experienced the greatest relative increases in this group, and it was the regions with the largest proportions of manual jobs which had the largest losses in this group. If London is excluded from the South East, then it is clear that this region still dominates the growth rates in all other regions. Third, analysis of the individual groups showed considerable differences between the manual groups. It is therefore necessary to refine the find- ings of Buck and Atkins (1978) and to suggest that if regional policy did influence the distribution of social classes, it is more likely to have affected the skilled rather than the semi- and unskilled. Finally, analysis of the largest cities showed these had far less favourable rates of change than the rest of the UK. This is particularly true of the skilled manual.

Regional intra-urban patterns of socio-economic change between 1961 and 1971

Thus far the analysis has identified two main spatial expressions of social change, namely decentralization and regional redistribution. There was decentralization of all socio-economic groups from cores to rings and the fastest-growing professional and managerial groups appeared to display the more rapid rate of decentralization. There are also regional changes with the largest increases or smallest decreases being in the South and Midlands. These regional changes are modified by the experiences of the largest cities, which grew less rapidly than the urban system as a whole; this was particularly important in the South East.

This section examines the relationship between these two spatial redistributions. Two questions are considered: first, whether the national decentralization trends are repeated in all the regions and second, whether the regional patterns for cores and rings, considered separately, are of the same relative magnitude as for the aggregate regional totals. Figure 6.2 illustrates these changes. For each social class all the regions are plotted against axes measuring percentage changes in cores and rings.

Taking the professional and managerial occupational groups first, it is observed that all the regions have increases of greater than 15 per cent in the rings while changes in the cores range between −1 per cent and +18 per cent. Excepting Scotland, the greatest increases are all in the South and Midlands. In all these regions there was decentralization, relatively in most cases but absolutely in the North West and Yorkshire/Humberside. The national pattern of relative decentralization is, therefore, replicated in most regions.

With the intermediate non-manual, the national pattern of decentralization is repeated even more faithfully. In all regions the trend of

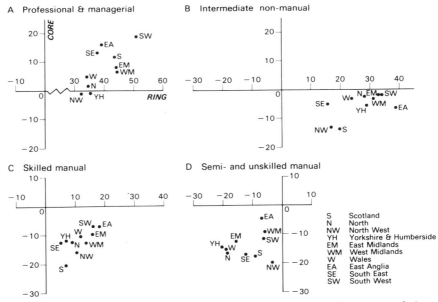

Figure 6.2 Percentage changes in the socio-economic groups in cores and rings aggregated to economic planning region level in Great Britain 1961–71

absolute decentralization is observed. The regional pattern is also evident with the greatest increases in the rings and the smallest decreases in the cores (excepting Wales and the North) tending to be in the South and Midlands. Almost exactly the same pattern is observed for skilled manual occupations, with the national pattern of absolute decentralization repeated in every region, and with the smallest losses in cores and largest increases in rings being observed in the South and Midlands.

With the semi- and unskilled manual the pattern is not so simple. The national trends were absolute losses in both cores and rings and this is repeated in all regions. However, as the national rates of change are similar, being −15.6 per cent in cores and −11.6 per cent in rings, it is not surprising that the pattern of decentralization is not regionally uniform. Decentralization occurred in Scotland, the North West, the West Midlands, the South East and the South West while centralization occurred in all the other regions. No obvious reason can be suggested for this peculiar pattern, and in view of the similar national rates of change, probably no great importance should be attached to it. In contrast, the regional pattern seems to be simpler, with the greatest decreases in both the cores and rings occurring mainly in the periphery.

The evidence therefore shows that the national patterns of decentralization are repeated almost perfectly in all regions for all socioeconomic groups except the lowest status. At the same time, the regional pattern of greater increases or lesser decreases in the South and Midlands generally holds true for both cores and rings. However, evidence on this latter point is by no means uniform. There are a number of minor exceptions and the South East constitutes a major exception. There, both cores and rings consistently had poorer growth rates than most of the South and Midlands, excepting the professional and managerial group. Given the intra-regional variation between London and the rest of the South East, noted earlier, this clearly deserves further examination. When the percentage change rates were recalculated for the South East excluding London, the latter was found to have exceptional growth rates. For all classes except the semi- and unskilled, the South East had far better growth rates in both cores and rings. In the middle status groups all regions experienced losses in the cores but the South East (excepting London) had increases of 13.4 per cent and 19.7 per cent in the intermediate non-manual and skilled manual. Therefore, rather than think in terms of a simple division between South and periphery, it may be necessary to think of a threefold division into periphery, South and Midlands, and the South East excepting London. Even this division may be too simplistic. Earlier, the exceptional changes in the largest MELAs were noted and it is clearly important to examine these cities. This could suggest further modifications to the intra-urban patterns already outlined. However, such changes are related to the important themes of inner city problems and social polarization and they will be examined in this wider context in the following section.

Decentralization and polarization in the Million Cities

This section considers the intra-urban patterns of decentralization in the Million Cities. At the scale of the individual MELAs, the question of centralization versus decentralization assumes particular importance. It has been suggested that differential migration rates for individual social classes has led to increasing social segregation between the inner and outer parts of metropolitan areas (Heidemann and Drewett, 1973). This has been termed social polarization and is usually, although not always, taken to mean the growing concentration of higher-status groups in outer areas and lower-status groups in inner areas. Polarization has been criticized as creating visible concentrations of deprivation, reducing social interaction between classes, and limiting the opportunities for social mobility (Harris, 1973). In recent years this argument has increased in importance because of its links with the debate on 'the inner city crisis'. Both the specially commissioned inner area studies (Department of Environment, 1977b, c, d) and a number of independent researchers (Eversley, 1975a; Hall, 1977) have identified the increasing concentration of lower-paid, lesser-skilled populations in poor environmental areas as a major symptom of the inner city crisis. A combination of housing and employment constraints is usually taken to account for the low migration potential of the less skilled who, therefore, seem to become 'trapped' in the inner city.

Given the importance of this debate, it will be useful to obtain a systematic analysis of the social class changes in the largest cities. Such analyses already exist for the GLC at both the levels of wards and enumeration districts (Harris, 1973; Hamnett, 1976). However, there have been no comparative studies of the major cities and no major analyses at the larger scale of the metropolitan labour areas. The cores of these labour areas do not, of course, correspond to the areas usually considered to be the 'inner cities'. For example, the core of London includes more than the entire GLC area. However, it is important to know whether polarization is occurring at this larger spatial scale, particularly as it has been suggested that characteristic inner city problems in London are beginning to spread to the 'outer' boroughs (Pahl, 1978; Bentham, 1978). The seven MELAs with populations greater than 1 million are especially suitable for this comparative study, as the London, Birmingham, Manchester, Liverpool and Newcastle MELAs are the locations of the seven *inner city partnerships*, while Glasgow has its own inner area redevelopment project, the Glasgow Eastern Area Renewal Project (Gray, 1978).

In actually measuring polarization, a number of definitions can be used. For example, polarization can be seen as affecting only one social class or two bipolar classes, as ongoing change or as a static state, and as occurring in only the inner areas or between inner and outer areas (Harris, 1973). This analysis will be concerned with polarization, only in so far as it affects the semi- and unskilled manual occupational group. Two definitions are used and polarization is said to exist if either:

1 A 'large' proportion of economically active males in cores are semi- and unskilled ('large' is arbitrarily defined as 50 per cent), or
2 Relative changes are leading to an increase in the proportion of core population who are semi- and unskilled manual workers.

The first of these definitions is a simple static form of polarization, while the second measure is of polarization as a trend, emphasizing the changing composition of the population resident in cores. The patterns resulting from these two forms of analysis are relatively simple. It was found that the semi- and unskilled do *not* dominate the social composition of any Million City core, with the proportions ranging from 22.6 per cent to 33 per cent in 1971. On the other hand, all except London's core had proportions higher than the nation-wide mean for the cores of 24.9 per cent. Thus, while no outright polarization appears to exist at this scale, there was a tendency for the semi- and unskilled manual to be relatively more important in the cores of the largest cities.

Examining the trend in polarization, it was found that changes between 1961 and 1971 had, in all but the case of Birmingham, led to a decrease in the proportion of core population who were semi- and unskilled manual workers. On the other hand, except for London and Liverpool, the decrease was less than the national average downward shift of 2 per cent. Therefore, the trend was against the increasing polarization of the lower status in the cores, but at a lesser rate than nationally. However, the changing levels of unemployment between 1961 and 1971, especially in the conurbations themselves, make it necessary to treat these findings with caution.

In summary, it is clear that the semi- and unskilled were generally decentralizing from the cores, were decreasing as a proportion of core population and did not constitute more than a third of core population in 1971 in any Million City. This is no evidence of polarization in terms either of static or changing distributions.

Perhaps the main conclusion which may be drawn from this analysis is that the overall character of the social structure (of low-status groups in core areas) has been affected by the all-pervasive national force of decline rather than by differential migration.

Speculative conclusions

Answers to the various questions posed at the beginning of this chapter have been provided in the relevant sections, but it is worthwhile to conclude with some speculations about recent developments in British class structure. The broad pattern of events since 1971 is of course well-known. Britain's manufacturing base has continued to decline and this trend has been intensified by the world recession which followed the 1974 increase in oil prices. Many of Britain's traditional manufacturing industries have been adversely affected by foreign competition which has led to a continuing decrease in skilled manual employment, especially in the inner areas of the large conurbations. In contrast, services have continued to grow but particularly those of a professional or scientific character (Manpower Research Group, 1980). Unlike the 1960s, however, the growth of the tertiary sector has not compensated for the decline of manufacturing. Indeed, the decline of traditional forms of 'blue-collar' service employment is seen as playing an important role in causing unemployment in many inner city areas (Townsend, 1977). Thus the limited evidence available suggests that the decline of blue-collar employment in the 1970s is proceeding at rates faster than most people initially anticipated (Leicester, 1978). The net effect of these developments is certain to be a continuation of the trend towards non-manual forms of employment (Gudgin, Crum and Bailey, 1979).

The spatial manifestations of these processes are rather more difficult to anticipate. The increasing costs of energy and hence mobility, the decline of investment in construction, and the general rundown of regional assistance and New Town policy would suggest a trend towards less dynamic spatial change than in the 1960s. Nevertheless, the preliminary results from the 1981 Census indicate the continued decline of the major British conurbations albeit at reduced rates in many cases (Office of Population Censuses and Surveys, 1981). Furthermore, the suburban rings and especially those in the south of the country are continuing to experience rapid change (Hall, 1980). Nevertheless, it does not seem likely that, at the scale of functional urban areas, future developments will lead to growing social polarization of manual workers in the cores. Polarization is much more likely to occur at smaller levels such as the street or block and this is an issue which requires future study. In any case it is not the particular social mix which is a cause for concern so much as the social conditions experienced by those at the bottom of the occupational hierarchy. In a period in which public sector services are under fierce political attack, and when technological developments look certain to increase rates of productivity and intensify occupational change, the most serious form of polarization in the future may be between those employed in well-paid technical managerial and skilled jobs, and those who are either unemployed or else in low-paid unskilled work. Another important development has been the increased rate of participation of females in the paid workforce. Projections suggest that the proportion of female workers may reach 45 per cent by 1991, although there is considerable controversy and uncertainty in these fields. Much of the work has been part-time and this may have important implications for future full-time employment (Leicester, 1978). Together all these developments suggests that future studies of the changing class structure will face increasing limitations in focusing upon the full-time economically active.

7

Population and employment decentralization and the journey to work

A. E. Gillespie

Introduction

THE JOURNEY TO WORK AND URBAN CHANGE

The unique characteristic of the journey to work in linking homes with workplaces has meant that many of the most important spatial aspects of social and economic restructuring have been reflected in the changing patterns and characteristics of such journeys. From a long-term historical perspective, the development of the journey to work as commonly experienced human activity was itself indicative of a major change in societal organization. Only with the industrial revolution and the associated development of wage labour did living and working become, on an appreciable scale, spatially separate activities. In these early stages, the urban fabric was conditioned by the need for pedestrian accessibility, and even in the largest cities journeys to work were local in nature (Schaeffer and Schlar, 1975; Boal, 1968; Bagwell, 1974). But as successive improvements in transport technology reduced the real costs of overcoming the friction of distance, so a successively greater proportion of urban residents were able to exercise some degree of choice in their residential location, with the result that journey lengths increased (Gillespie, 1980). This residential suburbanization phenomenon is of course still proceeding, facilitated by the yet greater locational flexibility made possible by the private vehicle, while the onset of decentralizing forces upon many types of employment is leading to greater complexity in journey-to-work patterns; the daily ebb and flow from suburb to centre is now but one component of emerging urban work travel systems.

In addition to highlighting changes in the spatial organization of society, the journey to work is an important activity for study in its own right. Many commentators have drawn attention to the time, resource and financial costs of commuting (for example, Liepmann, 1944; Westergaard, 1957; Lawton, 1963 and 1968). In the 1970s the costs of commuting became a particularly relevant issue as a result of the 'energy crisis', which has brought dramatically to an end the trend of falling real energy costs in the postwar period (Central Policy Review Staff, 1974). The transport sector accounts for over 20 per cent of fuel and energy final consumption (Advisory Council on Energy Conservation, 1976) and, more significantly, is almost totally dependent upon oil. It is now being asked whether in the long term individuals and society can afford to sustain the level of energy usage which developed during a period in which different cost relationships applied.

A further feature of the last decade which has served to push transport in general and urban passenger transport in particular to the forefront of public awareness has been the problems caused by public expenditure constraints. The state has always played an important role in the transport sector as an operator and/or in setting the rules of competition between different modes. In the sense of transport operator, the Callaghan government stated in the mid-1970s that constraints on public expenditure would necessitate 'first a painful re-appraisal of the priority to be accorded to transport as against the competing claims of housing, education and the social services, and secondly a ruthless re-examination of transport expenditure to ensure that it is actually achieving the social and economic ends in view' (Department of Environment, 1976b). As evidenced by the removal of new vehicle subsidies to public transport operators it is clear that the transport sector is not exempt from the further round of expenditure cut-backs now being implemented by the Thatcher government.

Thus from a number of perspectives – ranging from a desire to improve our understanding of urban spatial restructuring to a concern with the social and economic objectives of transport policy – it is important to document changes in the journey to work in recent years. The present study attempts such an exercise for the 1966–71 period, which it might reasonably be argued is already of mainly historical interest. Due to the short-sighted cancellation of the 1976 sample Population Census, however, this constitutes the most recent period for which journey-to-work changes can be related, in a consistent fashion, to the underlying changes in the location of homes and jobs within urban regions.

In order to meet this objective of describing the interrelationships between changing urban spatial structure and the characteristics of the journey to work, it is important to select a framework of areal units which is appropriate in terms of scale and definition for the phenomena being studied (Openshaw, 1978). Such a framework is provided by the 'daily urban system', a term coined in the American context by Berry (1967a) to describe the pattern of activities around urban areas on a typical working day. In this study we are interested in the journeys which link workers' homes to their jobs, and thus the most appropriate form of daily urban system is the urban labour market area (Goodman, 1970; Carmichael, 1978), which have been defined in a number of major studies in Britain (Hall *et al.*, 1973; Smart, 1974; Drewett *et al.*, 1975 and 1976; Coombes *et al.*, 1982). The present study uses the Metropolitan Economic Labour Areas (MELAs), with their constituent urban employment cores and surrounding commuting hinterlands, as described in the note on the spatial representation of urban and regional change on p. xx.

Changing journey patterns

THE NATIONAL CONTEXT

The best-documented trend in journey-to-work change has undoubtedly been that of increasing trip length. The Barlow Report (1940) on the distribution of industry in Britain condemned the economic and social consequences of an excessive journey to work and drew particular attention to this problem in the London conurbation. London has since received the most attention, building upon Liepmann's (1944) pioneering work on the 1921 Census data. Nevertheless, the tendency for journey lengths to increase has been a country-wide phenomenon (Lawton, 1963; Redcliffe-Maud Commission, 1969; Davies and Musson, 1978): Warnes (1972), for example, estimated that the mean distance of journeys to work in north-west England increased from 2.35 km in 1921 to 3.54 km in 1966.

Estimating journey distances from local authority area-based census data presents a number of problems, however, particularly as the majority of journeys to work do not cross local authority boundaries (see Warnes, 1972, for a discussion of this problem). An alternative indicator of changing journey length can be obtained by examining changes in the proportion of total journeys which cross such areal boundaries for, *ceterus paribus*, a tendency for journey lengths to increase will be reflected in an increasing proportion of inter-area relative to intra-area journeys. Thus as reported by the Redcliffe-Maud Commission (1969), between 1921 and 1966 the proportion of the active population in England (excluding

Greater London) who worked outside the local authority where they lived rose from 21 per cent to 34 per cent. These figures in fact underestimate the tendency for journey lengths to increase, for local government reorganization in the period reduced the number of local authorities by a quarter (which, if journey lengths had remained unchanged, would have reduced the proportion of journeys crossing area boundaries by 'internalizing' them within larger areal units; Smart, 1974).

In the present study of the 1966–71 period, changes in the importance of cross-boundary work travel can be examined at three spatial scales; the local authority, the constituent zone (i.e. urban core, urban ring or outer ring) and the labour market area as a whole. At each of these levels, journeys between areas grew at the expense of intra-area journeys, a consistent trend indicative of increasing journey-to-work lengths.

Journeys between local authority areas increased by 0.4 million (4 per cent), contrasting with a decline of 0.8 million in the number of journeys within these areas. As a result, the proportion of the nation's employed population working outside the local authority where they lived rose from 36 per cent to 38.2 per cent. As the spatial scale of analysis increases, the relative growth of inter-area movement becomes more marked; thus at the labour market area level, journeys between MELAs grew in number by 0.3 million (19 per cent), while journeys within MELAs declined by 0.8 million. Inter-MELA commuting consequently expanded its share of total journeys to work from 6.6 per cent in 1966 to 8.1 per cent in 1971. In spite of the substantial absolute decline in total travel within MELAs, trips between urban zones within these areas increased by 5 per cent, the overall decline thus being attributable to the contraction of within-zone journeys.

Although there is no explicit measure of journey distance in this type of analysis, the uniformity of the trends displayed at different spatial scales must lead to the conclusion that home–workplace separation increased in aggregate terms over the five-year period. Nevertheless, the direction of change should not be allowed to obscure the fact that, even in 1971, more than 60 per cent of the nation's employed population worked in their local authority area of residence.

How is this gradual and long-established trend toward increasing journey length to be explained? Lawton (1963) drew attention to the very marked decline between 1921 and 1951 in the number of local authorities in England and Wales with approximately balanced job and employed population totals, and a commensurate increase in the number of areas with net job deficits. The local authorities with net job surpluses (in the main the large towns and cities) remained relatively few in number, although their surpluses grew substantially in size. The causes of these changes were the growing urban concentration of employment on the one hand and a widespread dispersal of residences on the other, resulting in the extension and intensification of commuting hinterlands around the large urban areas. As Lawton (1963) put it, 'Clearly, changes in population and employment are not in harmony and the journey to work is, in part, an expression of their dissonance.' There is one very important difference between the processes leading to increasing trip lengths in the 1921–51 period described by Lawton and the processes evident in the 1960s – namely, the shift from employment centralization to decentralization. The 1950s effectively mark a transition period in this process (at this particular spatial scale); the rate of job growth in the nation's urban core areas was almost identical to the rate of ring area job growth (6.7 per cent and 6.6 per cent respectively; Department of Environment, 1976a, p. 61). In the decade which followed, this balance was firmly tipped in the direction of decentralization from cores to rings, the former recording a job-base contraction of 3 per cent and the latter an impressive 15 per cent increase (table 7.1).

Table 7.1 Change in resident employed population and employment by urban zone in Britain 1961–71

	1961–6		1966–71		1961–71	
	Employed population	Employment	Employed population	Employment	Employed population	Employment
Core	−70	+145	−869	−591	−939	−446
	−0.6%	*+1.0%*	*−7.0%*	*−4.1%*	*−7.5%*	*−3.1%*
Ring	+680	+512	+380	+197	+1060	+709
	+10.7%	*+10.8%*	*+5.4%*	*+3.8%*	*+16.7%*	*+15.0%*
SMLA	+610	+658	−489	−394	+121	+264
	+3.2%	*+3.5%*	*−2.5%*	*−2.0%*	*+0.6%*	*+1.4%*
Outer ring	+208	+175	+48	−39	+256	+136
	+6.0%	*+5.3%*	*+1.3%*	*−1.1%*	*+7.4%*	*+4.1%*
MELA	+818	+832	−441	−432	+377	+400
	+3.7%	*+3.7%*	*−1.9%*	*−1.9%*	*+1.7%*	*+1.8%*

Note: Figures in thousands, with percentage changes in italics

Even *within* the 1960s, however, there were marked changes in the spatial restructuring of employment. Between 1961 and 1966, the nation's urban cores experienced a slight increase in their job total, while the ring areas expanded vigorously (1 per cent and 11 per cent respectively). In 1961 20 per cent of national employment was located in the rings but these areas nevertheless captured 64 per cent of national job growth in the following five years. In the 1966–71 period, however, the worsening economic background translated net job growth into net decline, with a strong spatial differentiation in impact. Although the rate of ring employment growth was much reduced it was the cores that were particularly affected, suffering a loss of half a million jobs (table 7.1). Thus in national aggregate terms, the two halves of the 1961–71 decade were characterized by a shift from relative to absolute employment decentralization. It is this shift which sharply focused attention on the problems of the inner urban areas; although such areas had performed poorly in *relative* terms for a number of decades (Warnes, 1977), it was only when this poor performance took place in the context of a contracting economy that the trend began to be perceived as a serious problem.

With respect to the changing home–workplace relationship, it might be assumed that the onset of widespread employment decentralization would have reduced the 'dissonance' which Lawton commented upon for an earlier period. Paradoxically, however, such dissonance increased in the second half of the 1960s, due to divergence in the *rates* of employed resident population and employment decentralization. Whereas in the 1961–6 period both components had remained virtually static in the core areas and had grown at the same rate in the rings, between 1966 and 1971 employed population declined in cores at a faster rate than jobs (–7 per cent and –4.1 per cent respectively; table 7.1) and grew at faster rate in rings (5.4 per cent and 3.8 per cent respectively). The result of this divergence was an increasing net surplus of jobs in core areas, and an increasing net deficit in rings.

This trend towards a growing functional interdependency between urban employment cores and their surrounding commuting hinterlands can be demonstrated by reference to the 'net commuting ratios' of each zone type. The net commuting ratio is obtained by dividing the employed resident population of a zone by its employment. A ratio below 1.0 indicates an excess of jobs over employed residents and consequently a net inward commuting flow, while a ratio greater than 1.0 indicates a deficiency of jobs and hence net out-commuting from the zone. If a ratio is moving further away from 1.0, the zone is becoming relatively more imbalanced in net commuting terms. Between 1961 and 1966 the ratio for the nation's core areas became slightly more imbalanced moving from 0.88 to 0.86, but remained unchanged in the ring areas at 1.35. In the second half of the decade, however, the diverging rates of change in employed population and employment were reflected in the ratios for each zone type moving further away from 1.0 (falling from 0.86 to 0.84 in the core areas and rising from 1.35 to 1.37 in the rings). In the less functionally integrated outer ring areas a similar tendency is apparent, with a stable ratio in the first period followed by an increase from 1.05 to 1.07 in the second, produced by a small net increase in resident employed population and a small net decline in jobs. The outer ring areas are effectively one stage behind the ring areas, reflecting their greater distance from the declining core areas; they have begun to share the effects of residential decentralization, but by 1971 were still recording employment losses.

In summary then, the relative over-representation of jobs in core areas and under-representation in rings has not been reduced by the onset of employment decentralization. Indeed, such spatial imbalances have been accentuated due to the accelerating process of residential decentralization from cores to their hinterlands; that is, although home and workplace locational trends are now operating in the same direction, there are no signs at the national aggregate level that the trends are converging over time. As Thomas (1968) established for the largest urban areas, the essential feature of the spatial restructuring process is that workers are continuing to decentralize at a faster rate and in greater numbers than their jobs, resulting in a growing net functional interdependency between the constituent zones of urban areas.

The manner in which this increasing net interdependency is reflected in gross patterns of commuting is indicated in table 7.2, which shows the changing importance of the various origin and destination combinations of journeys within MELAs (which in 1971 constituted 88 per cent of total work travel in Great Britain). The dominant feature of the table is the contraction by 0.9 million journeys (−8.3 per cent) of the within-core component, resulting in its share of total intra-MELA work travel falling from 51.6 per cent in 1966 to 49.1 per cent in 1971, while the greater decentralization of employed population than employment in the period is shown by the growing importance of journeys from rings to cores. Such journeys increased by 111,000 (4.7 per cent), and by 1971 accounted for 11.9 per cent of the intra-MELA total compared with 10.9 per cent in 1966. Journeys *within* ring areas also expanded substantially in

Table 7.2 Flows within and between urban zones for journeys within MELAs 1966–71

Origin/Destination	1966 (000s)	1966–71 change (000s)	1966–71 % change	1966 % share	1966–71 change in share
Within core	11,105	−923	−8.3	51.6	−2.5
Core to ring	760	−26	−3.4	3.5	+0.0
Core to outer ring	73	0	+0.0	0.3	+0.0
Ring to core	2,354	+111	+4.7	10.9	+0.9
Within ring	3,840	+94	+2.5	17.8	+1.1
Ring to outer ring	140	+15	+10.7	0.6	+0.1
Outer ring to core	206	+42	+20.4	1.0	+0.2
Outer ring to ring	143	+37	+25.9	0.7	+0.2
Within outer ring	2,908	−128	−4.4	13.5	−0.1
Total	21,527	−777	−3.6	100.0	—

Note: Figures may not sum to totals because of rounding

number (94,000), but from a larger initial base. As a consequence, the proportion of total ring residents commuting into the urban cores increased slightly from 37.2 per cent to 37.6 per cent.

In the outer ring areas, the decline of local job opportunities resulted in the number of within-zone journeys falling by 121,000, but at the same time very high rates of growth were recorded in the centripetal commuting flows from outer rings to cores and rings (table 7.2). Consequently, they became more dependent on jobs located in the central zones of labour market areas; the proportion of outer ring residents working in the inner zones increased from 10.7 per cent in 1966 to 13.3 per cent in 1971. Although this rise in central dependency is marked in relative terms, the outer ring areas remain considerably less integrated with urban labour markets than the ring areas.

In summary, changes in the location of residences and workplaces and in the relationships between these elements, are leading to a restructuring of journey-to-work patterns. On the one hand, the decentralization of both homes and jobs is reflected in the massive absolute decline in the number of journeys within the nation's core areas and a much smaller but not insignificant expansion in journeys within ring areas. On the other, the differential rates of decentralization of the two elements helps explain the substantial increases in commuting into cores from their surrounding hinterlands. The first trend is reducing the overall degree of centrality of daily urban systems, while the second is in certain respects reinforcing this centrality by increasing the relative functional dependency between the constituent zones of urban labour market areas. The overriding impression then is one of increasing complexity in the pattern of journeys to work within the nation's MELAs.

VARIATIONS BETWEEN TYPES OF CITY

The above summary of trends at the national aggregate level disguises of course a wide range of variations in local labour market behaviour. In a report by the Urban Change Project (Department of Environment, 1976a), it was concluded that:

> decentralisation of population and latterly of jobs is a process which is coming to characterise most British cities, despite their size, region or relative location. What does vary is the *rate* at which the process is operating and the stage it has reached. Cities in the older industrial regions are decentralising more rapidly than free-standing towns in less populated regions. . . . Size of city is also an important explanatory factor.

This suggests that in terms of the relationship between home and workplace locational changes and the restructuring of journey-to-work patterns, many of the key variations in local trends can be identified by examining groups of labour markets with similar characteristics in terms of relative location and/or size. Using such criteria, a nine-group classification of labour market areas was devised, details of which can be found in Spence *et al.* (1982). The changes in the number of intra-MELA journeys to work beginning and ending in each zone type are aggregated for the nine labour market groups in table 7.3.

Table 7.3 Absolute changes in origins and destinations by urban zone for journeys within MELAs, by MELA groups 1966–71 (thousands)

MELA group	Core		Ring		Outer ring	
	Origins	Destinations	Origins	Destinations	Origins	Destinations
New Towns	+26	+28	+2	0	0	0
Secondary industrial	−54	−37	+6	−7	−28	−32
Retirement areas	−13	+4	+9	0	−2	−11
Peripheral free-standing	−31	0	+34	+21	−25	−44
Southern free-standing	−7	+4	+28	+22	+2	−3
Small Lancs/Yorks	−31	−19	+2	−9	−2	−2
London peripheral	−11	−4	+19	+14	+3	+1
Major industrial	−135	−111	+56	+38	+1	−5
Million Cities	−693	−634	+64	+25	+3	−17
Total	−948	−768	+221	+105	−49	−113

Note: Columns may not sum exactly to total due to rounding

Journey origins correspond to employed residents and journey destinations correspond to jobs, with the proviso that because the table is concerned only with intra-MELA journeys, employed residents working in other MELAs and jobs filled by residents of other MELAs are excluded from the accounting procedure. As the vast majority of journeys to work are within MELAs, however, the changes in zonal pattern of origins and destinations shown in the table represent very closely changes in the zonal location of residences and workplaces.

Table 7.3 firmly indicates the extent to which absolute population decentralization from cores to rings has come to pervade all parts of the country and all levels of the urban hierarchy. The number of journeys originating in core areas declined in every labour market group with the predictable exception of the New Towns, while the number of ring origins grew in all nine groups. Absolute employment decentralization is far less universally established, with only three groups recording core decline and ring growth in destinations. Indeed, the national experience of absolute employment decentralization is produced by just two groups of labour markets – the major industrial and the Million Cities, which together constitute the twenty largest urban labour markets. Nevertheless, the trends evident in the remaining groups are operating in the same direction, if not at the same stage or intensity, for in each case (New Towns excepted) the employment performance of the ring areas is better than that of the cores (i.e. larger growth or smaller decline). Thus although employment locational restructuring is not as far advanced as residential, *relative* decentralization from cores to rings is widely established.

A further common feature, which has particular importance with respect to journey-to-work change, is that within each group the zonal balances between workers' residences and jobs display a consistent relationship. That is, the employed population in core areas declined by a larger amount than employment (or declined while employment increased), and grew by a larger amount in ring areas. As a result, the job surpluses of cores and the job deficits of rings became larger. The trend observed at the national level towards a growing functional dependency in commuting terms between inner and outer areas is thus characteristic not only of the largest cities in the urban system but also of cities throughout the size spectrum and across a wide range of environments, from the heavily industrialized areas to the free-standing towns located peripherally to the main areas of urban Britain.

Because of the enormous size differential between the groups and their varying overall performances, it is difficult using absolute data to assess variations in the strength of the common trends identified above. Table 7.4 thus portrays changes in zonal origins and destinations for each group in relative terms – i.e. percentage points changes in share of the total. The table is ordered so as to represent a sequence from centralization (top) to strong decentralization (bottom). The New Towns are the

Table 7.4 Changes in the percentage share of total origins and destinations by urban zone for journeys within MELAs, by MELA groups 1966–71

MELA group	Core		Ring		Outer ring	
	Origins	Destinations	Origins	Destinations	Origins	Destinations
New Towns	+2.0	+2.5	−1.9	−2.4	−0.1	−0.1
Secondary industrial	−0.8	+0.1	+1.1	+0.4	−0.3	−0.5
Retirement areas	−0.9	+0.6	+0.9	+0.2	−0.0	−0.8
Peripheral free-standing	−1.3	+0.6	+2.3	+1.4	−1.0	−2.0
Southern free-standing	−1.4	−0.5	+2.0	+1.6	−0.6	−1.1
Small Lancs/Yorks	−2.1	−0.1	+2.1	+0.1	0.0	0.0
London peripheral	−1.8	−1.2	+1.6	+1.2	+0.3	+0.1
Major industrial	−2.5	−1.7	+2.2	+1.6	+0.3	+0.1
Million Cities	−3.3	−2.0	+2.8	+1.8	+0.5	+0.2
Total	−2.5	−1.3	+2.2	+1.3	+0.3	0.0

only group in which the core share of both origins and destinations increased at the expense of their hinterlands. The next three groups (secondary industrial, retirement areas and peripheral free-standing labour markets) are characterized by a declining core share of origins but a continuing increase in share of destinations (though at the expense of the outer rather than inner ring). In the southern free-standing and small Lancashire/Yorkshire labour markets relative employment decentralization is evident, with the inner rings recording increases in both origins and destinations at the expense of the other zones. Finally, the bottom three groups in the table (London peripheral, major industrial and the Million Cities) display the strongest decentralizing tendencies, with substantial core contraction in origin and destination shares and corresponding growth in inner and outer rings.

The manner in which these net changes in the locations of homes and workplaces within the labour market groups are translated into changing patterns of work travel is revealed in table 7.5: for each group, the percentage point changes in the share of total intra-MELA work travel accounted for by the nine zonal origin/destination combinations are shown. Concentrating first on journeys originating in core areas, the declining degree of overall centrality in daily urban systems finds expression in the falling importance of journeys contained within cores in eight of the nine groups. The strength of the trend varies considerably, however, with the largest relative contraction in this component occurring in the Million Cities (−3.4 per cent), in which the process of internal restructuring is furthest advanced. A decline of this magnitude – in absolute terms a fall of 0.7 million journeys in just five years – clearly has major implications for public transport operation in the conurbations, a point which will be returned to later when mode of travel changes are considered.

There is no such clear pattern in the considerably smaller commuting flow from cores to rings, even in the labour market groups in which job decentralization is furthest advanced. In the Million Cities, journeys from cores to rings slightly increased their share of total work travel, but this was due to a below-average rate of decline rather than a real increase – between 1966 and 1971 this type of journey fell by 11,000, despite increasing slightly in the 1961–71 period as a whole (Gillespie, 1977). Thus at this spatial scale, there is little evidence to suggest that reverse commuting is becoming a more important feature of urban work travel.

The influence of relative population and employment decentralization on journey-to-work patterns is indicated by the growing shares accounted for by both ring-to-core and within-ring journeys in all labour market groups but the New Towns (in which the intra-zonal component declined). The rate of growth in the two components, and the relationship between them, vary widely however. In the cities in which employment

Table 7.5 Changes in the percentage share of total flows within and between urban zones for journeys within MELAs, by MELA groups 1966–71

MELA group	Core to: Core	Ring	Outer ring	Ring to: Core	Ring	Outer ring	Outer ring to: Core	Ring	Outer ring
New Towns	+1.9	+0.1	+0.0	+0.6	-2.5	+0.0	+0.1	-0.0	-0.1
Secondary industrial	-0.9	+0.0	+0.0	+0.7	+0.3	+0.2	+0.4	+0.0	-0.7
Retirement areas	-0.8	+0.0	-0.0	+0.9	+0.0	-0.0	+0.5	+0.1	-0.7
Peripheral free-standing	-1.1	-0.1	-0.1	+1.3	+0.7	+0.3	+0.4	+0.9	-3.0
Southern free-standing	-1.5	+0.1	+0.0	+0.6	+1.3	+0.1	+0.3	+0.3	-1.2
Small Lancs/Yorks	-1.7	-0.5	+0.0	+1.5	+0.6	+0.1	+0.1	+0.0	-0.1
London peripheral	-2.1	+0.2	+0.0	+0.7	+0.9	+0.0	+0.2	+0.1	+0.0
Major industrial	-2.3	-0.2	-0.0	+0.5	+1.6	+0.1	+0.2	+0.2	+0.0
Million Cities	-3.4	+0.1	+0.0	+1.3	+1.5	+0.0	+0.2	+0.2	+0.1
Total	-2.5	+0.0	+0.0	+0.9	+1.1	+0.1	+0.2	+0.2	-0.1

decentralization is most firmly established, the net dependence of ring areas upon core jobs has increased marginally, if at all. In fact, in the Million Cities, the proportion of ring residents commuting to the cores rose only from 41.3 per cent to 41.7 per cent between 1966 and 1971, while in the major industrial group the proportion actually declined from 37 per cent to 35.9 per cent. In contrast, labour market groups at earlier stages of internal spatial adaption, particularly small labour markets and/or those peripheral to the main axis of urban Britain, experienced large relative increases in ring/core dependence in the second half of the 1960s. The level rose by around 2 percentage points for the peripheral free-standing and Lancashire/Yorkshire MELA groups, by 2.7 points for the retirement areas and by over 5 points for the New Towns group.

It can be hypothesized that during the 1970s the established trend will have been reversed in the ring areas of the largest cities, so that they will have become *less* dependent upon core jobs due to the continued relative decentralization of employment and a slow-down in population growth. It is already evident that the zone of most active population growth in these cities has moved to their outer rings, which are recording rapidly increasing levels of work travel integration with the urban labour markets. In effect, the outer rings of the conurbations are displaying trends which are characteristic of the inner rings of cities at less advanced stages in the 'life cycle'.

In summary, it has been demonstrated that changes in the location of homes and jobs are having substantial effects upon patterns of work travel within urban labour market areas. The growing inter-dependencies between urban zones and the intensification of commuting fields are not confined to a particular type of labour market area but are evident in groups with widely varying size, locational and functional characteristics. In the largest cities, the scale of relative employment decentralization from cores to rings resulted in little change in the *level* of dependency between the zones (although in absolute terms such interaction increased markedly); the outer rings of these cities, however, displayed imbalanced development due to a population influx not matched by job growth, and consequently centripetal commuting increased at a rapid rate. In the smaller cities and in those in which internal restructuring is at an earlier stage, the inner ring areas experienced strong growth in dependency upon the urban core zones due to the lag between residence and workplace shifts.

Mode of travel, car-ownership and spatial structure

The above section has been concerned with relating changes in journey length and orientation to changes in home and workplace location – i.e. viewing work travel as the outcome of or response to urban structure.

However, the relationship between structure and interaction is extremely complex, displaying characteristics which may be summarized as circular and cumulative causality. This is best illustrated with respect to another aspect of the journey to work, namely the mode of travel.

The five years between 1966 and 1971 witnessed a massive net shift from public to private road transport. Journeys within MELAs by bus contracted by 1.2 million (18 per cent), while car journeys increased by 1 million (16 per cent), and by 1971 the respective shares of total intra-MELA work travel stood at 27 per cent and 35 per cent, compared with 31 per cent and 29 per cent at the beginning of the period. How is the emergence of the private car as the dominant mode of travel to be explained?

The conventional explanation focuses on rising car ownership (in turn related to rising real incomes) because of the relationship between car ownership and car usage. Certainly, the growth of car ownership in the period under investigation was of an impressive scale. The number of journeys within MELAs made by people in households without cars fell by over 2 million (–21 per cent), while journeys made by members of car-owning households increased by 1.5 million (13 per cent). Particularly rapid growth occurred in the number of journeys made by members of households with two or more cars (38 per cent). As a result of these changes, by 1971 60 per cent of intra-MELA journeys were made by members of car-owning households, compared with only 51 per cent in 1966.

The reason why increasing car ownership would be expected to increase car usage is related to the difference in the mode of travel distribution between individuals in car-owning households and those in households without cars. Because of their constrained modal choice, members of households without cars rely very heavily on bus transport and on walking for the journey to work, with only 7 per cent travelling as passengers in cars owned by other households. This split contrasts strongly with households with one car, 50 per cent of whose members travel to work by car, with both bus travel and walking being considerably less important. In households owning two or more cars, the modal dominance is such that car journeys account for 64 per cent of the total, with bus travel being undertaken by a mere 8 per cent of employed household members. Thus there is little doubt that the net growth of car-owning households at the expense of households without cars is an important factor in explaining the switch from public to private motorized transport. At the same time, however, other rather more complex factors also need to be taken into account, for there is a marked tendency for car usage to have increased between 1966 and 1971 in each of the car ownership categories. Thus the propensity to travel to work by car increased from 46 per cent to 50 per cent in one-car households and from 59 per cent to 64 per cent in households with two or more cars.

While the trends are obviously related, in an accounting sense the shift to car travel for the journey to work can then be regarded as the product of two components; first, an effect due to rising car ownership resulting in a car being *available* to a higher proportion of the population, and secondly, an increasing propensity for *usage* when household car ownership is held constant. If we apportion the total increase in car commuting to each of these components, increasing ownership emerges as the more important, though the increasing usage propensity is by no means insignificant (57 per cent and 43 per cent respectively). It should be pointed out, however, that some care is needed in interpreting the latter figure. This is because the likelihood of an individual using a car within a car-owning household is not independent of the number of employed persons in that household; for example, a net shift towards single-worker at the expense of multiple-worker households might be expected to increase car usage within each ownership category, simply because of the different levels of car availability to individuals within the household types. While it is true that in the period under investigation single-person households became more important in relative terms, a countervailing tendency was the widespread growth of female activity rates, particularly so for married females (Thatcher, 1979; Manley & Sawbridge, 1980). There is thus little evidence to suggest that the increasing tendency for car usage can be explained by shifts in household composition.

There are of course a number of factors which account for this trend. Numerous studies have pointed to the attractions of car travel compared with bus public transport (see for example Hill and Martin, 1976; Munt and Woodhall, 1967; Wilson, 1967; Quarmby, 1967; Heggie, 1976): attractions such as journey time, reliability, comfort and frequently cost. Why, though, should usage increase during the five-year period within household car-ownership categories? Part of the answer would seem to lie in the deterioration of public transport quality and its increasing cost *vis-à-vis* private motoring a process in turn linked to increasing car ownership. Thus at the beginning of the period we have a proportion of the population living in households without cars and hence largely reliant upon either walking or public transport to get to work, while the remainder of the population within car-owning households have a degree of choice as to their mode of travel to work, a choice which will be reached by weighing up the benefits and disbenefits of the modal options (though the lack of 'choice' of secondary wage-earners in households with only one car should not be forgotten, as it is all too often by those who simplistically equate household car-ownership with car availability for all household members). By the end of the period, a significant number of households previously without cars have acquired cars, and modal choice can be realistically exercised by more individuals within these households.

Their decisions are likely to be more heavily weighted in favour of car usage than the car-owning group five years previously, for the balance of benefits and disbenefits of the competing modes has changed. A number have already made the decision to use the car for work travel purpose, which both increased the total number of vehicles on the road (and hence leads to impaired public transport journey times and reliability) and reduces the revenue of the public transport operators (who respond by increasing fares). This in turn affects the modal choice of car owners previously using public transport, who switch modes and the 'vicious circle' begins another revolution. Thus both components of car travel increase discussed above, the availability component and the propensity for usage component, can be seen as part of a process in which the attractions of private *vis-à-vis* public transport have been rapidly increasing.

The above simplified description of the changing basis of the modal choice decision is, however, only part of the reason for the decline of public transport and the growth of car usage in the journey to work. This is because we must also take into account the characteristics of the competing modes in relation to the types of journey which are being made, for each mode is more appropriate for some types of journey than for others (Meyer, 1968). At one extreme, for example, the commuter railway is appropriate in a limited range of contexts; the economics of operation dictate that it is only viable for transporting large numbers of people along fixed 'corridors'. This implies the existence of high travel demand along the corridor, generally of the pattern in which suburban or ex-urban residential concentrations are linked to a centrally located employment node of considerable size. It is consequently no coincidence that only in London is the railway (surface and underground) a major journey-to-work travel mode (accounting for 23 per cent of total intra-MELA work travel). At the opposite extreme, the private car requires no minimum number of commuters along a particular route to make the journey viable, although the quality of the road infrastructure will reflect the volume of travel. Further, the private car is not well-suited to the type of journey for which the commuter railway caters due both to the problems of road congestion where many radial routes converge on a limited range of destinations and to the parking limitations imposed by the density of development in the centres of large cities. The importance of spatial factors in influencing modal choice can be illustrated by examples of the modal split of journeys made in different types of environment and linking different types of origin and destination.

SCALE OF URBAN AREA AND MODAL SPLIT

The size of an urban area (in terms of the number of journeys made) is positively related to the proportion of those journeys that are made by public transport (the correlation coefficient being 0.33). With the exceptions of London and to a lesser extent Glasgow, public transport is virtually synonymous with bus. Of the seven largest urban areas in the British system, five appear in the 'top-10' ranking of public transport's share of total intra-MELA journeys, with Glasgow having the largest share of all (52 per cent of journeys being by public transport). It should, however, be stressed that city size is just one influence upon public transport's relative importance as a journey to work mode; as would be expected from the earlier discussion concerning the modal split differences between households with and without cars, MELAs with high levels of household car-ownership display low levels of public transport usage. Correlation between these two variables produces a coefficient (R) of −0.87, highly significant for the 126 cases in the analysis, while the strongest positive residuals (MELAs which have higher public transport shares than would be predicted from their levels of household car-ownership) tend to be the big cities, including London, Glasgow, Liverpool, Birmingham, Leeds and Sheffield. London provides the most extreme case, with public transport's share of total work travel being 18 percentage points above the level that would be predicted from the general form of the relationship between public transport usage and car ownership. This reflects two related factors; first the lower propensity for car usage among those with one available, and secondly the below-average level of car ownership in big cities generally (Hillman *et al.*, 1973). Both factors are indicative of the relatively favourable position of public *vis-à-vis* private transport in the major conurbations, due to an urban structure which has facilitated the development of rapid transit systems on the one hand and which serves to mitigate some of the advantages pertaining to car ownership and usage on the other.

Having established that the modal structure of journeys to work is influenced by the type of urban environment in which the journey takes place, how does this help us to understand the growth of private car journeys and the commensurate decline in public transport journeys? The problem, for public transport, is that the big cities in which the bulk of the infrastructure and 'appropriate' demand is located are declining in absolute and relative terms, part of a wider process of net decentralization from big cities to smaller towns. In London, for example, the number of journeys within the MELA declined by 6.4 per cent between 1966 and 1971. Even if there had been no change in the *share* of total travel accounted for by public transport, the number of journeys would have declined by 140,000 (i.e. 6.4 per cent of 2.18 million public transport journeys). In reality the number of public transport journeys fell by 220,000, indicating that in terms of the contribution to the overall change, the absolute decline in the total number of journeys undertaken was more important than the relative change in the proportion of total journeys made by public transport.

THE MODAL SPLIT IN RELATION TO ORIGINS AND DESTINATIONS

In the same way that the type of urban environment affects the balance between the competing modes, the nature of the journey *within* urban areas is also related to mode of travel structure. Using the ninefold classification of intra-MELA zonal origin and destination combinations which was used in table 7.2 to describe changes in journey-to-work patterns, considerable variation can be observed in the modal split between public and private transport.

Table 7.6 indicates for each of the nine flow-types in 1966 and 1971 the percentage of total motorized journeys (i.e. excluding walking and cycling) accounted for by public transport. By far the highest public transport share is found in the within-core component of urban work travel (59 per cent in 1971), while the lowest shares occur in the within-ring and within-outer ring components (33 per cent and 31 per cent respectively). Intermediate levels of public transport usage are occupied by the major centripetal work flows from rings and outer rings to cores.

Table 7.6 Public transport's share of total motorized work travel for intra-MELA origin/destination combinations 1966–71

Origin/Destination	1966 %	1971 %	1966–71 % change
Within core	66	59	−7
Core to ring	54	46	−8
Core to outer ring	44	34	−10
Ring to core	52	44	−8
Within ring	41	33	−8
Ring to outer ring	46	34	−12
Outer ring to core	50	38	−12
Outer ring to ring	49	36	−13
Within outer ring	40	31	−9

Even at the very crude spatial scale of urban zones, the characteristics of origin and destination zone and the spatial relationship between them can help explain the above variations in modal structure. The dominance of public transport for journeys made within urban cores, for example, reflects the same types of factor described in the previous subsection concerning the modal split differences between large conurbations and smaller towns and cities; i.e. it is in the centre of urban regions that travel densities are greatest and where consequently the bulk of the public transport infrastructure is located, and where by the same token the operation of the private car is least appropriate.

In the case of the centripetal commuting flows to the cores from the outer zones, the balance of public transport's advantages and disadvantages are less uniform, varying considerably according to the scale and characteristics of the urban area in which the journey takes place. London, for example, with its well-developed commuter railway network and huge concentration of jobs in the inner city and central business district has a very high public transport share, with a strong emphasis on rail rather than bus. The railway is of course particularly appropriate for long-distance commuting, because of its high average speed on limited-stop services (Munt and Woodhall, 1967). Indeed, the viability of an urban region of London's size and complexity, with well-above-average levels of home–workplace separation, is effectively predicated on the existence of rail mass-transit systems. In smaller towns and cities, in which public transport is virtually synonymous with bus, the private car captures a higher proportion of the inward commuting flows due to the different balance between the advantages and disadvantages of the competing modes.

The within-ring and within-outer-ring components of urban work travel, in which public transport's share of total motorized travel is lowest, reflect clearly the influence of spatial structure on journey mode. In such areas, where population and employment densities are considerably lower than in the urban cores and where origin–destination patterns are dispersed rather than nodal, public transport is least able to compete with the flexibility afforded by the private automobile. The modal dominance of the car in cross-commuting between suburbs was first observed in the United States context (see for example Taafe *et al.*, 1963; Burt, 1961), where this type of pattern is of relatively greater importance due to (interrelated) factors such as high car-ownership levels and widely dispersed employment locations (Ganz, 1968; Kasarda, 1976; Guest, 1975 and 1976). In the British context, the influence of workplace decentralization on mode of travel structure and change has been demonstrated by Wabe (1968) and Daniels (1970, 1972).

As with the big city/small city net redistribution, so the origin–destination combinations within cities that are most appropriate for public transport usage are those that are suffering absolute and relative decline, while journey types in which the private car is dominant are growing in importance. Thus within-core journeys declined in aggregate by 0.9 million, while centripetal and 'lateral' journeys in the outer zones recorded absolute increase, with the single exception of within-outer-ring journeys (table 7.2). At the same time the share of these flows accounted for by public transport was falling in each of the nine types though the shift in the modal split of intra-core journeys was the least marked (table 7.6). Thus public transport's problem is that it is of declining importance for all types of journey within urban areas, compounded by the fact that the only journey type for which it remains the dominant mode is contracting rapidly in numbers. The relative contribution of these two factors in the case of within-core journeys is such that 51 per cent of public transport's overall decline can be attributed to the decline of within-core journeys as a whole, while the remaining 49 per cent is attributable to the greater rate of decline in public transport journeys than in the competing modes.

In summary, this section has attempted to demonstrate that 'spatial factors' – such as the type of urban context in which journeys are made and the type of origin–destination combination within urban areas, in relation to the net redistribution of journeys *between* these general environments and flow combinations – are of substantial importance in explaining the scale of modal transfer in the second half of the 1960s. In other words, population and employment decentralization, operating at a variety of scales, has not only changed patterns of work travel but also contributed to the decline in public transport patronage and the growth of car usage. By implication, the argument can be extended one stage further by suggesting that the redistribution of homes and workplaces within and between urban areas can also be held partially responsible for the growth of car ownership. This is because as the separation of activities has increased and the suburbanization of both homes and workplaces has proceeded, so car ownership becomes more and more 'necessary' in order to maintain personal accessibility levels to workplaces, shops, and so on (Mogridge and Eldridge, 1970; Hillman *et al.*, 1973; Sammons and Hall, 1975; Thomas and Potter, 1977).

Although the above discussion has been presented on the basis of the mode of travel changes 'produced' by spatial restructuring, the direction and nature of causality are, in fact, considerably more complex. As Richardson (1971) has argued:

> within cities, everything seems to depend on everything else. Causation is rarely unidirectional, and interrelatedness is pervasive. This interdependence problem is found in a particularly striking form in the links between urban transportation, land use and the spatial structure of cities.

Thus whereas it is suggested above that changes in the spatial structure of urban areas have contributed to the growth of car ownership, this growth has itself facilitated changes in spatial structure by increasing the mobility levels of car owners and by encouraging the development of spatial forms which are more suited to car usage (i.e. low density). In other words, processes such as the decentralization of homes and jobs, changes in work travel patterns, the growth of car ownership and changing modal split are all causally realted to each other. Nor is the system closed; car-ownership growth and suburbanization can be understood only in the context of rising incomes and the changing aspirations of society (Kain, 1967; Warnes, 1972). Further, the role of public policy in spheres as diverse as road construction and housing finance in influencing the spatial structure of cities and the competitive position of the various modes of travel needs also to be taken into account. This will be returned to in the final section, but first consideration will be given to some of the developing problems or disbenefits concerning accessibility levels that are associated with the restructuring of urban space and the attendant decline of public transport.

Spatial restructuring and the implications for mobility and accessibility

PROBLEMS

Recognition of the distinction between mobility and accessibility is crucial to an understanding of the nature of 'urban transport problems'. Mobility in this context refers to 'the ease with which a person can move about or the amount of movement he [sic] performs' (Independent Commission on Transport, 1974, p. 106). There is little doubt that levels of individual mobility within urban areas have been increasing for a considerable period of time, due to successive transport improvements and the falling real costs of transport (Webber, 1973). Improvements in personal mobility have not of course been distributed evenly between social classes (or between men and women), but over much of this century the 'base' level of individual mobility has risen. However, the objective of transport, of making a journey, is not mobility but accessibility. Travel is not undertaken as an end in itself, but to provide access to other people or to facilities such as workplaces, shops, pubs, etc. Accessibility is affected not only by changing levels of mobility, but also by changes in the spatial organization of activities.

There are grounds for suggesting that spatial restructuring trends are detrimentally affecting the accessibility levels of certain individuals and groups within society. Virtually all changes in the spatial organization of society have distributional implications (Harvey, 1973). For example, the development of out-of-town hypermarkets, made possible by suburbanization and growing car-ownership, is, clearly, likely to be of benefit to suburban car-owners. If, however, the development is associated with contraction in the number or range of retail facilities in inner urban areas, then disbenefits may be experienced by inner urban residents, particularly if they do not have access to a car.

In terms of the journey to work, it is important to gauge (both on welfare *and* economic efficiency grounds) whether spatial restructuring is detrimentally affecting the access to workplaces of certain groups within society. For a number of reasons, most concern has been expressed at the present or developing job access problems of inner city resident manual workers. Inner urban areas have suffered particularly from a contracting job base, particularly in manufacturing and blue-collar services; white-collar jobs have not experienced the same decline, due to the secular growth in the office sector compensating for the less marked relative decentralization of such employment. Although we have seen that the absolute decentralization of total jobs has lagged behind the decentraliz-ation of workers, such that total job surpluses in 'core' areas have actually risen, it can be argued that the operation of both private and public hous-ing markets is likely to have restricted the suburbanization of manual workers in general and unskilled workers in particular, leading to a 'mismatch' of homes and workplace locations and a consequent fall in accessibility levels.

Before considering the validity of this hypothesis in the British context, mention should first be made of the experience of US cities, where the inner city 'accessibility crisis' has been the subject of much academic and political concern and where the scale of the problem is considerably greater. On the one hand, the decentralization of employ-ment away from inner urban areas has been longer established, while on the other the operation of the housing market, combined with zoning regulations, have 'trapped' Black workers in the inner urban ghettos (Kain, 1967; Gold, 1972; Muller, 1976). The explicitly racial dimension in the US case is indicated by the fact that the issue first became of wide-spread concern in the aftermath of the race riots in Watts, Los Angeles, in 1965. The report of the McCone Commission, 'Violence in the City', declared that the cause of the riots was the extremely high level of un-employment in Watts, which it directly linked to the inadequacy of public transportation services to the suburban job centres (Kidder and Saltzman, 1973).

The work by De Vise (1976) on Chicago has indicated that the rate of job decentralization from inner to outer city was more than double that of employed residents in the period from 1960–70, and that the accessibility to jobs of inner city blue-collar workers was markedly reduced – indeed, by 1970 there was actually a net commuting *outflow* of blue-collar workers from the inner city (i.e. fewer jobs than workers) and reverse commuting had become a major feature of Chicago's travel patterns. Various transport schemes have been introduced in US cities to facilitate reverse commuting (Collura and Schuster, 1971), but opinion is divided as to their success (Ornati, 1969; Goering and Kalachek 1973). Muller (1976) has concluded that:

> It is interesting to note that demonstration project experiments have shown the accessibility crisis to be a surprisingly complex problem, one apparently incapable of simple solution by merely providing direct transport between inner city and suburban industrial parks.

While the problem may be difficult to solve, the basis of the problem at least seems fairly clear – i.e. the increasing spatial mismatch between unskilled workers' homes and the location of job opportunities. Can the same be said for the emerging situation in British cities?

At the urban zone scale of analysis there is little evidence to suggest that manual workers resident in cores are becoming disadvantaged due to workplace shifts. While it is true that the number of manual jobs declined substantially in core areas, the number of resident manual workers declined by a larger amount and at a faster rate, and core job surpluses consequently increased slightly between 1966 and 1971 (Gillespie *et al.,* 1978). Reverse commuting from cores to rings by semi- and unskilled manual workers declined in number by 14 per cent, an identical rate of decline to the number of semi- and unskilled workers as a whole. For skilled manual workers, however, the reverse flow from cores to rings increased slightly in relative importance (although contracting in absolute terms), and the propensity for skilled manual workers residing in core areas to work in ring areas remains higher than for the other social groups (though the differences are not dramatic). These findings relate to core zones in aggregate, but it is to be expected that reverse commuting would be of greatest importance in the big cities, where job decentralization is furthest advanced. Jarvis (1976) has examined the socio-economic group structure of in- and out-commuting across the Greater London Council boundary for 1966 and 1971, and his findings lend support to this assertion. The outward flow displays a very different socio-economic structure to the inward, with skilled manual workers being strongly over-represented in the former. However, in terms of changes in reverse commuting, increases were considerably more marked for non-manual workers than for manual (9 per cent and 53 per cent for skilled manual and professional workers respectively; see also Das, 1978, for comparable findings from the other conurbations).

While these studies do not lend much support to the 'accessibility crisis' hypothesis, the spatial scale at which they were undertaken (i.e. urban zone and county) could be obscuring problems which are manifest at the specifically inner city scale. There remain grounds, however, for arguing that this is not the case. A mismatch between the skills of an area's workforce and the level of skills demanded by the area's workplaces does not in any way prove the existence of a problem which is amenable to 'transport solutions', *unless* other areas in the city have surpluses of the type of job that is under-represented in the area in question. If the latter condition does *not* apply, then the problem is one of occupational imbalance rather than spatial mismatch and different solutions would be appropriate such as job creation or labour force retraining. While the necessary condition *does* apply in American cities (or, at least, Chicago), as the work of De Vise (1976) has indicated, there is no evidence to suggest that British inner areas have job deficits while the outer areas have job surpluses. Thus Gillespie *et al.* (1979) have shown that inner London (in this case the ward-based Department of Environment's definition thereof) has more jobs than employed workers for all eighteen occupational groups, and that as a consequence there is a net journey-to-work flow from the outer to inner city for all groups. Similarly, Bentham (1978) has examined the distribution within Greater London of the supply (including the unemployed) and demand for male general labourers; while the inner rings in total do indeed have more economically active residents classified as labourers than equivalent jobs, the outer ring of Greater London is almost in balance. He concludes, 'The potential for improving the job prospects of unskilled inner city residents either by residential mobility within the conurbation or by an increase in reverse commuting appears to be small'.

Thus while the available evidence up to 1971 does not support the 'accessibility crisis' model, it needs to be stressed that the economic problems of inner city areas have magnified over the last decade (Lever *et al.*, 1980) and that the situation may indeed be following the American experience; this remains to be seen. In one important respect, however, the British spatial restructuring situation differs from the American, thereby perhaps contributing to the development of different kinds of accessibility problem. In British cities, one of the major features of postwar development has been the proliferation of non-central or peripheral council housing estates. The accessibility problems of residents of these decanted estates are likely to be more severe than those of inner city residents, due to the considerably poorer provision of public transport (Town, 1977). As would be expected, car ownership is closely related to social class; where in 1971 86 per cent of professional and managerial workers were members of car-owning households, only 43 per cent of semi- and unskilled manual workers fell into this category (Gillespie *et al.*, 1978). As a result, modes of travel to work also vary considerably in importance between the socioeconomic groups; National Travel Survey data for 1975/6, for example, reveals that 64 per cent of unskilled manual workers reach work on foot or by bus, compared with only 16 per cent of professional workers (Das, 1978). The increasing separation of homes and workplaces may then be leading to accessibility problems for people without cars; in this respect, the contraction of public transport services and increasing fares give serious cause for concern. As we have seen, one result of emerging forms of urban spatial organization is that car ownership and usage are becoming increasingly necessary – in one sense, space is being structured by and for car-owners. Where then, does this leave people without cars, who have no effective modal choices except for walking or a declining public transport system?

Before turning to possible policy options for preserving the accessibility levels of people without cars, it is necessary to dispel two myths.

The first is that the oil crisis has changed everything to the benefit of public transport. There is no evidence at all to support this assertion. Between January 1974 and mid-1975, for example, the price of petrol more than doubled yet average mileage travelled fell by only 5 per cent (Thomas and Potter, 1977). This very low price elasticity of car usage partly reflects its necessity with present forms of spatial organization, while additionally it is often overlooked that the costs of private motoring have risen by less than have public transport fares. Certainly according to successive National Travel Surveys, the trend of declining public transport usage for journey-to-work purposes and the associated growth of car usage continued unabated during the 1970s. The second myth, based on the opposite premise, is that the admitted problems of people without cars will in the future be of limited importance due to the small minority of the population which will be without access to a car. Yet even on the Department of the Environment's own highly criticized forecasts of car ownership, some 30 per cent of households will still not own a car by 2010, to which must be added those members of car-owning households who do not have access to the car (either by inability to drive or because the car is being used by another household member, a particularly likely occurrence in the case of the journey to work). As Mayer Hillman (1978) has put it,

> Let us not forget that even if the millennium envisaged by the DOT's forecasts of 28 million cars in 2010 is reached . . . there would still remain a further 28 million or so people without a car of their own and they would no doubt still benefit from the availability of public transport.

The question remains then of how public transport is to be preserved for the *majority* in the face of the changing nature of home–workplace relationships and the linked deterioration in public transport services. While a topic of such complexity is beyond the scope of this essay, a few brief comments are apposite.

POLICY RESPONSES

Two broad types of policy response to developing mobility/accessibility problems can be distinguished. The first is to try and improve existing public transport systems and to modify them in order to take account of changing spatial patterns of demand. The difficulties of making inside-out journeys and lateral inter-suburban journeys by conventional public transport have already been alluded to. To an extent, this reflects the failure of public transport operators to come to grips with changing patterns of demand. Ornati (1969), for example, in a study of transport needs of the poor in New York, highlighted the extent of the problem:

> The New York Metropolitan Transport Authority proudly reported in September 1968 that it had set up an integrated computerized model on which it was simulating different subway speeds, frequencies, loads, etc. Meanwhile, the Authority's buses run on the same routes as the horse-drawn trolleys of 1908.

While there is clearly some scope for public transport solutions to emerging work travel situations, such as attempting to facilitate the accessibility of low-income workers in peripheral estates to suburban job opportunities, the difficulties inherent in this type of approach are substantial. The root of these difficulties lies in the fact that the forms of urban spatial structure which optimize the advantages of car ownership and usage also 'optimizes' the deficiencies of public transport. Specifically, low trip densities between any pair of origins and destinations conflicts with the viability of conventional bus services. While some of these problems can be overcome by demand-actuated systems such as 'dial-a-bus', such systems are labour-intensive and hence very expensive to operate (Roos, 1973).

The second broad type of policy response to emerging problems tackles the 'root cause' rather more directly, and as a consequence is more controversial. Before considering these options, it needs to be stressed that public policy has played a considerable role in encouraging the growth of different transport modes and new forms of spatial organization (Glaister, 1976). Even in the previous century of 'unrestrained' free enterprise, mention can be made of the development of working-class suburbs which followed the Cheap Trains Act of 1883 (Dyos, 1955 and 1961) or the rapid expansion of electric tramways and the associated wave of new urban development which occurred largely in response to the Light Railways Act of 1896 (Bagwell, 1974). In more recent times, government has encouraged the growth of car ownership and usage at the expense of public transport, and, by implication, has facilitated intra-urban decentralization (to which might also be added the implicit suburbanization effect of tax relief to owner-occupiers). This encouragement stems from the initial premise that the objective of transport planning is to satisfy the demand which it is projected will occur (Bruton, 1975). Whether or not the projected changes are desirable does not enter the calculation – if the forecasts predict that demand will increase, supply must be adjusted to cope with it. This line of reasoning, which was employed in the influential report by Buchanan ('Traffic in Towns', 1963) has a number of major pitfalls, particularly the question of how demand can be predicted in any meaningful sense except in relation to supply and to price. That it cannot is indicated by the universal tendency for new traffic to be generated whenever a new road is built. Attempting to 'meet demand' is consequently a self-fulfilling prophecy – road-building generates new demand which necessitates more road-building, and so on. The reason for this 'bottomless pit' effect is the inadequacy of the road-pricing mechanism. Although the full cost of building and maintaining roads is met by the taxation on road users (i.e. vehicle excise and fuel duty), the congestion costs which peak-hour road users impose upon other motorists (and bus users) are completely unpriced (Beesley, 1973; Schaeffer and Schlar, 1975; Willeke and Baum, 1971). The importance of this lack of adequate road pricing has been demonstrated by Glaister (1976) in a mathematical simulation exercise on the effect on model split and travel costs of introducing a full marginal social cost pricing policy for both public and private transport:

> Car travel becomes prohibitively expensive and dies out rapidly. . . . Average travel costs are much lower and there is a dramatic increase in road speeds. The phenomenon of decay in service quality is completely absent. The bus service earns a substantial profit.

While full marginal social cost pricing is unlikely to come about, serious consideration is being given by policy-makers to 'congestion-tax' measures such as supplementary licensing (Department of Environment, 1976b, vol. 2, annex 3). However, while it would seem logical to assume that any scheme to restore the competitive position of public transport would be of benefit to people without cars, the complex relationship between transport and urban spatial structure could produce rather different outcomes, as Collins and Pharoah (1974) have suggested:

> The long and short-term effects of road pricing on land prices, land use, densities, public transport and road investment have not been thoroughly investigated, nor have its social implications. On the one hand, for example, the high cost of car use in densely built-up areas might encourage urban sprawl and the dispersal of activities, but on the other hand the elimination of congestion could allow the development of a sufficiently attractive public transport system to retain the relative advantages of urban concentration.

If the range of policy options remain contentious, and the outcomes uncertain, the fact remains that the inter-linked changes in urban spatial structure, in journey-to-work patterns and in modes of travel to work, which have formed the subject of this chapter, are intrinsically bound up with past policy decisions. In other words, the 'do-nothing' option is itself a policy decision; before any such decision is reached, the social and economic implications of current trends deserve wider consideration.

Population trends in the 1970s

A. G. Champion

Introduction

The context for population redistribution in the 1970s was different in
many ways from that of the two decades which preceded them, both for
Britain and for many other countries. In particular, the decade featured
the most severe and prolonged economic depression since the late 1920s,
partly associated with the rising real cost of petroleum and other natural
resources. Demographic phenomena also exhibited major contrasts with
previous experience, particularly a reduction in the scale of international
migration, a decline in birth-rates to below the levels recorded in the
early 1930s and a turnaround in the net migration balance of many non-
metropolitan areas. This last observation has been highlighted dramatically by Vining and Kontuly (1978), who showed that during the first half
of the 1970s a large number of advanced countries had seen a marked
reduction in the apparent attractiveness of their densely populated core
regions or even a reversal in the direction of net population flow in favour
of their sparsely populated, peripheral regions. In their analysis no clear
evidence was found to suggest that Britain was sharing in this major
reversal of past trends, though qualifications were made concerning the
reliability of the data.

A major task for this chapter, therefore, is to explore whether
Britain has indeed been bypassed by these developments, though this
investigation is set in the context of a broader review of population trends
in the 1970s. Indeed, an equally important aim, as with the other essays in
this volume, is to demonstrate that a spatial perspective can help our
understanding of national as well as more local events and that the
selection of the spatial scale of analysis can influence the nature of the

findings and conclusions. In the study by Vining and Kontuly, for instance, the densely populated core region was defined as the area made up by the standard regions of the South East, the South West and East Anglia. It may be that different conclusions would have been reached in that study if the core had been defined differently, so as perhaps to include the West Midlands and even the North West, which with the South East have the highest regional population densities in England, or so as perhaps to build up a more accurately defined core from smaller geographical units, omitting the more remote rural zones of East Anglia and the South West.

This analysis begins by outlining the context of the 1970s. Clearly, in demographic and broader social-economic terms, the 1970s exhibit some major differences from the 1960s at national level, which may have their counterparts in the more local distribution of population, involving differences not only in the magnitude of trends but also in their direction in some cases. Next, after a statement on the nature and reliability, census data supplemented by the official population estimates are used to describe the major features of population change in the 1970s and to draw comparisons with the previous two decades. The dramatic reversals observed by Vining and Kontuly in other countries are found equally for Britain, dating from the late 1960s at a broad regional level but affecting some non-metropolitan zones rather earlier. Rather than being revolutionary, these events can be seen as part of a longer-term evolution of metropolitan space which has been unfolding in Britain for at least twenty-five years. The concluding discussion, nevertheless, focuses on the extent to which these trends are likely to continue; an issue raised by the fact that during the later 1970s the scale of non-metropolitan population growth fell substantially from the unprecedentedly high levels reached in the first few years of the decade.

Underlying patterns and processes

The central question concerns the extent to which the experience of the 1950s and the 1960s continued through the subsequent decade. Many studies have shown that the main processes producing changes in the aggregate patterns of population distribution during the twenty years up to 1971 were long-term in nature and therefore it is natural to suggest that they are likely to have played a significant role in fashioning the spatial facets of population change more recently. Set against this hypothesis, however, is the fact that since the mid-1960s major changes have taken place in Britain's demographic, economic and social milieux including a much reduced birth-rate, higher unemployment, restricted capital flows, and a higher divorce rate. This section of the chapter outlines the demographic background of the long-term trends in the national space-economy, goes on to describe the principal features of contrast between the 1970s and the previous decade, and attempts an *a priori* assessment of their likely significance on the long-term spatial trends.

THE EVOLVING PATTERN OF POPULATION REDISTRIBUTION

Most accounts of the 1950s and 1960s are in substantial agreement in highlighting two major components of population redistribution in Britain, distinguished principally by the scale at which they operate. Data presented at the scale of the ten standard regions have been shown by the Office of Population Censuses and Surveys (1978a), Lawton (1977) and Department of Environment (1971) to reveal a broad shift of emphasis from north to south. This pattern is part of a long-term process of readjustment to the eclipse of the export-oriented coal-based heavy industries which gave rise to the rapid growth of northern conurbations in the nineteenth century and marks something of a return, under very different circumstances, to the pre-industrial dominance of southern Britain in terms of population density (Osborne, 1964). Though no regions actually declined in population size during the 1950s and 1960s, inter-regional migration was sufficiently large to produce the continuation of this shift, with the five more northerly regions (including Scotland and Wales) seeing their share of the British population fall from 44.5 per cent to 42.3 per cent between 1951 and 1969 (Department of Environment, 1971).

Meanwhile, at the much finer grain of the local authority district, Lawton (1974) and Champion (1976), among others, have observed a much more complicated pattern of population changes, for which the largest single explanation can broadly be labelled as decentralization from the main urban centres. To some extent, this process is a relative one resulting from the spillover effects of the lateral expansion of towns in growth areas, but increasingly during the postwar period as Hall *et al.* (1973) and Craig (1975, 1980) have shown, it has involved an absolute loss of population from the older urban cores in favour of the newer suburbs or surrounding towns. Thus, despite the continuing southward shift in Britain's population, Greater London's population fell by over 200,000 in 1951–61 (2.5 per cent) and by as many as 540,000 in 1961–71 (6.8 per cent). Other major cities experienced similar tendencies; Liverpool lost 18.2 per cent of its population in the 1960s, Manchester 17.9 per cent, Newcastle upon Tyne 17.6 per cent and Birmingham 8.6 per cent, rates of population loss which moreover were at least twice, and in some cases over three times, as large as those recorded in the 1950s (Champion, 1976).

The intermediate scale of the metropolitan labour market (Hall, 1971) helps to put these local shifts into their broader regional context, as well as to identify more clearly the patterns of redistribution associated with movements between the standard regions. It also provides an integrated framework for summarizing the major spatial changes of the period 1951–71 (Department of Environment, 1976a). Over 90 per cent of the British population and three-quarters of its land area lie within a total of 126 metropolitan areas, which, in aggregate, have traditionally gained population at the expense of non-metropolitan space. Though some of these metropolitan areas stand directly by themselves, many are arranged in close-knit regional clusters, where a major labour market such as London, Birmingham, Manchester and Glasgow is surrounded by smaller city regions. These regional clusters vary in their overall growth rates according mainly to their relative economic performance, while within each the smaller surrounding areas were gaining at the expense of the major labour market. Finally, within individual areas, the same process of decentralization was reducing the importance of the metropolitan core in terms of the proportion of local residents and, in many cases, of local employment (Department of the Environment, 1976a).

Set within this simplified urban and regional framework, the relative importance of these four types of population shift can be seen to have changed during the course of the 1950s and 1960s. The southward shift between regional clusters was more strongly marked in the 1950s than in the next ten years, which among other things saw the reinvigoration of regional policy. By contrast, decentralization of residential population within individual metropolitan areas increased in the 1960s, stimulated by rising real incomes and accelerating slum clearance. Thirdly, spillover from major metropolitan labour markets to surrounding metropolitan areas also accelerated in terms of both numbers involved and distances traversed, as both private development and the New Towns programme looked further from the main centres for available sites. Finally, it was in the second decade that some of the non-metropolitan areas changed their migration balance from loss to gain, though the absolute numbers involved in these low-density zones were relatively small compared with the other three types of redistribution (Champion, 1976; Department of Environment, 1976a).

THE CONTEXT OF THE 1970s

There are clear grounds for suggesting that these broad trends continued into the 1970s and that the changes of emphasis which took place between the 1950s and the 1960s proceeded further. One line of evidence is that outlined in the introduction, namely the loss of momentum of the major core regions of many countries and a shift in migration flows in favour of peripheral zones (Vining and Kontuly, 1978). More detailed studies of the USA, Canada and Australia indicate that, as in Britain, certain non-metropolitan areas had experienced a reversal in their migration balances by the late 1960s, but that the process accelerated so rapidly in the early 1970s that non-metropolitan areas in aggregate recorded a net inflow (Beale, 1975; Beale and Fuguitt, 1976; Bourne and Simmons 1979; Australian government, 1977). Moreover, these studies are at pains to point out that, while rural areas adjacent to metropolitan zones experienced the highest growth rates, it was the more remote areas which recorded the greatest change in growth rate. For instance, between 1960–70 and 1970–4 the entirely rural counties of the USA changed their overall performance from a 0.4 per cent a year decline to a 1.4 per cent increase, achieved entirely through a complete reversal of migration flows from −1.2 per cent to 1.0 per cent a year (Morrison and Wheeler, 1976).

On the other hand, many of the circumstances bearing directly or indirectly on the rate and distribution of population change underwent a profound change in the UK. The brash confidence associated with the push for new technological progress in the 1960s, with the schemes for major new cities and estuarine developments and with the perceived advantages accruing from possible membership of the European Economic Community was overwhelmed by a series of events which the exploitation of North Sea oil did little to compensate for. The true character of the decade revealed itself fairly suddenly after 1974, though several features had appeared earlier and in some cases can be traced back into the previous decade. The main components of this new demographic context can be identified from the Office of Population Censuses and Surveys (1978a) and from more recent issues of *Population Trends*; they can be summarized under the following headings:

Lower levels of international migration

A major change had taken place in the early 1960s, when anticipation of tighter immigration controls had stimulated a massive influx from New Commonwealth countries, followed by a return to the long-established pattern of net emigration. The 1970s, however, did see further reductions in overseas migration levels, with annual numbers of immigrants below 200,000 (except for 1972 owing to the sudden arrival of 25,000 Ugandan Asians) and with emigration declining from over 300,000 in 1967–8 to under 200,000 by 1978. The net figures (including the Irish Republic) averaged an outflow of 0.07 per cent a year in 1971–7, compared to a rather larger loss of 0.13 per cent in the late 1960s.

Fall in birth-rate

Live births declined from a postwar peak of just over 1 million in 1964–5 to 655,000 in 1976–7, a lower figure than any recorded for well over a century. As a result, the substantial population growth forecast by demographers in the mid-1960s did not take place on anything like the scale envisaged. Indeed, the rate of natural increase dropped from nearly 400,000 in 1963–4 to virtually zero by the mid-1970s, thereby reducing its significance as an influence on population change both nationally and locally and enhancing the relative importance of migration.

Increase in the elderly population

This long-standing feature continued through the 1970s, as the large birth cohorts of the period immediately before the First World War moved into old age. Particularly rapid growth was recorded in the numbers aged 75 years and over, which saw their contribution to the total population rise from 4.8 per cent to 5.6 per cent during the decade. The numbers of over-pensionable age (65 for men, 60 for women) increased at a slower rate than previously, rising from 9 million to 9.8 million (16.3–17.4 per cent of the UK population).

Smaller average household size

Sample data collected by the General Household Survey reveal an acceleration in the fall in average household size since 1971, declining from 2.91 persons to 2.71 persons in 1977. This fall of about 7 per cent in only six years was equivalent to the change experienced over the previous twenty years from 1951 when it stood at 3.14 persons per household. Lower birth-rate and the increasing proportion of elderly persons can be held partly responsible for this dramatic acceleration, while other factors include the increasing numbers of single people living away from home, greater household fission resulting from divorces, and the growing tendency for elderly couples and widows to live by themselves rather than with their children. The proportion of one-person households, for instance, rose from 17 per cent to 22 per cent of all households between 1971 and 1978.

Turning to the economic situation of the 1970s, at least three aspects are likely to have had significant effects on population redistribution trends. First, economic recession normally has the general effect of reducing migration flows owing to the lower level of job vacancies. Second, the 1970s depression appears to have had a disproportionately severe effect on the core industrial regions in contrast to less urbanized regions which have recorded some net increase in manufacturing jobs (Keeble, 1976). Finally, the rate of new house construction, which peaked at over 425,000 dwellings in 1968, averaged only three-quarters of this level in the 1970s, with production under 280,000 in 1974 and even lower by the end of the decade. As well as the general effects of inflation and credit restrictions on house-building levels, housing improvement policy shifted from its 1960s emphasis on slum clearance and redevelopment programmes to the rehabitation and conversion of older property.

IMPLICATIONS FOR POPULATION DISTRIBUTION

The above account of the major developments of the 1970s and the longer-term evolution of the UK's population patterns helps us to restate the central questions of this chapter in more detail and provides a stimulus for hazarding an answer on theoretical grounds before examining the data. Clearly some major contrasts can be identified between the 1970s and the previous decade, particularly in birth-rate, household size, house-building activity, unemployment levels and international migration. Are these features of such a nature and scale as to produce fundamental changes in the patterns of population redistribution which were evolving in the 1950s and 1960s? In particular, do they suggest a significant centrifugal surge as involved in the counter-urbanization process described by Berry (1976) and documented by Vining and Kontuly (1978)? Finally, to what extent are these developments likely to cancel out the effects of each other instead of operating in unison? The remainder of this section attempts to answer these questions in the context of the simplified spatial framework introduced earlier, arguing from theory and thereby providing hypotheses which can later be tested by reference to the data.

As far as broad *regional* shifts are concerned, most considerations point to the further erosion of regional differentials in population growth rates. With high levels of unemployment nation-wide, net movements of working-age people from north to south can be expected to have become less significant, while some increase in the level of return migration by disillusioned job seekers may also have taken place. With the continuation of an active regional policy through virtually all the 1970s and with those outside the labour market (retired and unemployed) tending to flee the high-cost areas, both the industrial and the non-metropolitan parts of the periphery should have seen at least some relief from their traditional pattern of population loss, though marked changes of fortune would be required to offset the effect of declining birth-rate.

Redistribution of population between labour markets in each broad regional group (the *intermediate* scale) depends principally on the capacity of the largest metropolitan centre to retain its population. As a general rule, falling household size means that existing areas with a given stock of dwellings will not be able to maintain their population levels unless recourse is made to redevelopment at higher dwelling densities or to the conversion of large single-family dwellings into multiple units. On the other hand, the cut-back in house-building can be expected to limit the opportunities for overspill to the smaller cities which hem in the conurbations. The traditional reception areas may have been more severely affected than elsewhere, since the capacity of private sites has been becoming saturated and as new town schemes have passed through their rapid-growth phase.

The *local* scale of shifts within individual metropolitan areas provides further evidence for a slowdown in decentralization, particularly since 1974. The elderly age structures and high crude death-rates of the inner city and other older urban areas point to further substantial population reductions in the cores, aggravated by the nation-wide plunge in birth-rate since the mid-1960s. On the other hand, the general reduction in mobility caused by the economic depression of the mid-1970s is likely to have forced more to stay on in the inner city, while the completion of housing redevelopment schemes and the switch towards rehabilitation will have slowed down the shrinking of the inner city housing stock. Moreover, local studies suggest that the change in housing improvement policy, allied with the replacement of an ageing population and the encouragement of owner-occupation, has made these areas more attractive to certain groups such as young professionals.

In sum, it seems fairly clear that the broad shift between north and south should have become gradually less significant over time, continuing the trend begun in the 1960s. On the other hand, the redistribution of population around the major metropolitan centres seems to be subject to contradictory forces which may cancel each other out in aggregate terms, but which may affect more localized areas in different ways and at different times. For instance, the fall in household size in inner urban areas may have been compensated for by the change in housing improvement policy since 1974. The lower level of immigration could aggravate the loss of population in the major cities or, by easing the pressure on their housing markets, lead to a reduction in overspill needs. The lower birth-rate could be associated with a reduced need for suburbanization in search of family-size housing and, simultaneously, with the metropolitan core shifting from overall growth to a situation of population decline. Experience at the most local scale depends, of course, on a wide range of factors such as attractiveness to employers, spare capacity in the housing market and local planning authority attitudes, but even at broader scales the interrelationships of the major factors are too complicated to allow a confident prediction of trends. Instead, to get an impression of the overall effect of these factors on the space economy, it is necessary to turn to an alternative approach.

The recent evidence on population redistribution

The cancellation of the census planned for 1976 meant that, until recently, studies of population trends had to rely on estimates, but fortunately the preliminary results of the 1981 Census are now available and provide a sounder bench-mark for the examination of the main features of the past decade. The mid-year estimates produced annually by the Office of Population Censuses and Surveys (OPCS) for England and Wales and by the Registrar General for Scotland, however, still have an important role to play, because they can indicate the phasing of developments during the decade. The following study therefore makes use of both these sources in taking both regional and sub-regional perspectives on population change in the 1970s and its trends since the previous decade and begins with a closer look at the available data and the constraints which they place on the analysis.

THE DATA

The Census of Population provides data which are valuable in providing a more reliable picture than the mid-year estimates but which, at the time of writing, are relatively crude and not as accurate as they will be in their final form. To date (January 1982), only the preliminary results relating to enumerated population are available for the whole of Britain. These allow the tentative calculation of the change in the total enumerated population for local government districts and aggregation of these either to the official levels of the county and region in England and Wales and the region in Scotland or to other types of groupings. This is possible in spite of the reorganization of local government boundaries in the early 1970s, because population totals for 1971 have been revised to fit the new areas. Similar revisions have also been made for 1961 in order to compare trends experienced in the 1970s with those recorded in the previous decade. Because registration records provide details of births and deaths, it is also possible to disaggregate the changes for the two intercensal decades into their two main components of natural change and net migration, though it is important to remember that the latter is a residual element and will reflect any inadequacies in the preliminary 1981 results.

The mid-year estimates provide a much more complete record over time, but are recognized to be generally less accurate and to decline in accuracy as they move further forward from the latest full enumeration. They comprise an annual series of 'home population' totals for officially recognized areas down to the scale of the local government district, as well as an unpublished breakdown of the twelve-month changes into births, deaths, net civilian migration and other changes, the last relating to prisons, residential educational establishments and armed forces. The key problem in their accuracy lies with the estimation of the migration component – a problem which is greater at more local scales as the significance of migration as a factor in population change increases. During the 1970s, however, various improvements in the method of estimating migration were made (OPCS, 1978b) and a check against the preliminary results of the 1981 Census has led the Office of Population Censuses and Surveys to conclude that, 'The methods used in making the annual estimates seem to have worked out reasonably well though with some exceptions' (OPCS, 1981, 10). As regards spatial units, the mid-year estimates have been revised on the basis of the current local government boundaries back to 1961 for England and Wales, but for Scotland the revisions for the new boundaries have been taken back only to 1971 and moreover the mid-year estimates for the 1960s there have not been revised in the light of the 1971 Census results.

The two data sources thus provide a useful complement to each other, with the census expected to be the more accurate but with the mid-year estimates furnishing a more detailed temporal perspective. Both, however, suffer from a significant drawback in that the smallest spatial unit for which data are currently available is the local government district. This means that the present study cannot be based on the framework of 'metropolitan areas' used by the Department of Environment (1976) and Spence *et al.* (1982) or on the 'functional regions' developed for eventual use with 1981 Census data by Coombes *et al.* (1982), because both these are built up from pre-1974 districts and thus cannot be used in the present context until the small area statistics of the 1981 Census are available. In the analysis which follows, therefore, attention is focused initially on the scale of the economic planning regions and then is forced to stay with the officially recognized local government units for the sub-regional perspective.

TRENDS IN REGIONAL PERFORMANCE

For the purpose of this stage of the analysis Great Britain is divided into ten statistical units. The key features of population change for these areas in the 1970s and the main points of comparison with the 1960s can be seen from table 8.1. The most rapid rate of population growth between the 1971 and 1981 Censuses was recorded by East Anglia, followed by the South West and the East Midlands. Lower rates of growth were registered by Wales and the West Midlands, while Yorkshire and Humberside's population was virtually stationary. Finally, the South East, North West, northern region and Scotland experienced population declines of up to 3 per cent for the ten-year period.

This pattern of regional performance presents some immediate contrasts with the trends of the 1960s (table 8.1). Most noticeable is the fact that, whereas five of the ten regions saw population decline between 1971 and 1981, no region had experienced an overall loss of population over the previous ten-year period. Moreover, the most dramatic changes in fortune are found to have taken place in the two regions which are

Table 8.1 Great Britain: intercensal population changes and shifts 1961–81, by regions and regional groups (in percentages)

Regions and regional groups	1961–71 change	1971–81 change	Total shift	Shift attributable to Natural change	Shift attributable to Migration and other changes
Great Britain	5.3	0.3	−5.0	−4.9	−0.1
Scotland	1.0	−2.1	−3.1	−5.5	2.4
Wales	3.3	2.2	−1.1	−3.6	2.5
Northern	0.7	−1.4	−2.1	−4.9	2.7
Yorks & Humb.	3.7	−0.1	−3.8	−5.0	1.2
North West	2.6	−2.9	−5.5	−4.8	−0.8
East Midlands	9.4	4.8	−4.6	−4.9	0.3
West Midlands	7.4	0.5	−6.9	−5.8	−1.1
East Anglia	13.6	11.7	−1.9	−3.8	1.9
South East	5.9	−1.2	−7.1	−4.8	−2.3
South West	10.6	6.0	−4.6	−4.7	0.1
South East, South West and East Anglia	7.2	1.0	−6.2	−4.7	−1.5
Rest of Britain	3.9	−0.3	−4.2	−5.0	0.8
Difference	3.3	1.3	−2.0	0.3	−2.3
South East, West Midlands and North West	5.3	−1.3	−6.6	−4.9	−1.7
Rest of Britain	5.1	2.0	−3.1	−4.8	1.7
Difference	0.2	−3.3	−3.5	−0.1	−3.4

Source: Calculated from OPCS (1981), Registrar General Scotland (1981) and provisional analyses by component provided by OPCS and Registrar General Scotland

traditionally associated with relatively rapid economic growth and the so-called 'drift to the South East'. Both the South East and the West Midlands were affected by a downward shift of around 7 percentage points in their population growth rates between the two decades (table 8.1). By contrast, Wales, East Anglia, the Northern region and Scotland, though experiencing some reduction in growth rate between the two decades, nevertheless all achieved a strong improvement in performance relative to the national average. In particular, the rate for Wales dropped by only a fifth of the shift registered by Britain as a whole, raising it from seventh to fourth place in the ranking of the ten areas. The South West and East Midlands retained their positions as the second and third fastest growing regions after East Anglia, with negative shifts marginally below the national average, but the North West suffered worse than average and replaced the Northern region as the least dynamic area in the 1970s.

The direct explanations for these patterns of shifts between the 1960s and 1970s can be identified by reference to the components of population change (table 8.1). The general pattern of slower population growth can be traced to the reduction in natural change rates between the two decades, resulting entirely from the fall in birth-rate mentioned earlier. The downward shift in natural change is relatively consistent across the regions at around 4.7–5 percentage points, except for the West Midlands where natural increase had previously been well above average and for East Anglia where the reduction was ameliorated by the continuing high level of in-migration of young families. With the exception of these two cases, therefore, it is very largely the trend in migration balance which is responsible for the second main observation, namely the altered ranking of regional performances. The improvements in overall population rates relative to the national average recorded by Wales, the Northern region and Scotland, as well as by East Anglia, are associated with a positive shift of 2–3 percentage points in these regions' migration balances between the two decades. Meanwhile, the North West, West Midlands and South East saw a deterioration in net migration levels by 1–2 percentage points, leading to the erosion of their positions in the ranking of the regions by growth rate.

These observations seem to suggest that, contrary to the conclusions of Vining and Kontuly (1978), Britain is indeed sharing in the population turnaround involving a shift of growth forces away from the traditional core areas, which they identified for a number of other advanced countries. The present analysis admittedly covers a longer time-span and uses a more reliable data source than the mid-year estimates which Vining and Kontuly were forced to use, but that does not account for the divergence of the findings. Instead, the key lies in the way that the country's core and periphery areas are defined. As mentioned at the beginning of this chapter, Vining and Kontuly defined the core as comprising not only the South East but also East Anglia and the South West, two essentially rural regions which have experienced rapid growth only in the last twenty or thirty years, while at the same time their definition excluded the West Midlands, the most important twentieth-century core area after the capital region itself.

The importance of the definitional question can be seen if population change rates are calculated for alternative groups of regions. If the core area is considered to comprise the three most southerly regions of Britain, then it is indeed found to be increasing its share of the country's population, for its population grew by 1.1 per cent between 1971 and 1981 in contrast to an overall decline of 0.3 per cent for the remainder of the country. Even on this definition, however, this difference of 1.4 percentage points in the performance between core and periphery represented a considerable reduction on the 3.3 point difference recorded in the previous decade. If the core is redefined to comprise the three regions which constitute the traditional urban and industrial spine of the country, namely the South East, West Midlands and North West, the population turnaround appears to have advanced much further, as the region-by-region analysis suggested. Even in the 1960s their average growth rate of 5.4 per cent was only marginally higher than the average for the rest of the country, while for 1971–81 these three more heavily urbanized regions experienced a loss of 1.3 per cent, a rate which was 3.3 percentage points below the increase of 2 per cent achieved by the other seven regions together. Thus, while the north–south difference in population trends grew narrower in the 1970s, a new dimension of regional differentiation has appeared with the dramatic change of fortunes experienced by the more heavily urbanized central spine of the country, on the one hand, and the less metropolitan zones which flank it on the west, east and north.

It is tempting to conclude from this comparison of the two intercensal periods that this major change in the geography of Britain's regional population redistribution was accelerating over time. The more detailed time perspective afforded by the mid-year estimates, however, suggests that this was not the case. Instead, as shown in table 8.2, it appears that the major changes in this direction had been completed by the early 1970s and that subsequently there has been some move back to the previous patterns. It can be seen that the three southern regions recognized as the core by Vining and Kontuly (1978) came closest to being overtaken in growth rate by the rest of the country in the period 1971–4, but by 1977–80 the gap had almost returned to the level found in the early 1960s. The scale of retrenchment is just as marked for the alternative grouping of regions which distinguishes the three most urbanized regions from the rest. The South East, West Midlands and North West had seen their combined change rate fall below the national average in the later 1960s and move into decline in 1971–4 whereas the rest of the country actually managed to increase its growth rate between 1966–71 and 1971–4 against the national trend. The 0.49 percentage point difference found between the latter two groups of regions for 1971–4 had, however, fallen back to 0.13 by 1977–80 (table 8.2).

The rates for the individual regions, also shown in table 8.2, provide a starting point for explaining both the earlier shift away from the traditional growth pattern and the subsequent return towards it. At this level the most impressive features of the first half of the period covered are the acceleration of growth rate between 1966–71 and 1971–4 in East Anglia and the South West, contrary to the national trend, and the much greater than average downward shift registered by the South East and West Midlands. Equally significant in terms of the current discussion, however, is the relative lack of change in certain regions. While the national rate of population change fell from 0.64 per cent to 0.19 per cent a year between

Table 8.2 Population change in Great Britain 1961–80, by regions and regional groups (in percentages per year)

Regions and regional groups	1961–6	1966–71	1971–4	1974–7	1977–80
Great Britain	0.64	0.39	0.19	−0.04	0.05
Scotland	0.07	0.07	−0.01	−0.13	−0.27
Wales	0.45	0.22	0.42	0.11	0.11
Northern	0.08	0.08	−0.07	−0.16	−0.36
Yorks & Humb.	0.56	0.25	0.15	−0.10	0.06
North West	0.41	0.19	−0.12	−0.30	−0.35
East Midlands	1.00	0.79	0.78	0.24	0.29
West Midlands	0.77	0.71	0.32	−0.11	−0.00
East Anglia	1.16	1.41	1.74	1.06	0.97
South East	0.81	0.33	−0.12	−0.19	0.12
South West	1.12	0.86	0.97	0.57	0.50
South East, East Anglia and South West	0.89	0.50	0.21	0.04	0.26
Rest of Britain	0.47	0.32	0.17	−0.10	−0.10
Difference	0.42	0.18	0.04	0.14	0.36
South East, West Midlands and North West	0.71	0.36	−0.04	−0.20	−0.01
Rest of Britain	0.56	0.42	0.45	0.15	0.12
Difference	0.15	−0.06	−0.49	−0.35	−0.13

Source: Calculated from mid-year estimates supplied by OPCS and Registrar General Scotland

1961–6 and 1971–4, the rate for Wales dropped by only 0.03 percentage points, that for Scotland by only 0.08, and that for the Northern region by only 0.15 (table 8.2). In these latter two developments – the setback suffered by the three most urbanized regions, particularly the South East, and the relative improvement in the more peripheral areas of the west and north – lies the major part of the explanation for the shift in regional differentials away from a straightforward north–south dimension.

The reappearance of this dimension in the later 1970s partly follows a mirror image of the previous developments. Three of the traditionally slow-growing areas (Scotland, Wales and the Northern region) experienced a sharp downturn in their fortunes after 1971–4 despite holding up so well against the national trend until then. Since 1971–4, too, the two fastest growing regions of East Anglia and the South West recorded sharp cut-backs in their growth rates, but their effect on the overall growth rate for south and east Britain was completely offset by the resilience of the South East, so that the three regions combined suffered a smaller fall in growth rate than Britain as a whole through to 1974–7 and subsequently grew more quickly than the national average. The return of the South East to a more dynamic position, however, stands in marked contrast to the experience of the other two heavily urbanized regions, for in the West Midlands the slight recovery in 1977–80 was insufficient to compensate for the slump in growth rate registered over the previous three-year period and the North West shifted further into a negative balance contrary to the national trend. The recent experience of the West Midlands and North West, along with the setbacks to the traditional peripheral areas and the resilience of the South East, thus provide the keys to understanding the renewed importance of the north–south distinction and the waning of the urban–rural dimension in British population trends in the second half of the 1970s.

The mentions made above of movements relative to the national average are required largely because of the trend in natural change rate, which fell steadily through to 1974–7 and then stabilized for the remainder of the decade. As with the intercensal analysis described above, therefore, it is useful to distinguish the natural change and migrational components of population trends and, as before, it is found that, though the regions differ somewhat in their natural change rate at any particular time, they share very similar trends in natural change over time and thus leave migration to account for the changes in relative regional performance during the period under study (figure 8.1). Over the first three periods recognized in this analysis, two features stand out even more dramatically, now that the effect of falling natural increase is removed from the analysis. The first is the steady improvement in Scotland and the Northern region, where the severe net migration losses of the early 1960s had ameliorated considerably by the early 1970s. The second is the massive surge in net in-migration rates registered by the less urbanized regions of the southern half of Britain. In East Anglia this constituted a consistent acceleration through to the early 1970s, but in the East Midlands, South West and Wales it involved a resurgence following small reductions in 1966–71. Meanwhile, the South East shifted steadily from a positive migration balance in the early 1960s into substantial migration loss by the early 1970s, reflecting its greater net losses to the adjacent more rural regions as well as lower net gains from Scotland and the Northern region.

Against this background, the developments since 1971–4 seem less consistent and somewhat more difficult to interpret. The period 1974–7 not only saw a further improvement in the migration balances of Scotland and the Northern region, but also witnessed a reversal in the deterioration of the position in the North West and South East, the latter being in marked contrast to the experience of the West Midlands. Meanwhile, the East Midlands, East Anglia, the South West and Wales shared a reduction in their rates of net migration gain. For East Anglia, the South East,

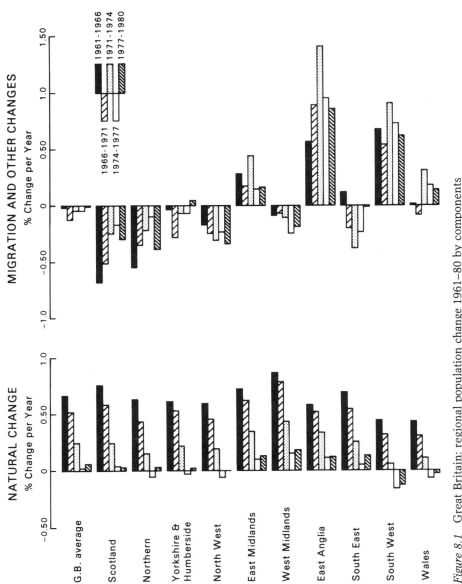

Figure 8.1 Great Britain: regional population change 1961–80 by components

Source: Mid-year estimates supplied by OPCS and Registrar General Scotland

the South West and Wales, the trends between the early and mid-1970s were continued into the last three-year period, with the South East putting in the most impressive change and almost regaining a balance between in- and out-migration. Further north, however, the last part of the 1970s saw a reversal of the previous trend and a return to less favourable migration balances, with the Northern region receiving the most severe jolt but recording a rate of migratory loss for 1977–80 not much greater than those for Scotland and the North West.

The interpretation of these more recent trends depends on the weight attached to the last three-year period as opposed to 1974–7. One possible explanation, which fits the experience of the southern half of the country reasonably well, is that the early 1970s constituted a period of high mobility and that subsequently the general propensity to migrate has fallen. Certainly in 1974–7 all regions except the West Midlands saw their net migration levels fall back towards zero, but this explanation does not fit the experience of most northern areas in 1977–80. For an alternative and more specific explanation, it is useful to focus on the experience of the South East. Its improvement in 1974–7 must be closely related to the reduction in net migration into the more rural regions of southern Britain, but in the last three-year period the South East must also have benefited from the return to higher migration losses by the north of the country.

A fuller explanation of these more recent developments requires more detailed data, particularly on gross migration flows. Fortunately, the analysis of National Health Service data by Ogilvy (1980, 1982) has produced estimates of the gross migration flows into and out of each region on a two-year moving average from 1971–3 to 1977–9. Four observations are particularly relevant in the present context. First, there was indeed a progressive decrease in the overall level of inter-regional mobility through the 1970s. Second, the element which contributed most significantly to this reduction was a marked fall in the numbers leaving the South East for other parts of the country, beginning early in the decade according to this data source but accelerating after 1974–6. Third, all regions appear to have suffered from the lower level of outward movement from the South East, particularly to the adjacent regions but also the more northerly areas. The latter are now seen to have benefited from the higher mobility early in the decade, which by bringing them more in-migrants narrowed the migration deficit or even converted it to a surplus in some regions for a time, but the later years witnessed a more rapid decline in in-migration than out-migration, widening the gap again. Fourth, however, the timing of these changes came earlier nearer the South East, thereby allowing Scotland and the Northern region to maintain their improvements later in the decade than elsewhere.

The major developments in regional populations in the 1970s, therefore, carry further the trends evolving in the 1960s, but at the same time give some sign that the decentralization process had passed its peak. Early in the decade migration produced a marked acceleration in the swing against the three most heavily populated regions in favour of the adjacent regions including Wales, but by the mid-1970s some amelioration in this pattern is evident, with all regions in southern Britain seeing their net migration rates move back towards a balance. In the north the fortunes of the periphery, characterized by high net losses to the south in the early 1960s, improved steadily up till the last part of the 1970s, when the north–south distinction strongly reasserted itself. Overlying these migration shifts was the dramatic decline in natural change since the mid-1960s and its subsequent stabilization towards the end of the 1970s. Since this downward trend was shared to a broadly similar extent by all regions, this did not noticeably distort the changing pattern of relative regional performance produced by migration, but it had a major effect on overall growth rates, being particularly significant for regions experiencing net out-migration.

A SUB-REGIONAL PERSPECTIVE

A more detailed spatial scale can help to shed more light on the main features which the regional-level analysis has shown, particularly the greater importance of the urban–rural dimension in the 1970s than in the 1960s but also the move back towards more traditional patterns of population redistribution by the end of the 1970s. The important question is the spatial extent of the population turnaround in the 1970s; whether it was concentrated in one or two parts of the regions which were involved and, if so, whether in the more remote parts or merely across the boundary from more populous regions. Another question concerns the background to the changes in the heavily urbanized regions, particularly which areas contributed most to the cut-back in growth in the late 1960s and early 1970s. A third relates to the nature of the developments which helped the return to population gain of the South East in the later 1970s.

Figure 8.2 presents the main results of an analysis which tackles the first two questions. The patterns are relatively clearcut, both for overall population change and for migration which is clearly the dominant force behind it, but do not perhaps produce the commonly expected picture in all cases. Least surprising is the distribution of areas which experienced high overall population decreases and net out-migration in the 1970s, comprising Greater London, West Midlands county, Greater Manchester, Merseyside, Tyne and Wear and Strathclyde (figure 8.2 A/B). At the same time, however, it is apparent that the traditional suburban counties surrounding these conurbations, which had grown rapidly in the previous two decades, were generally relatively subdued in their growth performance in the 1970s, with Surrey even failing to maintain its population level.

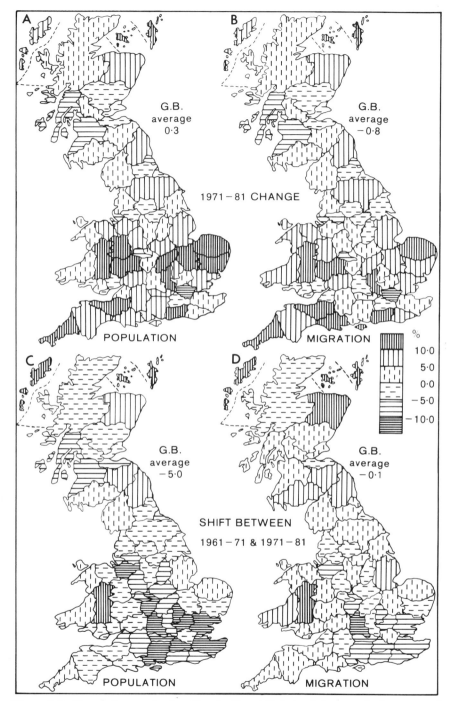

Figure 8.2 Population and migration in Great Britain: intercensal changes and shifts 1961–81, by counties (England and Wales) and regions (Scotland)

Source: Provisional 1981 Census data supplied by OPCS and Registrar General Scotland

Most of the main ring of counties round Greater London, together with Warwickshire and Cheshire, recorded growth rates in the 1970s which were 10–15 per cent lower than for the 1960s and net migration changes some 5–10 per cent lower (figure 8.2 C/D). The downturn in the performance of the three most heavily urbanized regions in the 1970s can thus be attributed as much to the cut-backs experienced by the suburban counties as to any further deterioration in the position of the conurbations themselves.

The main areas of rapid population growth and net in-migration in the 1970s tend to lie just beyond the traditional suburban counties. Thus in south-eastern England they describe a broad arc round the north of the home counties stretching from Norfolk to Northamptonshire and Buckinghamshire and reappearing in West Sussex, while for the West Midlands the fastest growth appears to have been recorded by the areas to the west of the conurbation and extending across the national boundary to include Powys (figure 8.2 A/B). Areas lying further away from the major metropolitan centres tend to have grown rather less rapidly than these intermediate locations, except for Cornwall and the Scottish areas most closely associated with North Sea oil development. While the dominance of these intermediate locations may suggest that the counter-urbanization process had advanced only a limited distance from the country's core areas, a rather different impression is obtained from figure 8.2 C/D, where it appears that it was indeed the most remote areas which saw the greatest change in fortune between the two decades. Not only Cornwall and northern Scotland but also western Wales, the counties bordering the Wash, and the more rural parts of northern England and southern Scotland all experienced a significant improvement in their net migration balance and an upward movement in their rates of overall population change contrary to the downward shift of the national average by 5 per cent. Indeed, over most parts of the country, the shift between the rates of the 1960s and 1970s presents a relatively regular pattern, graduating from the largest positive movements in the more remote areas to the largest downward shift in rates for the counties immediately surrounding the conurbations. Only the conurbations themselves break this overall pattern for they generally experienced cut-backs little more than the national average and in some cases improved their relative position.

This relatively clear-cut zonation of the country based on the analysis of census data presents a similar pattern to that derived by Champion (1981). The latter was based on a classification of counties according to their migration experience over the period 1961–77, using the mid-year estimates, and can be used to summarize the trends at more frequent stages across the two decades than is possible with the census data. The only limitation is that this framework can be used here only for the counties of England and Wales because of the absence of revised mid-year estimates for Scottish regions for before 1971. As well as indicating the character and composition of the five types of counties recognized, table 8.3 shows their rates of population change per year caused by net migration and other changes for five periods and set these data alongside the rates of natural change and overall population change.

According to the mid-year estimates it was the Type 3 counties which experienced the most rapid population growth and highest net in-migration rates in the 1960s (table 8.3). These comprise the traditional suburban counties adjacent to Greater London and the metropolitan counties and lying broadly within the main urban spine of England running from the South East to the North West. Their strong performance contrasts markedly with that of the conurbations (Type 1) and the other older industrial and mining areas (Type 2), groups composed of counties characterized by net out-migration through all or most of the five periods. Types 4 and 5 recorded population growth and net in-migration at much lower rates than Type 3 in the 1960s, though the gap narrowed with the latter's growth rate falling back as the decade proceeded.

With the early 1970s, however, came the major shift in net migration gain in favour of the more remote areas which has been suggested above by the regional analysis and by the intercensal analysis at sub-regional level. Between 1966–71 and 1971–4 the zone of most rapid migration gain jumped from the Type 3 counties to Type 5, though in overall population growth terms it was the Type 4 counties which took over the lead because of their higher rate of natural increase. This evidence confirms that it was the traditional suburban counties rather than the older urban areas of Types 1 and 2 which experienced the parallel downward shift in net migration balances. Indeed the latter two groups appear to have managed some net improvement in their migration balances after the deterioration of the late 1960s, but clearly London and the metropolitan counties remain the principal generating force behind this increasingly more pervasive pattern of counter-urbanization. Moreover, with the nation-wide fall in natural change rates, the Type 1 counties are seen to have plunged much deeper into overall population loss in the early 1970s (table 8.3).

The classification of counties used in table 8.3 also gives some insight into the more recent developments by distinguishing two further three-year periods through to 1980. The nation-wide decline in migration propensities noted since the 1970s by Ogilvy (1982) is generally evident from the migration component of the mid-year estimates, but it has not had a consistent effect on all five types or over time. In particular, the attractiveness of Type 4 counties for net in-migration dropped markedly after 1974, but appears to have achieved a measure of recovery by 1977–80, as too does the migration balance of Type 3 (table 8.3). From this evidence it appears that, though the actual rate of net in-migration

Table 8.3 Population change in England and Wales 1961–80, by components, for groups of counties classified according to net migration experiences (in percentages per year)

County type	1961–6	1966–71	1971–4	1974–7	1977–80
A *Migration and other changes*					
Type 1	−0.74	−0.91	−0.88	−0.66	−0.58
2	−0.09	−0.19	−0.11	−0.19	−0.08
3	−1.11	0.73	0.32	0.21	0.35
4	0.63	0.59	0.84	0.47	0.52
5	0.40	0.39	0.94	0.77	0.55
B *Natural change*					
Type 1	0.68	0.53	0.23	0.01	0.08
2	0.73	0.56	0.30	0.08	0.11
3	0.77	0.65	0.36	0.11	0.16
4	0.52	0.44	0.19	−0.03	0.01
5	0.38	0.27	0.04	−0.16	−0.11
C *Overall population change*					
Type 1	−0.06	−0.38	−0.64	−0.65	−0.50
2	0.64	0.37	0.19	−0.11	0.02
3	1.88	1.38	0.68	0.32	0.51
4	1.15	1.03	1.03	0.45	0.53
5	0.78	0.67	0.98	0.61	0.44

D *Classification of counties*

Type 1: Net out-migration in all four periods: Gter London, Gter Manchester, Merseyside, S. Yorks, Tyne & Wear, W. Midlands, W. Yorks.

Type 2: Net out-migration in at least three periods (other than those in Type 1): Cleveland, Humberside, Notts; Gwent, Mid-Glamorgan, S. Glamorgan, W. Glamorgan.

Type 3: High net in-migration in 1960s, but lower in 1970s: Avon, Beds, Berks, Bucks, Cheshire, E. Sussex, Essex, Hants, Herts, Kent, Oxfordshire, Staffs, Surrey, Warwicks.

Type 4: Net in-migration in at least three periods but no overall trend (i.e. excluding Types 3 and 5): Derbys, Gloucs, I. o. Wight, Lancs, Leics, Norfolk, Northants, Salop, Suffolk, W. Sussex, Wilts; Clywd.

Type 5: Significant improvement in migration balance in early 1970s after net out-migration or low levels of net in-migration in 1960s: Cambs, Cornwall, Cumbria, Devon, Dorset, Durham, Hereford & Worcs, Lincs, Northumberland, N. Yorks, Somerset; Dyfed, Gwynedd, Powys.

Source: Calculated from mid-year estimates supplied by OPCS and Registrar General Scotland

recorded by Type 5 counties fell in the mid-1970s, these generally more re-mote areas in fact increased their significance in the counter-urbanization process relative to the other types of counties. This remoteness factor, however, seems to have been short-lived, because by 1977–80, with the futher cut-back in migration gains of Type 5 and the considerable recovery of Type 3, a relatively narrow margin separated the migration balances of all three of the less urban categories. Indeed, when natural change is taken into account, it is the Type 3 and 4 counties which were vying for the highest rates of overall population growth. Population redistribution from the more urban to the more rural zones obviously continued throughout the decade, but by these later years the rate of change had slowed down considerably and the lead taken by the more remote rural areas earlier in the decade had been very largely pulled back by the counties located closer to the major metropolitan centres.

This observation that counter-urbanization had slowed down but was not a completely spent force is reinforced by an analysis of district-level data for England and Wales, with the 402 districts separated into six equal-size classes according to their 1971 population density (table 8.4). The first part shows that the density class experiencing the most rapid

Table 8.4 Population change, 1961–79 for districts of England and Wales by density groups

A *Actual annual percentage rate (linear and weighted)*					
Density classes	(N)	1961–6	1966–71	1971–5	1975–9
Highest Class 1	(67)	−0.35	−0.70	−0.81	−0.75
Class 2	(67)	1.03	0.68	0.12	−0.06
Class 3	(67)	1.14	0.77	0.32	0.17
Class 4	(67)	1.90	1.47	0.94	0.63
Class 5	(67)	1.75	1.57	1.17	0.83
Lowest Class 6	(67)	0.69	0.84	1.20	0.58
National average		0.64	0.39	0.13	−0.01
B *Annual percentage rates standardized to the national average*					
Density classes	(N)	1961–6	1966–71	1971–5	1975–9
Highest Class 1	(67)	−0.99	−1.09	−0.94	−0.74
Class 2	(67)	0.39	0.29	−0.01	−0.06
Class 3	(67)	0.50	0.38	0.19	0.18
Class 4	(67)	1.26	1.08	0.81	0.64
Class 5	(67)	1.11	1.18	1.04	0.84
Lowest Class 6	(67)	0.05	0.45	1.07	0.59
National average		0.00	0.00	0.00	0.00

Source: Calculated from mid-year estimates supplied by OPCS

Note: The 402 post-1974 districts of England and Wales are grouped into six categories with 67 cases each on the basis of 1971 population density. The national average rates relate to Great Britain

rate of overall population growth shifted from Class 4 in 1961–6 to Class 5 and then in 1971–5 to Class 6, the lowest density category. In the later 1970s, this distinction reverted to Class 5, with a marked reduction in the performance of Class 6. Even so, the latter remained well above the national average rate in 1975–9, in marked contrast to its position in the early 1960s, as shown by the second part of table 8.4. If the assumption is made that the lowest density areas tend to be the most rural and remote, as more detailed inspection of the data largely confirms, then it is clear that the surge outwards towards the periphery built up progressively through the period until it peaked in the first half of the 1970s and subsequently suffered a significant retrenchment. Also, recognizing the highest-density category to comprise the major metropolitan districts, these data confirm the improvement made in their relative performance since the late 1960s and particularly in 1975–9.

Finally, figure 8.3 indicates the geographical patterns which have produced the recent changes in the performances of the conurbations, the more remote counties and the areas lying in-between. Based again on the mid-year estimates, it reflects most noticeably the overall decline in the role of population redistribution between 1971–4 and 1977–80, because most of the areas which the 1981 Census suggests were net recipients of migrants over the previous ten years witnessed a downward shift in their rate of in-migration during that decade, while several of the traditional suppliers of migrants (Greater London, Merseyside, Tyne and Wear and Strathclyde) saw an improvement in their migration balances. The pattern of downward shift explains why the Type 5 and Class 6 areas of tables 8.3 and 8.4 respectively had lost their places as the fastest growing areas of the country by the end of the decade. It appears from this evidence that some of the areas which had experienced the largest upward surge in migration between the 1960s and 1970s (figure 8.2 D) had also suffered some of the largest cut-backs between 1971–4 and 1977–80; in particular, parts of northern Scotland, north and west Wales, the far South West, East Anglia and several counties lying between the main population centres of the Midlands and South East. Within the South East region itself, lastly, is located the main concentration of counties which significantly improved their migration balance during the course of the 1970s, comprising not only Greater London but also virtually all the adjacent counties. Herein lies both confirmation of the recovery of the South East in 1977–80 noticed in the regional-level analysis and an indication that this feature was recorded widely through the region, being experienced by both the conurbation and the surrounding counties and not confined to one or the other. This recovery contrasts particularly with the experience of the remoter areas in southern Britain and also with that of much of northern England and Scotland, helping to produce the reopening of the contrast between north and south noted earlier.

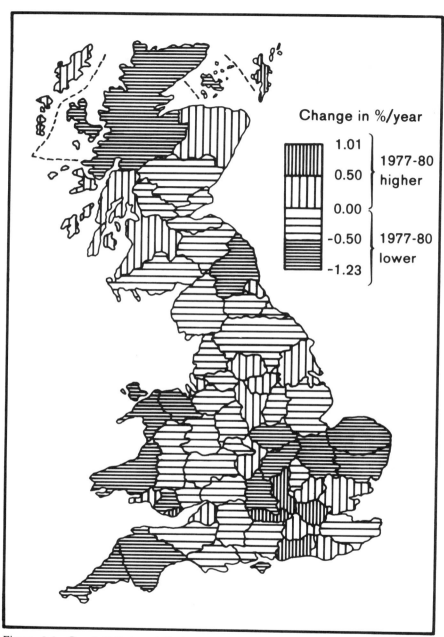

Figure 8.3 Great Britain: shift in net migration rates between 1971–4 and 1977–80, by counties (England and Wales) and regions (Scotland)

Source: Mid-year estimates supplied by OPCS and Registrar General Scotland

Concluding observations

This chapter is seeking to answer two main questions, namely the extent to which patterns of population change in the 1970s differed from those of the previous decade and how far such deviations can be explained in terms of changes in wider national circumstances. Amongst the latter were specified the reduction in gross international migration flows, the decline in birth-rate, the increasing numbers of elderly, the accelerating reduction in average household size, the lower level of house-building activity and the general depression in economic conditions. A further question relates to the value of regional and sub-regional perspectives in shedding light on major changes taking place in the demographic, economic and social characteristics of the nation.

The regional level is particularly valuable in indicating the nature and significance of the single most conspicuous change of the 1970s – the decline in birth-rate. It confirms, first of all, that this was a nationwide phenomenon and has been experienced relatively evenly across the country, thus having a fairly insignificant effect on relative regional performances. For individual regions, however, the implications of lower rates of natural change have been highly significant, particularly for those regions where natural increase was no longer sufficient to compensate for net migration loss. Four of the eleven regions fell into this category by 1971–4, seven by 1974–7.

In terms of our understanding of relative regional performance, however, the value of the regional perspective is less significant relative to the insight offered by the sub-regional level. The traditional distinction between northern and southern halves of the UK encapsulates a much smaller proportion of the population shifts experienced in the 1970s than it did in the 1950s or even the 1960s. The gap in overall growth rates between the two halves grew progressively narrower until the late 1970s though the south was still maintaining a small advantage as noted by Vining and Kontuly (1978).

Closer inspection of the regional data, instead, reveals that changes in population distribution were becoming increasingly dominated by the influence of the major metropolitan centres. The central spine of England, extending between the South East and North West regions, appears to act as the pivot around which adjustments are taking place, with decentralization sending net flows of migrants to the less heavily populated regions in the east and west of the country. These urban-centred patterns are, however, more correctly described and explained at a sub-regional level, preferably within a purpose-designed framework of metropolitan areas but in this paper, given the limitations of recent data, at the level of the counties of England and Wales and their equivalent 'regions' in Scotland.

The sub-regional perspective provides strong evidence for the tendencies towards counter-urbanization recognized for other countries. The situation is particularly clearly-cut in Scotland, where the more remote areas experienced a major improvement in their migration balances in the 1970s. The north-eastern parts were stimulated by the economic activity associated with North Sea oil, but the southern borders also experienced more modest improvements. The geographical patterns in England and Wales are distorted by the more complicated nature of the urban system, but a comparison of the migration rates for the 1960s and the 1970s reveals a continuum of experience ranging from considerable upward shifts in more remote areas to marked downward shifts in the areas adjacent to the main metropolitan centres.

The examination of sub-regional changes on a more detailed time-scale, however, raises some qualifications and questions about the nature and causes of this apparent counter-urbanization trend. First, the improvement in migration balance in peripheral areas did not take place progressively, but involved a marked surge in the early 1970s, only to fall back significantly by the middle of the decade. Second, the major metropolitan centres, though characterized by heavy net out-migration throughout the study period, did not, in aggregate, experience any acceleration in migration loss after 1966–71 and indeed saw a significant reduction in the rate of loss in the mid-1970s. Rather than the direct fuelling of the peripheral surge by increased conurbation losses, it was the metropolitan rings of counties which experienced the parallel deterioration in migration balance.

The previous studies of population trends reviewed at the start of the chapter throw up a number of possible explanations for these three linked observations. The reduction in the attractiveness of peripheral areas in the mid-1970s could equally well be attributed to the rapid saturation of their limited spare housing capacity and building land, to the temporary effects of economic depression on the mobility of households and perhaps jobs, or to the hypothesis that the early 1970s provided a unique combination of favourable conditions which will never be repeated. The stabilization and subsequent reduction in net migration losses from the conurbations can, by virtue of their timing, be attributed only partly to the economic difficulties of the mid-1970s; instead, explanations can also be sought in the improvement of the size and quality of the housing stock, resulting from the completion of redevelopment schemes and the shift in emphasis towards rehabilitation.

The progressive decline in the positive migration balances of the traditional suburban counties through to 1974–7 seems comparatively easy to understand. The capacity of these areas must have become increasingly saturated, as development used up the available sites both within and beyond the metropolitan green belts. At the same time, average household size will have fallen faster in these areas than nationally as the children of the young couples who settled there during the 1950s left school and moved to other areas for jobs and houses. To some extent the latter may have contributed to the improvement in the conurbations' migration balances, but the experience of these suburban counties also raises a query about the nature of the apparent counter-urbanization trends.

The query arises from the definition of counter-urbanization and the associated process of rural rejuvenation, for the North American literature makes clear that this phenomenon concerns a different type of settlement rather than an extension of the traditional type; hence the emphasis on remote rural areas rather than on the lateral spread of existing metropolitan areas. The Type 5 counties in table 8.3 comprise not only the remoter parts of England and Wales but also counties like North Yorkshire, Hereford and Worcester, and Cambridgeshire which are directly open to metropolitan influence. Indeed the small scale of the UK, relative to New World countries, raises the question of the extent to which any parts can be considered immune from spillover effects from the major conurbations, whether these involve migrants directly from the conurbations or step-wise movements through their rings. The need for an answer to this type of question is made all the greater by the developments which took place during the last three years of the decade in the South East. The return to high net in-migration rates by the counties round London must have been produced as much by a redirection of London overspill to nearer rather than more distant locations as by increased inter-regional migration gain.

Satisfactory answers to this question and the others raised in the previous two paragraphs require more detailed information about gross migration flows, about the characteristics of the migrants and about their reasons for moving. Analysis of the changing economic conditions and studies of the housing stock and availability and cost of building land in more localized areas are also essential. Both are beyond the scope of the present chapter and, moreover, the former cannot be attempted on a comprehensive basis until the detailed results of the 1981 Census have been analysed.

Acknowledgements

The author gratefully acknowledges the co-operation of the Office of Population Censuses and Surveys and the Registrar General Scotland in providing unpublished data on the components of population change at regional and county level and giving permission for their data to be published in this form. He is also indebted to John Craig for his helpful comments on an early draft of this chapter and to Jim Milne for assistance in the computations.

Migration within and between labour markets

S. R. Kennett

Introduction

Population redistribution is the most fundamental aspect of change in the urban system. At sub-regional scales, as noted in the previous chapter, migration is the more important and variable determinant of population change. Of the British population in 1971, more than 6 million (or one in eight) were recorded as moving at least once during the previous year. About 17.5 million moved in the five-year period 1966–71, equivalent to more than one-third of the total population or about the size of all the conurbations together. Nevertheless, for various reasons outlined in the first section, the importance of migration has tended to be underestimated. This chapter then outlines some of the features of population movement in the urban system, concentrating on the characteristics of differential migration. This leads to a discussion of the implications of population decentralization for local government fiscal issues, a topic which illustrates the pervasive importance of migration trends.

The study of migration in the urban system

The migration mechanism itself should be seen as a process rather than a set of independent, unrelated actions. Ideally, it should be viewed through a hierarchically ordered, interacting urban system, instead of a number of discrete towns, cities and rural areas. The temporal dimension is also vital. The influence of previous population distributions and movements should not be overlooked in an analysis of recent trends. The essential characteristics of the present *regional* population distribution were shaped in the period between the mid-eighteenth century and the

First World War. Changes since then have predominantly affected intra-regional population patterns. Despite the similarity of these statements, a number of significant, and in some ways insuperable, implications emanate from them for research strategies.

The importance of migration has been underplayed by much of the literature. Two complementary themes have conspired to produce this position. First, the 'economic health' of regions (and, latterly, of inner cities) have usually been studied in terms of indicators such as unemployment, wage rates or skill levels. Migration has frequently been seen as a side effect of these phenomena. Its true role, however, is integral, relating to causes as well as effects of an area's economic growth or decline. Perhaps since government policies which influence population distribution have been uncoordinated, confused with their impacts and, therefore, difficult to monitor, research has tended to concentrate on themes where the objectives of government policy are more clearly defined.

The second reason why the importance of population redistribution processes has been underestimated lies in the nature and availability of the data. The census, although offering the best available view of population movement, only presents a 'snap-shot' of this dynamic phenomenon. Thus, for example, the interrelationship between contemporary and earlier moves is lost. The problems of using census data are particularly severe for estimating return migration and life-cycle patterns of movement; hence the value of research which has adopted a longitudinal approach following the migration of individuals through their lifetime (Kiernan, 1979). A related difficulty in the use of census data is the loss of details concerning people moving more than once within the time period spanned by the question on place of residence at an earlier date.

Though these shortcomings may exacerbate the misunderstanding of migration processes, even within a descriptive framework of the kind employed in this chapter, the migration data in the census provide a valuable source of information on the dynamics of urban change. Indeed within the census itself the data are unique in incorporating aspects of both temporal change and spatial interaction. Only the occupational mobility question also specifically involves change over time, while the properties of interaction between areas are shared with journey-to-work data.

In the analyses which follow, these data are organized on the basis of the Metropolitan Economic Labour Area (MELA) system described at the beginning of this book. This form of city-region or labour-market framework is valuable in depicting national, regional and daily levels of the urban system, thereby allowing assessment of the linkages among the structural tiers of the economy on the one hand and its spatial areas on the other. Since the MELAs can be disaggregated into their constituent zones of cores, rings and outer rings, this approach has the

intrinsic advantage of aiding the study of the context of inner city problems as well as regional problems, though under this definition the core
encompasses a much wider area than those generally used to study inner
city areas.

Only recently have estimates of flows and characteristics of migration become available for the component zones of MELAs (Spence
et al., 1982). Such information facilitates a more detailed assessment of
decentralization within and between labour markets than has previously
been possible. Hitherto, discussion of migration flows was restricted to
inter-SMLA (Standard Metropolitan Labour Area) streams (see Johnson,
Salt and Wood, 1974, for the 1965/6 interval) and population dynamics
within MELAs had been assessed by use of decennial net migration
estimates (e.g. Department of Environment, 1976a). Age or socio-economic
characteristics of migrants had previously not been considered on an
MELA basis although research had been conducted on social polarization
which combines the effects of social mobility with those of selective
migration (Hall *et al.*, 1973; Goddard and Spence, 1976). Before examining these aspects of migration, however, the next section outlines the
background to recent population movements within the MELA framework.

POPULATION DYNAMICS IN THE URBAN SYSTEM

The patterns of total population change and migration flows may be summarized briefly, as they have been the subject of previous discussion (e.g.
Department of Environment, 1976a; Drewett, Goddard and Spence 1975,
1976a, 1976b; Kennett, 1977, 1979). Although there were important
variations between cities, the population of urban cores increased during
the 1950s by approximately 500,000 people. Some losses were however
being experienced by the biggest cities. During the 1960s such declines
increased both in volume and area, spreading to most of the urban cores.
By 1971 85 per cent of SMLAs were decentralizing and the net population
loss for cores during the decade reached 750,000. In contrast the rings
experienced continuous growth, accommodating over 4 million people in
two decades. Since the Second World War population loss has been
predominantly, but not entirely, associated with the urban cores. Unclassified areas suffered the traditional process of rural depopulation into
the 1950s, although for the zone as a whole this had halted by the 1960s.
Additionally, many individual outer rings and some rings lost population
throughout the 1951–71 period.

Nevertheless, the dominant feature has been the flight from the cities.
There was a clear tendency for decentralization to commence earlier in the
conurbations. Indeed, some inner areas have incurred population decline

since about 1900. Most nineteenth-century cores are currently accommodating a smaller proportion of their total city-region population than they had in 1951. This decline would have been still greater but for the natural increases in the cities up until 1971. Thus, by net migration, the 126 urban cores lost some 900,000 people to the rest of Britain between 1966 and 1971.

Although the rings received more than 700,000 of these core outflows, the scope of decentralization has, more recently, extended to the outer rings and beyond. Between 1966 and 1971 the rings themselves directed net outflows to both the outer rings (80,000) and the unclassified zone (14,000). Consequently, the outer rings and not the rings received net gains by exchanges with each of the other urban zones in this period, although their growth was not as rapid as the rings.

In the light of this discussion, it is easy to become overawed by levels of net decentralization. Yet when streams of migrants are considered on an origin–destination basis, moves from rings to urban cores in fact comprised almost 1 million people between 1966 and 1971 (table 9.1). Whilst this was easily offset by the corresponding outflow of nearly 1.9 million, the ring-to-core flow was nevertheless almost twice the volume of the third largest of sixteen inter-zonal streams (that from cores to outer rings). Furthermore, on a proportionate basis, the percentage of the cores' population moving to rings in the period was only fractionally higher than the proportion of the rings' population moving to cores. (In the USA counterstreams on this basis are proportionately greater than the outflows (see Alonso, 1978.)

By use of individual migration streams, it is also possible to discriminate the deconcentration of population within and between city regions. Not surprisingly, given the well-known negative relationship between migration and distance, the vast majority of core-to-ring flows took place within individual MELAs. Nevertheless, although the relative strength of

Table 9.1   Inter-zonal migration 1966–71 (thousands)

Origin	Destination				
	Core	Ring	Outer ring	Unclassified areas	Total
Core	794	1865	530	115	3304
Ring	963	640	494	90	2187
Outer ring	335	416	235	87	1072
Unclassified areas	82	76	87	10	255
Total	2175	2997	1345	302	6819

Note: Columns may not sum to totals because of rounding

the counterstream increased with migration length, net movements away from cores were still recorded over the longest distances.

A slightly different picture is presented by the outer rings. This zone achieved marginally larger net gains from inter-MELA interactions. Moreover, inter-MELA increases there were both relatively and absolutely larger than the rings' inter-MELA increases, despite the latter's much larger total population. This feature is due to the largest cities beginning to decentralize their populations into the outer rings of neighbouring labour areas.

The implication from the study of migration dynamics within and between city regions is that the pattern is not simply a case of city loss and hinterland gain as is so often presented in the literature: it is a much more complex set of events. Within these general trends the conurbations play a crucial role and attention is now briefly turned to the importance of these areas.

DECENTRALIZATION FROM THE CORES OF MAJOR CITIES

From a detailed analysis of migration trends among the MELAs it is possible to suggest that the major urban areas were decentralizing both more rapidly and more widely than their smaller counterparts. Consequently, major cities were directing migrants not only into their own commuting hinterlands but also further afield between the MELAs into their neighbours' outer rings.

The major city systems are thus the key to understanding national patterns of migration. The seven largest MELAs or Million Cities (London, Birmingham, Manchester, Glasgow, Liverpool, Leeds and Newcastle), incurred rapidly rising population losses from their cores during the 1950s and early 1960s (figure 9.1). These continued unabated into the early 1970s despite the completion of postwar urban renewal programmes. Furthermore, since their peak growth rates between 1961 and 1966, the Million City rings have experienced diminishing rates of expansion. The London ring has even recorded population decline since 1971. Similarly, the 1970s have seen reduced rates of increase in the outer rings (figure 9.1). In part this reflects the declining birth-rate which has affected almost all areas in Great Britain. However, the slackening pace of growth in outer rings may also be a reflection of falling migration propensities. Nevertheless, the declining birth-rate of the late 1960s and early 1970s has served to increase the comparative importance of the migration component as a determinant of patterns of population change.

Only two of the seven Million Cities' outer rings experienced increased rates of population growth in the early 1970s: Glasgow and Newcastle. Unlike the other cities these MELAs are not tightly bounded by other labour markets. Therefore, their extensive outer rings facilitate lower levels of population decentralization into neighbouring MELAs.

POPULATION CHANGE

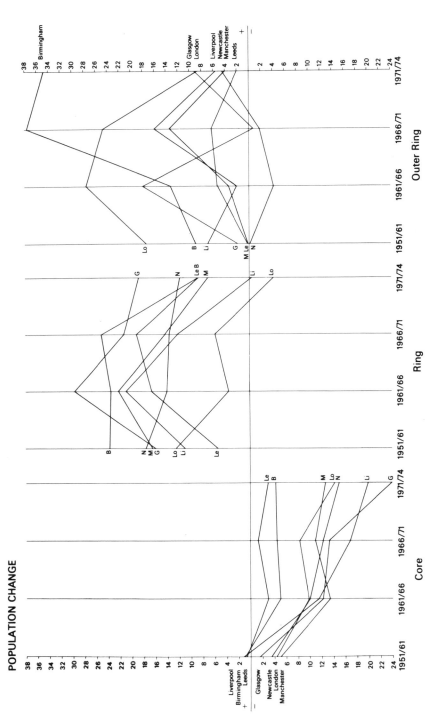

Figure 9.1 Million City population changes 1951–74 (decennial rates)

Although the Registrar General's estimates may be used to assess the post-1971 shifts of population, the change of local government system in 1974 has prohibited the use of the MELA concept after this date. The most recent population shifts are however discussed by Tony Champion in the previous chapter and by Kennett and Spence (1979).

Analysis of population changes in the cities between 1951 and 1974 places the detailed migration flow data for the 1966–71 period in perspective. In simple terms the major cities were all suffering large losses due to inter-MELA movement during this five-year period. However, considerable differences are evident in the nature of their inflows and outflows. First, the conurbations were much more important in terms of sources of migrants to other cities than they were as destinations. As suggested earlier, the Million Cities' most important out-migration streams were directed to neighbouring satellite MELAs. Secondly, of those moves between the Million Cities themselves, the most southerly, London, derived net inflows from each of the other six and their performance steadily deteriorated moving northward, with Glasgow incurring net deficits by exchanges with each of the cities. (For elaboration of these points see Kennett, 1977b.)

It is therefore upon relatively recent inter-urban trends that the long-established southward shift of population and economic activity remains superimposed. Many of the problems of Britain's traditionally declining regions now also appear to be urban problems exacerbated by changes in the intra-regional distribution of population. Hence the decline of large cities in more prosperous regions – e.g. London and Birmingham – have heightened intra-regional variations and contributed to the continued dampening of regional contrasts which has frequently been noted in the recent literature (e.g. Moore, Rhodes and Tyler, 1977).

The effect of the extension of migration fields from the large cities, which still contain more than 40 per cent of the nation's population, has been a net shift of people into intermediate and smaller-sized settlements in parts of the country which previously had much lower proportions of the industrial base. Most notable recipients have been East Anglia and the South West. Thus there has been considerable change in the status of towns peripheral to the largest cities with many developing as significant employment centres in their own right. However, one implication of this trend might be a future increase in the oscillation of settlements up and down the urban hierarchy reflecting more varied and rapid fluctuations of the fortunes of local economic bases due to the smaller labour markets' greater dependence on individual firms and industries compared with the largest cities.

It is also worth noting at this point that there appears to be a subtle but important difference between population and employment decentralization. Whilst migration is the dominant element within population change at the spatial scales utilized here, the same is not true of employment. Recent evidence suggests that differential birth- and death-rates amongst firms are the more important component in the decentralization of employment when compared with net out-migration of jobs (Dicken and Lloyd, 1978; Bull, 1978).

CENTRALIZATION–DECENTRALIZATION: A CONTINUUM OF PERFORMANCE

Despite the importance of the large cities and associated population movements, attention should not be solely restricted to this theme. Within the urban system there exists a continuum of performance linked by time and space. This continuum has frequently been portrayed as a city life cycle (Department of Environment, 1976a) the phases of which are associated principally with population size and location. The cycle has as its initial phase population centralization. A few MELAs (e.g. Hereford and Perth) had, by the 1966–71 period, still not advanced further than this stage. At the other end of the spectrum, decentralization from both core and ring to the outer ring and neighbouring MELAs has been experienced by a few of the major cities.

Thus, although when MELAs are aggregated to the regional level, decentralization appears ubiquitous, a number of labour markets still possess growing cores and declining hinterlands, usually representing the last vestiges of the long-standing pattern of rural depopulation. It is important to remember that these local economies, few as they are, will also therefore suffer from socio-economic problems which in their own way are no less severe than those resulting from more common features or urban population decline.

POPULATION TURNOVER AND THE LOCAL LABOUR MARKET

It has already been suggested that the process of decentralization within the city region may be viewed differently when the volumes of inflows and outflows are considered. Similarly, net movements between entire labour areas represent only a small proportion of the total exchanges involved. Thus, as with the internal dynamics of MELAs, net migration changes are not composed of a simple dichotomy between gainers and losers (or more formally, that in-migration rates are inversely related to levels of out-migration) as hypothesized by the 'push–pull' migration models (Lowry, 1966). In reality the system seems to approximate the notions of Ravenstein (1885 and 1889) almost a century ago: that each migration flow has its own counterstream and consequently there is a strong direct relationship between in- and out-migration.

Whilst Cordey-Hayes and Gleave (1973) first applied such notions in the British context by relating per capita in- and out-migration rates for twenty city regions developed by Fielding (1971), the strength of this relationship also deserves consideration at the MELA level. By using simple linear regression, for descriptive rather than causal purposes, out-migration (Y) was related to in-migration (X) (figure 9.2). The resulting correlation coefficient 0.87 was high for 126 observations and the value of the standard error was low. The regression equation suggests that each percentage increase in the level of out-migration is likely to be accompanied by a considerably greater increase in population inflows. Thus the higher the rate of population turnover, the higher the net surplus of in-migrants.

Why do the areas suffering highest net in-migration rates also incur the highest per capita outflows? One suggestion is that population turnover may be stimulated in a healthy economic environment because risks attached to job-motivated migrations are relatively low. In environments suffering economic duress labour turnover rates may be less due to the greater risk (perceived or real) that is associated with job change. Rees (1978) has depicted the reluctance of population in one such community, the Upper Afan Valley in South Wales, to resort to labour migration. Interestingly, the valley's neighbouring MELA, Rhondda, has the nation's lowest per capita migration inflows *and* outflows. Greenock, Hartlepool and Sunderland, three other members of the secondary industrial MELAs, and Sheffield, one of the major industrial MELAs, also display low turnover rates (figure 9.2). The only group to average net migration deficits, the Million Cities, tends to have slightly higher rates of interaction. This is especially true of London which receives disproportionately large numbers of long-distance young migrants and directs slightly older, wealthier individuals and families to neighbouring labour markets. (This theme is discussed in more detail in this chapter.)

Between 1966 and 1971 the London MELA lost more than 400,000 people to the rest of Great Britain. Of these, 325,000 remained in the South East. Thus the MELAs surrounding the capital in the 'London periphery' and 'New Town' groups have the highest turnovers and associated net migration gains (figure 9.2). Among the former, Aldershot in particular stands out because of unexpected net migration losses, due presumably to the decline in the armed forces which are heavily concentrated in this area. Within the latter category, Basingstoke has high net inflow rates, not reciprocated by outflows. This feature may be attributed to the town's very rapid expansion during the study period. Consequently, this is likely to be a once and for all phenomenon. Note also the relatively high in-migration rates accruing to the resort group of MELAs, particularly those with cores actually lying on the coast (figure 9.2). This illustrates one implication of these places' special role in the migration process – their function as retirement centres (Kennett, 1975).

If, as suggested here, population turnover is in part attributable to

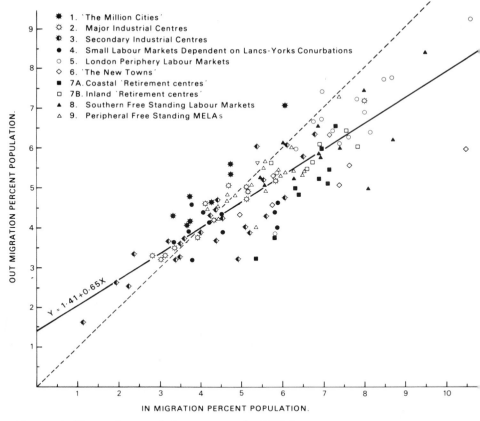

Figure 9.2 Per capita population turnover by MELA 1970–1

the 'economic health' of individual areas, what are the likely temporal effects of this phenomenon? Since the early 1970s the decline of the national economy is likely to mean that voluntary quit rates from jobs and associated labour migration will be lower than for the early 1960s. However, this important dimension has so far not been formally considered and deserves attention in future research initiatives.

In summary, labour markets with very high inflows per capita will incur almost equal outflow rates. Consequently vigorously growing areas will still be losing a high proportion of their younger, more footloose people. The implication is that a subtle shift in job opportunities could lead to a substantial fall of in-migration rates. In the short term these might not be matched by a similar fall in the less variable levels of out-migration. Areas like New Towns might be particularly vulnerable to such shifts. If government were to intervene and substantially reduce the population decline of inner cities, it is possible to envisage a scenario where the 'problem' of out-migration might effectively be transferred to those centres currently expanding most rapidly.

This example, hypothetical though it may be, does serve to emphasize the need for integrated rather than piecemeal approaches to solving population (and economic) problems in the space economy. Hitherto this has not occurred. Britain has a national regional policy and is currently developing a programme for inner cities. Additionally, the New Towns still receive support, despite the fact that their original rationale of tackling problems of population concentration is now apparently regarded as outmoded by central government. Rather than pursue a battery of seemingly uncoordinated policies, the high level of interdependence and interaction in the urban system (exemplified here through the migration process) emphasizes that what is required is an integrated strategy for the whole urban system.

Characteristics of migrants in the urban system

Broadbent (1977) has noted that decentralization from larger cities 'is far from being a neutral phenomenon'. How does population redistribution affect the age and socio-economic structure of labour markets? How does selective migration operate *within* daily urban systems? From census data it is possible to estimate some effects of net migration for various socio-economic and age subgroups at the MELA and constituent zonal level. Whilst there are a number of critical problems associated with this information, especially concerning the relationship between age, socio-economic grouping and direction/length of migration, they are too technical to be discussed in the present context. Deficiencies relating specifically to data used in this chapter have been covered by Kennett (1978b).

Shortcomings relating more generally to migration information are discussed by Willis (1974) and Rees (1976).

AGE-SPECIFIC MIGRATION

Turning first to the effect of differential migration by age, table 9.2 reveals the age composition of the net changes by urban zones. Urban cores suffered outflows in each cohort, whilst both rings and outer rings incurred ubiquitous net gains. Urban cores appeared to be polarizing by net migration change, suffering particularly severe outflows of the 15–44-year-old cohorts. By comparison, low rates of those of pensionable age were directed from cores between 1966 and 1971.

Table 9.2 Net gains and losses of migrants by age and urban zone 1966–71

Age	Cores		Rings		Outer rings		MELA*	
	(000s)	*(%)*	*(000s)*	*(%)*	*(000s)*	*(%)*	*(000s)*	*(%)*
5–14	−192	(−17.0)	146	(18.1)	42	(15.5)	−3	(−6.2)
15–29	−316	(−28.0)	276	(34.1)	48	(17.5)	8	(+ve)
30–44	−280	(−24.3)	214	(26.5)	58	(21.2)	−8	(−14.9)
45–pension age	−197	(−17.4)	119	(14.7)	57	(21.0)	−21	(−37.8)
Pensioners	−143	(−12.7)	53	(6.6)	68	(24.7)	−22	(−41.2)

Notes: * Net exchanges between MELAs and unclassified areas
Figures in brackets denote the proportion of each urban zone's overall gain (or loss). Figure omitted where net flow is in the opposite direction to the overall trend for the zone

Broadly speaking, the rings provide a mirror image of core outflows. Net in-migration was recorded in each age cohort, with particularly rapid inflows of 15–29-year-olds. Together, the inflow of the 15–29 and 30–44 cohorts represented more than 60 per cent of the rings' increase. Thus the rings are becoming younger by selective migration. This is in marked contrast to the outer rings, where those over 45 years moved in the most rapidly. Smallest inflows accrue to the 5–30-year age band. Whilst in absolute terms the level of overall gain by the outer rings is smaller than that for the rings, the net inflow of those of pensionable age is, in fact, greater.

The exchanges between MELA units and unclassified areas by age group produce four net outflows from urban Britain and one net inflow. The age group still centralizing was predictably the 15–29 age cohort (table 9.2). Relatively large outflows left urban Britain in the two most elderly cohorts. These findings corroborate the contention that unclassified areas were increasingly becoming the destinations of retirement migrants whilst they continued to lose their younger populations to the cities. Clearly, relatively small absolute changes by migration are likely to have an important impact for these small communities in terms of demand for and provision of local facilities.

The impact of age-selective migrations is not, of course, identical upon all MELAs. Figure 9.3 demonstrates once again the overriding importance of the Million Cities. These are the only group to suffer population loss in each cohort. During 1966–71 decline ranged from just over 100,000 of their population between 5 and 14 to more than 150,000 of those aged between 15 and 29. Out-migration from the Million Cities thus fuels the net in-migration recorded by every age cohort of the other eight MELA groups except for the small net outflow of those of pensionable age in the Lancashire/Yorkshire MELA category.

Despite the virtually ubiquitous in-migration to all age cohorts in the other MELA groups, there was a considerable difference in the proportional composition of these streams. Five MELA categories record highest inflows within the 15–29 age cohort representing the attraction of this age group to the South East and major industrial cities. The age-specific net migration profile for the secondary industrial group is unique as it revealed roughly equal-sized inflows for the three cohorts under 45 and did not experience the usual 'peaking' among the 15–29 age group. Only small inflows of the young economically active cohorts were drawn to the peripheral free-standing MELAs. Thus these city systems were ageing by selective migration, although the volume of inflow was approximately evenly distributed between groups over 30 years.

The resort MELAs of course revealed particularly prominent inflows among those of retirement age. Less than 10 per cent of this group's net migration gain were aged between 15 and 29. Retirement migration and the identification of retirement areas have come under increasing consideration in the literature (Law and Warnes, 1975 and 1976). Retirement areas (predominantly coastal areas) are peculiar not only because their proportion of elderly population is high but also because they are associated with high female sex-ratios (Clarke, 1960). This is partially due to the longevity of women and the relatively rich female employment opportunities generated in these areas by tourism and service provision for the elderly. Consequently, with the relatively greater and specialized demands on medical provision by the elderly (Department of Health and Social Security, 1976), these areas require special attention in terms of resources and service allocation. Yet, with the notable exception of the Centre for Urban and Regional Studies (1968), little detailed policy-oriented research has been undertaken in this field.

The preceding discussion has centred upon selective age migration

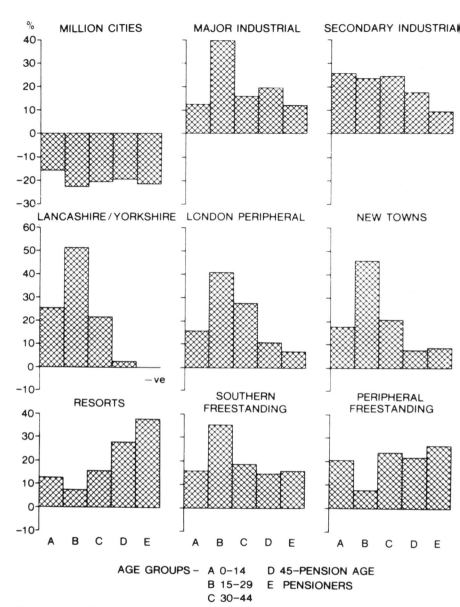

Figure 9.3 Relative contribution to net migration change by age and MELA groups 1966–71

for either MELA categories or urban zones at the national level. Differentiation of trends among the urban zones at the MELA group level has also been undertaken (Spence *et al.*, 1982). One of the most prominent features within inter-regional migration exchanges is London's continuing net inflow of 15–29-year-olds. Whilst the long-distance inflows in this cohort are easily offset by net outflows to other MELAs within the South East region itself, the continuing attraction of young workers to the capital is now a unique phenomenon among large cities (although net decline within this age group is frequently lower than expected in major cities). The Department of Environment (1975) suggested that for inner areas of the conurbations the rise in the proportion of 15–24-year-olds in the inner areas' population was much lower in the 1966–71 period when compared with the previous five-year period. Nevertheless, for the core areas of Million Cities there has been a tendency for working-age population to fall proportionately, and in most cases absolutely.

THE IMPACTS OF DIFFERENTIAL MIGRATION BY SOCIO-ECONOMIC GROUP

As for age-structure data, there are no details of gross migration flows by socio-economic group for MELAs, or the pre-1974 local authorities which constitute their building blocks. Conurbations and regional remainders are the lowest spatial order for which published material tabulates both total and migrant population according to their own socio-economic group. These data have been used by Kennett and Randolph (1978) to investigate differential decentralization from conurbations in the 1966–71 period. This work showed that, in terms of migration propensities, decentralization is considerably less important for manual groups compared with white-collar workers. However, turnover was also found to be higher among the professional and managerial group so that the volume of inflows to conurbations was greater than might otherwise have been expected. The analysis of individual migration streams suggested that the South East, excluding London, has acted as a magnet for migrants in white-collar occupations. Even the capital, despite its massive outflows, lost lower proportions among these groups than might have been expected and indeed continued to attract a small net inflow of female professional workers.

At the MELA level, the data available only allow us to view net flows of persons by the head of family's socio-economic group. Nevertheless, complementary perspectives may be added to the analysis of migration flows for conurbations. For example, figure 9.4 shows that, like Greater London, Million City labour markets as a whole were losing relatively low proportions of their total migration outflow within the managerial and professional groups. It may be suggested that slight

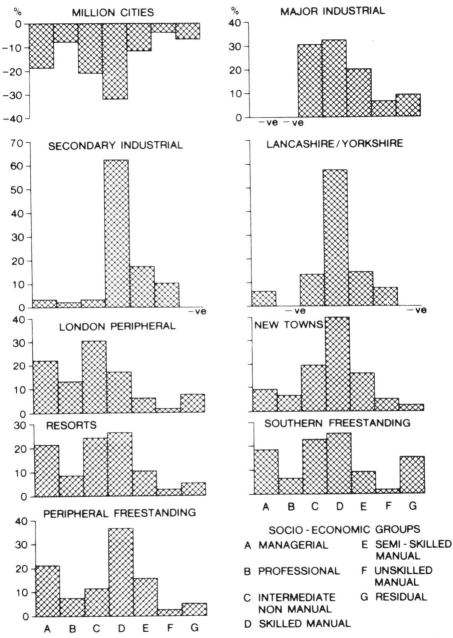

Figure 9.4 Relative contribution to net migration change by socio-economic and MELA groups 1966–71

polarization, already noted in terms of differential age migration, is also evident for socio-economic structure. However, the unknown import-ance of migration's twin component, social mobility, should limit strong assertions about this process.

Other MELA groups revealed net overall gains by migration. How-ever, more variation in performance is encountered among individual socio-economic group aggregates. The net out-migration of managerial and professional families from the major industrial MELAs is particularly interesting, possibly denoting the first signs of a more general deconcen-tration out of these labour markets. The professional group is also shown to have been leaving the Lancashire/Yorkshire MELAs, probably a reflection of the relatively low levels of opportunity for such workers in these areas. This contention is supported by our earlier observation of the out-migration of the younger age cohorts from these MELAs.

The London peripheral and New Town labour markets have con-sistently shown similar features in their net migration and population patterns in the previous analyses. However, they display considerable divergence among net inflows of migrants by socio-economic character-istics. Whilst the London peripheral MELAs draw in large proportions of those categorized as managerial, professional and intermediate non-manual, the New Towns have particularly high attraction for the blue-collar sector (figure 9.4). Inflows of persons in managerial families exceed those of the skilled manual in the London peripheral towns, whilst the latter represent 40 per cent of inflows in New Towns. Thus, the funda-mental differences between planned and unplanned deconcentration from the capital is depicted here, complementing the recent detailed survey studies by Deakin and Ungerson (1977).

The resort, southern free-standing and peripheral free-standing MELAs also draw relatively large proportions of managerial and pro-fessional group in-migrants (figure 9.4). They display low levels of attraction of the young economically active groups. The influx of manual workers (especially the skilled group) is more important in the peripheral free-standing MELAs closely paralleling the experience of major and secondary industrial MELAs. On the other hand, the resort and southern free-standing categories resemble the London peripheral MELA profile.

The study of selective migration has indicated that the south of Britain has seen disproportionate gains in white-collar groups. Whilst migration is only one component of socio-economic changes in the characteristics of the population, studies of these broader features of change in the urban system suggest that those regions with fastest growth in white-collar populations were those in which such populations were already concentrated, particularly in the South East (Spence *et al.*, 1982). This conclusion is of course in line with studies of other phenomena. These have shown the South East as having for example the highest incidence of research and development activity (Buswell and Lewis, 1970); the greatest concentrations of office functions in general and those of high status in particular (Goddard, 1978b); the most rapid increases in concentrations of high-order decision-making functions of firms and of corporate headquarters of organizations (Goddard and Smith, 1978; Leigh and North, 1978a) and increasing concentrations of high-status employment generally (Westaway, 1973; Frost and Spence, 1978b).

Yet, while all these themes portray a complementary picture and are undoubtedly part of the same process, there has been no formal attempt to link shifts of population with employee occupation or industry sub-groups. The growth of high-status jobs in the South East may well motivate labour migration to this region, due to the relatively small number of people with appropriate skills combined with wider job search areas. The net shifts of manual or clerical employment is, however, much less likely to stimulate migration flows. The movement of low-order routine functions (Goddard and Spence, 1976; Massey and Meegan, 1978; Frost and Spence, 1978b; Fothergill and Gudgin, 1979b) is more likely to be filled by untapped indigenous populations. Whilst some analysis has been attempted to link occupational and geographic mobility (Gleave and Palmer, 1977, 1979) so far it has not been possible to show that high-turnover occupations were directly associated with low migration propensities. Clearly, research which integrates these diverse but interrelated processes should be a future priority.

Differential migration between aggregate MELA zones is also an important influence on population changes. As with age-specific migration, urban cores suffered decline in each individual socio-economic group (table 9.3). The losses amongst the intermediate non-manual and managerial groups were particularly significant – the remaining groups each comprising less than 10 per cent of the total outflow. Both rings and outer rings made net overall gains in each socio-economic group but, as with age-specific migration, the profile of their gains vary. The inflow of migrants to the rings virtually mirrors the core outflows in age composition. However, in the outer rings a higher proportion of the net gains were attributable to the managerial group with commensurately lower proportions for the professional, intermediate, non-manual and skilled families.

These trends provide more indirect evidence for the importance of a longitudinal or lifeline perspective to the process of population decentralization. The young and intermediate non-manual workers may be thought to move to central cities after leaving home to get their first job. The time of marriage coincides with the most rapid decentralization rates to rings. Later in their life cycle, as professional and even managerial workers, they move still further from the city being able to afford the higher costs of the longer journey to work, finally reaching the outer

Table 9.3 Net gains and losses of migrants by socio-economic group and urban zone 1966–71

Socio-economic group	Cores		Rings		Outer rings		MELA *	
	(000s)	*(%)*	*(000s)*	*(%)*	*(000s)*	*(%)*	*(000s)*	*(%)*
Managerial	−248	(−19.4)	155	(17.3)	64	(22.5)	−29	(−30.4)
Professional	−115	(−9.0)	80	(9.0)	24	(8.4)	−11	(−11.2)
Intermediate non-manual	−263	(−20.7)	200	(22.3)	52	(18.1)	−11	(−12.1)
Skilled	−430	(−33.7)	315	(35.0)	91	(32.0)	−24	(−25.7)
Semi-skilled	−121	(−9.5)	84	(9.3)	30	(10.6)	−6	(−6.6)
Unskilled	−32	(−2.5)	22	(2.4)	8	(2.7)	−3	(−3.2)
Residual	−67	(−5.2)	41	(4.6)	16	(5.6)	−10	(−10.6)

Notes: * Net exchanges between MELAs and unclassified areas
Figures denote numbers of migrants allocated to socio-economic group of family head
Figures in brackets denote the proportion of each urban zone's overall gain (or loss).

rings. This notion is further supported by interaction between MELAs and unclassified areas. The managerial groups, along with the professional workers, form relatively large proportions of the remote rural areas' total inflow. Table 9.3 demonstrates that the managerial group exceeds the skilled workers in terms of absolute net out-migration from the urban system.

This highly simplistic model of life-cycle decentralization should not be taken to imply a fixed number of migrations in an individual life-span. Of course, any number of moves might have been made but after the age of about 25, the contention is that their net direction is likely to be away from the city centres. With this in mind it is worth noting the indirect support for this model generated by studies casting light on the 'ripple effect' in migration (Forbes and Robertson, 1978; Harris and Kennett, 1978).

Discussion: the implications of population redistribution for local government finances

Relatively little attention has been devoted in the literature to the impacts of migration upon other phenomena. This is nowhere more true of the interaction between differential population change and local authority revenue and expenditure needs. The dual objectives of this final section are: first, to introduce this theme as an example of the pervasive importance of migration change in the British urban system, and secondly, to highlight how little is currently known of the precise nature of these interrelationships.

The hypothesis that local authorities with declining populations suffer because reduction in rateable values depletes the local revenue base has been proposed by Eversley (1972a, 1972b). He suggested that the presence of static or declining rateable values makes it more difficult for administrative areas to finance their own operations from local inhabitants' contributions. Eversley claimed that differential out-migration from these areas means that, unless much higher increases in rate poundages are imposed on the relatively poor community, their derived income will fall.

Developing this argument, it is possible to suggest that migration declines might themselves be cumulatively exacerbated by increasing rate bills and the associated drop of standards of community service (caused by the inability of large cities to service their functions). Evidence for such events is lacking in Britain, although a pilot analysis in the Leeds area has been undertaken by Aronson (1974). However, the importance of these processes have been recognized in the United States for some time (Bradford, Malt and Oates, 1969; Bradford and Kelejian, 1973; Bradford and Oates, 1974). Earlier in this chapter it has been demonstrated that differential migration is causing particularly rapid rates of loss among the managerial and professional groups, as well as the younger more able workers, from British cities in general, and the conurbations in particular. Eversley (1972a) and more recently Caulcott, as Secretary of the Association of Metropolitan Authorities, have argued that 'when people leave an area . . . it is the old, sick, lonely and unemployed who remain' (Caulcott, 1977). Thus, expenditure per capita is likely to rise in areas of population decline. Stone (1978) has also argued that depopulation will lead to a decline in the locally derived revenues of conurbations. An important caveat on such contentions concerns the relative importance of selective migration and social mobility. Hamnett (1976), for example, argues that social mobility is the more important component, although this has been disputed by Eversley (1975b).

It is certainly the case that changing patterns of rateable value resemble those of migration change, as can be shown by an analysis at the urban zonal level. The evidence in table 9.4 supports Eversley's contention that areas outside the urban cores are likely to be better able to support themselves because of the greater buoyancy of their rateable value. This applies to the industrial and commercial components of rateable value as well as the domestic component (table 9.4). The cores, meanwhile, will have to raise their rate poundages by relatively higher levels to bring in similar levels of increase in revenue. An analysis of the relationship between rates of net migration change and rateable value increases at the MELA scale yields relatively high correlation coefficients, as seen in table 9.5. The implication is that increasing proportions of central government grants will be needed to support the local

Table 9.4 Rateable value (RV) change by urban zone, England and Wales 1966–71

	Total Rateable Value 1966: £m.	Total RV Change % 1966–71	Domestic RV Increase % 1966–71	Commercial RV Increase % 1966–71	Industrial RV Increase % 1966–71
Cores	1321	10.1	9.2	11.7	4.0
Rings	568	18.7	18.8	24.6	13.2
Outer rings	255	18.7	21.3	16.3	16.2
MELAs	2144	13.4	13.9	13.9	7.4
Unclassified areas	51	21.7	21.0	13.3	74.7
England and Wales	2195	13.6	14.1	13.9	8.1

revenues of cities (Jackman and Sellars, 1977; Kennett, 1980). If such subsidization is diminished, however, the cities might well have to increase their local rates which, in turn, may trigger the self-feeding process of selective out-migration by the richest and highest ratepayers on the lines of the American model.

The failure of the cities to meet national growth rates in rateable values applies to all, and not solely the domestic, components (table 9.4). Whilst the domestic rateable value represents about two-thirds of the total, the almost static industrial rateable values should also be seen as significant. Nationally 'the yield of non-domestic rates has been increasing faster than that of domestic rates, and faster than that of other taxes borne by commerce and industry' (Layfield Report, 1976, 153). But population has led first manufacturing and now service industry out of the core areas.

Stone, like Eversley, has argued that, in addition to higher per capita costs resulting from differential migration decline, some services operate at fixed rates and thus local authority costs generally do not decline proportionately with populations and economic activity. 'Generally, once

Table 9.5 Correlation coefficients between net migration change (per cent) and rateable value (RV) increases (per cent) 1966–71

	Cores	Rings	Outer rings	MELAs
Net migration and Total RV	0.73	0.44	0.46	0.69
Net migration and Domestic RV	0.82	0.58	0.44	0.71
Net migration and Commercial RV	0.64	0.33	0.37	0.55
Net migration and Industrial RV	0.38	0.06	−0.00	0.36
No. of observations	115	108	84	115

a settlement is established, growth increases costs less than in proportion while revenue increases in proportion. The opposite is true for a settlement in decline ' (Stone, 1978, 117). With the demand for more and better services, local authorities have found themselves in the invidious position of being squeezed between increasing costs and a source of taxation which is increasingly unable to provide the necessary finance. This has resulted in an inability to promote the desired improved environment and local services, lack of which stimulates the outward migration of households and firms. More research needs to be undertaken of the relationship between population decline from big cities and the nature of urban costs.

At the same time, it could be suggested that areas with relatively low and contracting rateable values may in fact be able to spend more rather than less. According to Jackman and Sellars (1977), 'Low rateable values mean low rate payments and, faced with relatively low rate burdens, people may be more ready to support a higher standard of local government services. This is particularly so because only a small part of the additional costs will fall on the ratepayers, the remainder being financed from the resources element' (of the rate support grant). However, despite the fact that the cities' rateable value increase is much lower than the nation as a whole, many urban areas, particularly central London, have very high levels of rateable values. Hence, while the Jackman and Sellars argument may have applied to some smaller metropolitan cores with lower per capita levels of rateable value and thus may in turn have tended to stem the outward flow of their populations, it is unlikely to operate in the central London boroughs. The change from the rate support grant system to the new block grant in 1980 may have closed this particular inconsistency. Nevertheless, it seems doubtful whether the underlying problems with the distribution of rateable values will have been resolved, though verification of this is a research priority.

Whilst the use, and increase, of government grants may in some cases help to stem the self-feeding tide of out-migration that has been seen in America, the erosion of the importance of locally based revenues does diminish 'accountability' as seen by the Layfield Committee. The latter argued that the body which spent the funds on local services should also be seen to be actually raising the revenue for them. Hence, the relative erosion of rateable values by out-migration may result in lowering (rather than raising, as the Layfield Committee desired) the levels of local accountability.

Related to this is the question of areal scope of local authorities. If a declining population leads to diminishing revenue, or at least diminishing accountability through the proportionate rise in central government grant, should not areal units be employed which reduce this problem to a minimum? Is there any suggestion concerning the form of such areas? Two apparently conflicting notions present themselves.

The first is based on the idea that local government resources should be drawn from the whole commuting area of a city rather than from separate fragments within it (Lady Ursula Hicks, 1973). In this way spillovers would be reduced. Such a proposal is analagous to the kind of reallocation process that was operating within the Greater London Council (GLC) area for some time (the 'equalization scheme'). The GLC, however, is much too strictly defined to represent 'the London region'. Even the London MELA will fail to incorporate the longest-distance commuters who of course tend to be among the most wealthy. An extension of this reasoning is the suggestion that many labour markets bordering the capital's MELA might meaningfully be combined into one resource-sharing unit. Thus some of the London periphery and New Town labour areas, which are attracting an increasing number of migrants continuing to work in London, could be amalgamated with the capital under such a scheme. The problem, as always, is where to draw the line. As documented in chapter 7, there has been a substantial growth of inter-MELA commuting, such that it could well be argued that a realistic resource-sharing area would be one that covered the urban heartland or 'Megalopolis Britain', if not the whole urban system. In so doing, the scheme argues against 'local' taxation in any form!

Even if it were possible to define areas which reduced spillovers to a minimum, a second strand of thought suggests that the problems of local authority finances resulting from population redistribution might not be overcome. Although there is little to be seen of Derek Senior's 'city regions' within the districts created by the Local Government Act of 1972, a number of created authorities did combine areas of population loss with those of rapid gain. The Centre for Environmental Studies (CES) Review has noted the plight of Cheshire, where internal migration *within* the county is responsible for recent high expenditure: 'For example, though there is ample school accommodation in some parts of the county, new schools will be needed in Runcorn. The RSG formula [did] not allow for effects of internal migration.' (CES Review, 1978, p. 4). The new block grant system has not changed the position. A similar factor has been noted within the new borough of Oldham (NWIG, 1974). Hence, in summary, whilst it appears valid to reduce spillovers by amalgamating poor and wealthy areas, it would appear equally logical to reduce the size of districts which receive financial grants reflecting population loss. Perhaps one solution would be the expansion of the resource gathering unit (as a form of precept) and the reduction of the areal scale at which central government grants are allocated.

We have here then a virtual but not a complete paradox. Issues such as these should be regarded as urgent research questions which should be satisfactorily resolved before a further round of local government reform ensues especially after the recent dramatic upheavals in the system of central government finance. Nevertheless, reform has increasingly been propounded (Marshall Report, 1978; Labour Party, 1978; Hall, 1978; *The Economist*, 1978). What is needed in this interim period is constructive research on these and related themes in order to fuel, or dampen, this rapidly growing debate.

10
Unemployment change
M. E. Frost and N. A. Spence

Introduction: contexts of convergence and policy

Current studies of unemployment characteristics for different areas of the country can be set in two powerful and interconnected contexts. The first arises from the growing realization that the simple division of the country into the 'peripheral', slow-growing assisted areas contrasted with the more healthy and buoyant economies of the 'core' areas of the South East and the West Midlands is no longer tenable and is unlikely to regain its former power in an era of rising national unemployment and slow or negative economic growth. The generally harsh economic conditions of the 1970s and even harsher 1980s have highlighted weaknesses in the economic structure of the country and, in the national sense, these weaknesses have not been restricted to those areas which have traditionally been the recipients of industrial grants and other forms of government assistance. These changes have produced rates of unemployment in non-assisted urban areas that are in many cases at least as high as those found in the development areas if not higher. It has been possible to show also that, at the level of the economic planning regions, the differences between the areas of traditionally high unemployment in Scotland, Wales and the North and those areas characterized by lower rates in the rest of the country narrowed from the mid-1960s to the mid-1970s (Chisholm, 1976; Manners, 1976). The figures for the 1980s, as will be considered later, exhibit similar characteristics.

The inevitable response to this situation has been a call for some fundamental reconsideration of the role of regional policies (Townsend, 1977, 1980, 1981). Reference is made to the competing needs of the inner city areas of the country recognized by the inner urban area legislation of 1977–8 (Department of Environment, 1977a; Inner Urban Areas Act, 1978). Reference is also made to the declining fortunes of hitherto more buoyant regions of the country where the length of time available for adjustment to high levels of unemployment has been short. The purpose of this chapter is to provide a review of research on British unemployment characteristics over the recent past which will serve as a framework within which such responses can be assessed.

The need for such assessment is strengthened by the second context in which this work is set. This consists of the government's reaction to the existence of regional inequalities in economic performance and their patterns of change over time. Levels of unemployment and the disparities between these levels in different areas of the country have traditionally been important in influencing the application of restrictions and grants to modify patterns of industrial activity. Whilst it is clear that the rate of unemployment in an area is only one of many possible indications of its 'economic health' these rates have acquired a particular political significance that frequently ignores the complexities and practical difficulties involved in the calculation of these apparently simple measures. The emphasis placed on unemployment comparisons has clearly varied from time to time since 1945; however, the Thatcher government brought it sharply to the fore with their review of regional assistance. In this it is clearly stated that their objective is to concentrate on those parts of the country with the most intractable problems of unemployment (Department of Trade and Industry, 1979). Their list of amendments to the previously existing broadly defined assisted areas clearly selects the predominantly urban centres of existing development areas which were suffering from relatively high rates of unemployment as the focus for the application of their policies in the future. If this level of importance is to be given to unemployment rates in the operation of public policies then it reinforces the need for some careful consideration of the setting in which such decisions are made (Frost and Spence, 1980, 1981a).

In these twin contexts this paper attempts to describe and interpret the nature and patterns of unemployment rate changes in Great Britain over the period since 1963.

Unemployment in Britain and British regions

To provide a meaningful setting for some of the research on regional unemployment time series it is useful to consider briefly some of the basic aspects of the levels and rates of unemployment applicable over the period. Figure 10.1 shows the changing national rates of unemployment for both males and females. Generally the rates are on the increase save for the troughs apparent for both series reaching their bases in mid-1966, early 1974 and early 1979. A consistent upward sloping trajectory is apparent, steeper for males, for the period from early 1967 to early 1972.

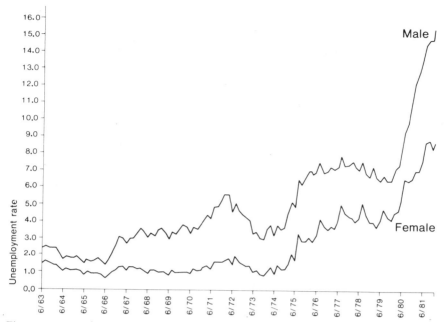

Figure 10.1 Male and female national unemployment rates 1963–82

There is a sharp rise in rates from the bottom of the second trough reaching a plateau and culminating in the last rather shallow trough. This is then followed by the unprecedented acceleration of unemployment rates to heights that surely could not have been conceived of at the start of the series. The overall shape of the series then consists of a rather weak cyclical form projected on to a more consistent upward trend.

In actual figures for males the series begins at around 2.5 per cent and terminates at slightly over 15 per cent. This reflects some 345,000 and 2,123,000 people out of work respectively. For females the equivalent figures are around 1.5 per cent and 8.5 per cent, again in absolute terms 115,000 and 833,000 respectively.

The national economic business cycle is of course the primary factor influencing these graphs but the slightly differing responses of male unemployment compared to female unemployment are interesting to consider. Several aspects are apparent, the first is the much greater response of male unemployment to the economic downturn from June 1966 to February 1967, where a rise of 1.5 per cent unemployment was twice as high as that for females. This proved to be an important and long lasting differential. The winter of 1971–2 also saw a similar lack of female unemployment responsiveness to recession. Exactly as to why these differences are apparent has been a matter for some considerable debate

(Gujarati, 1972; Cheshire, 1973). It has been suggested that the greater responsiveness of male unemployment for given levels of economic activity in the main reflects productivity increases which is not so apparent in the continued trends for increased levels of female employment (Department of Employment, 1976). Related to this could be the widespread substitution of female for male labour throughout the economy. In the winter of 1971–2 for example the recession has in the main been attributed to budgetary control which primarily affected and coincided with a downturn in the steel and steel-using (engineering) sectors of the economy (National Institute of Social and Economic Research, 1972). These sectors of course employ relatively little female labour. The penultimate downturn to be considered also poses some interesting male–female differences. This, by far the deepest recession of the 1970s, hit female unemployment rates probably harder than those for males. Exactly why this occurred is a matter of conjecture.

One of the confusions behind this lack of explanation arises from the critical weakness that affects male but, more particularly, the female statistics used here. This concerns the problem of registration. Department of Employment unemployment counts relate only to individuals registered for unemployment benefit or those in a comparable position with respect to other Government benefits. The extent to which these figures provide an unbiased guide to involuntary worklessness has been the subject of extensive debate (Allen and Yuill, 1978; Civil Service Working Party, 1972; Metcalf and Richardson, 1972) and it is certainly true that the lack of registration affects the female figures more than the male. It has also been shown recently (Department of Employment, 1976) that the rise in levels of unemployment since 1974 has been accompanied by a much increased flow of females both on and off the unemployment register. This change means that in 1976 around 130,000 females registered as unemployed each month (with about 120,000 leaving the register) whereas in 1970 a figure of about 80,000 per month was typical. The simplest explanation of this is that female workers were making more use of the employment services, and particularly unemployment benefit, in a period of falling employment prospects and living standards resulting from national economic factors. A more indirect argument might be that some of this increased registration arose because the mid-1970s economic downtown affected more than before the type of jobs in which females tend to be employed. This implies that the service sector has been affected more severely than before. This has some attractions as an explanation particularly in terms of the productivity-increase arguments used previously to explain upward shifts in male unemployment. The rise in female unemployment could therefore partly reflect increased automation of the service sector, especially office jobs. As yet it is not possible to evaluate all of the potential explanations of fluctuations in female rates but the complexity of the issue is further illustrated by the most recent recession figures. Female rates reacted markedly to the onset of the latest recession in the last few months of 1979 and this persisted until mid-1980. Since then, if anything, male unemployment rates seem to have been more responsive to the economic crisis no doubt related to the disastrous fortunes of the vehicles, mechanical engineering and metal manufacturing and goods working sectors.

So much for the national trends, what of the sub-national breakdown of the statistics? A simple indication of the levels and rates of unemployment for the nation's regions can be seen in figure 10.2. Two cross-sections of the time series have been selected to illustrate change – January 1972 and January 1982 – both corresponding to peaks in the cycle (optimistically assuming improvement at the time of writing). With just under 1 million persons unemployed in January 1972, the South East accounted for the highest absolute regional total – some 30,000 more than in the whole of Scotland. Scotland, however, was the region of greatest relative intensity of unemployment recording over 7 per cent. The North, Wales, North West and West Midlands, in that order respectively, followed Scotland in relative levels of unemployment. In contrast the region of lowest relative levels of unemployment was the South East followed by East Anglia and the East Midlands. This then is the by now traditional pattern of British regional unemployment.

Not so traditional is the most recent regional picture. With just under 3 million persons unemployed in January 1982 the South East again accounted for the highest absolute regional total. But by this time the figure was around 350,000 higher than in Scotland, well over double Scotland's number of unemployed. The North assumes the role of worst-hit region in relative terms followed respectively by Wales, Scotland, the West Midlands and the North West. The unemployment rate in the West Midlands, and almost that reached in the North West, now matches the rate for Scotland at 15.3 per cent. The region of lowest relative levels of unemployment is still the South East, followed again by East Anglia and the East Midlands but relative difference in both rates and levels between these regions and the rest of the country has altered markedly over the ten-year period. On these cross-sectional figures alone the regional unemployment convergence hypothesis seems to be particularly strong. There are now more persons unemployed in the West Midlands than in all the then development areas of Great Britain in 1972, and more than twice as many in the South East.

Such is the level of change viewed cross-sectionally; let us consider next briefly, and perhaps superficially, some of the fluctuations from year to year. Tables 10.1 and 10.2 record the June unemployment rates for the nation's regions and major cities for each year since 1970 (January in 1982). In addition these unemployment rates are expressed as a ratio of

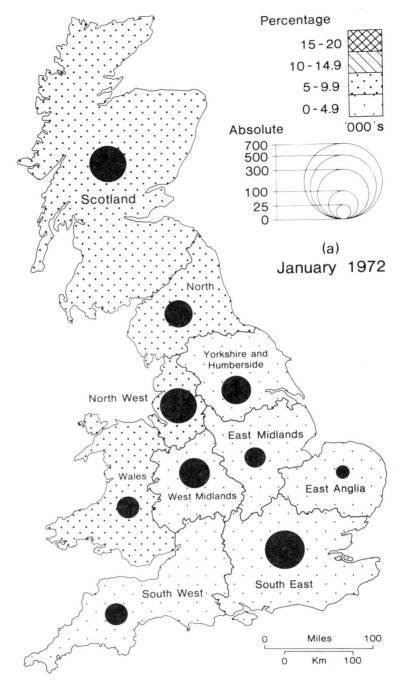

Figure 10.2 Unemployment levels and rates in British regions (a) January 1972 (b) January 1982

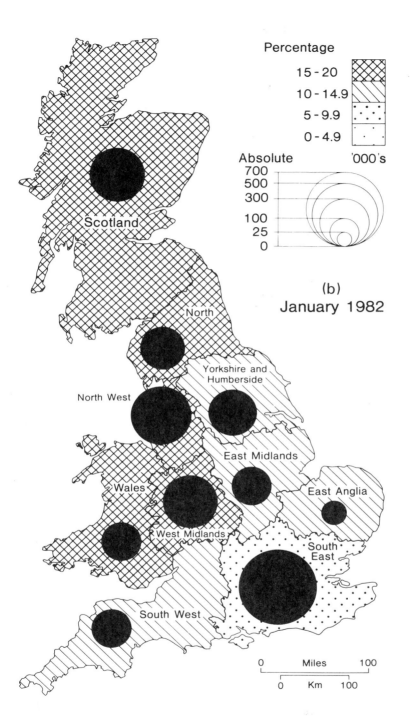

Percentage

15 - 20	(cross-hatch pattern)
10 - 14.9	(diagonal line pattern)
5 - 9.9	(dense dot pattern)
0 - 4.9	(sparse dot pattern)

Absolute   '000's

700
500
300
100
25
0

(b)
January 1982

Scotland

North

Yorkshire and
Humberside

North West

East Midlands

Wales

East Anglia

West Midlands

South
East

South West

0   Miles   100

0   Km   100

Table 10.1 Unemployment rates (a) and relatives (b) in Britain and British regions

	June												Jan
	70	71	72	73	74	75	76	77	78	79	80	81	82
(a)													
South East	1.5	1.8	1.9	1.3	1.4	2.5	4.1	4.4	4.1	3.5	4.2	7.7	9.2
East Anglia	1.8	2.8	2.5	1.7	1.7	3.2	4.9	5.4	4.9	4.2	5.2	8.8	10.4
South West	2.4	2.9	3.0	2.2	2.2	4.2	6.2	6.7	6.2	5.4	6.0	9.5	11.2
West Midlands	2.4	3.2	3.4	2.0	1.9	3.6	5.5	5.4	5.3	5.2	6.9	13.2	15.3
East Midlands	2.2	2.9	2.8	2.0	2.0	3.3	4.8	5.2	5.1	4.7	6.1	10.3	11.2
Yorks/Humb.	2.6	3.7	3.8	2.6	2.3	3.5	5.6	5.7	5.8	5.5	7.2	11.9	13.3
North West	2.5	3.6	4.4	3.3	3.0	4.9	7.1	7.5	7.5	7.1	8.8	13.5	15.2
North	4.3	5.3	5.7	4.4	4.1	5.5	7.8	8.6	8.9	8.6	10.5	14.9	16.4
Wales	3.4	4.2	4.5	3.3	3.2	4.9	7.0	7.6	7.9	7.3	9.1	13.9	16.2
Scotland	3.9	5.6	5.9	4.3	3.6	4.7	6.6	8.6	8.3	8.1	9.9	13.5	15.3
Britain	2.4	3.2	3.4	2.4	2.3	3.7	5.5	6.0	5.9	5.4	6.7	10.9	12.3
(b)													
South East	63	56	56	54	61	68	75	73	69	65	63	71	75
East Anglia	75	88	74	70	74	86	89	90	83	78	78	81	85
South West	100	91	88	92	96	114	113	112	105	100	90	87	91
West Midlands	100	100	100	83	83	97	100	90	90	96	103	121	124
East Midlands	92	91	82	83	87	89	87	87	86	87	91	94	91
Yorks/Humb.	108	116	112	108	100	95	102	95	98	102	107	109	108
North West	104	113	129	138	130	132	129	125	127	131	131	124	124
North	179	166	168	183	178	149	142	143	151	159	157	137	133
Wales	142	131	132	138	139	132	127	127	134	135	136	128	132
Scotland	163	175	174	179	157	127	120	143	141	150	148	124	124
Britain	100	100	100	100	100	100	100	100	100	100	100	100	100

Table 10.2 Unemployment rates (a) and relatives (b) in Britain and selected British cities

| | June | | | | | | | | | | | | Jan |
	70	71	72	73	74	75	76	77	78	79	80	81	82
(a)													
Birmingham	2.6	3.3	4.1	2.6	2.3	4.4	6.5	6.2	5.8	5.7	7.3	13.8	16.5
Liverpool	4.2	5.5	7.2	6.6	5.6	8.2	10.9	11.4	11.8	12.3	13.6	17.2	18.7
Manchester	2.1	3.1	4.1	2.9	2.4	3.7	5.7	6.2	6.2	5.4	6.9	11.6	13.0
Greater London	1.3	1.5	1.7	1.3	1.3	2.2	3.8	4.0	3.8	3.4	4.1	7.3	8.9
Glasgow	4.6	6.5	7.7	5.8	4.7	5.5	7.6	9.8	9.5	9.1	11.4	15.1	16.5
Tyneside	4.9	6.0	6.5	5.2	4.6	5.8	8.2	9.0	9.5	9.2	10.8	14.0	15.4
Britain	2.4	3.1	3.4	2.4	2.3	3.7	5.5	6.0	5.9	5.4	6.7	10.9	12.3
(b)													
Birmingham	108	106	121	108	100	119	118	103	98	106	109	127	134
Liverpool	175	177	212	275	243	222	198	190	200	228	203	158	152
Manchester	88	100	121	121	104	100	104	103	105	100	103	106	106
Greater London	54	48	50	54	57	59	69	67	64	63	61	67	72
Glasgow	192	210	226	242	204	149	138	163	161	169	170	139	134
Tyneside	204	194	192	217	200	157	149	150	161	170	162	128	125
Britain	100	100	100	100	100	100	100	100	100	100	100	100	100

Source: Department of Employment Gazette

national rates for comparative purposes. What are the general trends to be seen in the figures? The early period of the regional table shows a slight widening of unemployment rate differentials with the situation in Scotland especially worsening. The middle period shows a coming together of the regional rates, reflected by a slight worsening in the South East and East Anglia but marked improvement in the development areas. The late 1970s then brought a slight widening of the relativities. Then finally the last and deepest recession phase has brought renewed convergence, with the improvement in the relative status of the development areas reaching mid-1970s levels and the dramatic decline in the fortunes of the West Midlands being most noteworthy. The picture then, when not viewed cross-sectionally, appears more complex. Added complexities are also apparent when the scale selected changes to major cities. Here the changes taking place are perhaps more extreme than in the regional case, although similar periods of widening and convergence can be detected.

Clearly, drawing conclusions concerning regional convergence of unemployment rates is a hazardous exercise – or at least has been over the last decade or so. Perhaps the safest comment that can be made is that proof of the convergence hypothesis does vary according to the dates chosen. Furthermore it does seem to be related to the national business cycle. There is no doubt that the rates of regional unemployment do seem to move together during the early periods of economic downturn, but also seem to move apart during the trough and recovery which follows. That there is an important difference between the beginning and the end of the period is, of course, clear but whether the terminal date shown in tables 10.1 and 10.2 is at all meaningful remains to be seen.

Sensitivities, trends and cycles in British regional unemployment

Although well-exhibiting rates and levels of unemployment in Britain's regions and cities at certain times over the period, the series so far considered say little in precise terms of trends and sensitivities to national events calculated over a period of time. A range of techniques and models have been designed to add just that precision. Most certainly they are not without their critics (Clark, 1980), and sensibly so, but nevertheless are useful in certain contexts. The standard method in the field was first proposed by Brechling (1967) for use on British standard regions and has been used in a variety of contexts since. Basically this method attempts to represent the unemployment time series of an area by a number of compositional factors which correspond to certain hypothesized influences. The first of these measures the sensitivity of the area's fluctuations in unemployment to national levels and changes in unemployment. The second isolates the effects of structural change in an area's economy or quite simply the lack of an area's ability to generate demand for labour for whatever reason. This is in fact a trend term which reflects any tendency for rates of unemployment to change systematically over time, having allowed for its average response relationship with national events – its sensitivity. Lastly, the purely regional effect may be considered as the variation in each area's performance that could not be accounted for by any of the other specified components. The whole model is simply calibrated using regression methods, the residuals corresponding to the regional effect. In addition to these main components it is also possible to adapt the approach to recognize timing differences in the response of an area to national changes and to allow for possible seasonal effects.

King and Clark (1978) used the approach to analyse unemployment trends in Canadian economic regions in a monthly series from 1966 to 1975, while Jeffery and Webb (1972) applied the model to unemployment in Australian regions in a monthly series from 1955 to 1970. A more relevant application in this context is that by the Northern Region Strategy Team (1975), who used the model on unemployment in small areas in the northern region as a monthly series from 1958 to 1975.

The present authors have undertaken some similar research on an extensive scale in Britain (Frost and Spence, 1981b). The data used are the unpublished unemployment rates collected by the Department of Employment for individual employment office areas for the whole country. They are analysed at two spatial scales; first at the level of subdivisions of the economic planning regions and second at the level of the travel-to-work area (Smart, 1974). The first set of areas are the pre-1974 planning sub-regions of Britain which, although not functional in the labour market area sense, do provide a convenient disaggregation of the national space into some 61 areas and will be focused upon here. The actual data were collected for a bi-monthly time series of 77 observations between June 1963 and February 1976, the terminal date representing the most recent data available at the time of collection.

Before considering some of the findings on sensitivities and trends it may be useful to mention briefly timing. Brechling's original research on British standard regions, supported by other studies at the more local scale, pointed to small but nevertheless detectable differences in the timing of cyclical movements of unemployment rates (Brechling, 1967; Bassett and Haggett, 1971; Haggett, 1971). Without making over-optimistic claims, Haggett concludes that awareness of leads and lags existing in various parts of the regional system may play some valuable role in long-run disaggregated simulation models capable of testing effects of alternative policies.

Similar studies searching for leads and lags were undertaken for the current data series. The principal findings are reported on in detail elsewhere and so will only be summarized here (Frost and Spence, 1981c). The findings are extremely negative. At both the scales of the planning sub-regions and the travel-to-work areas an almost complete lack of timing differences was found. The main method used to search for leads and lags was admittedly rather simplistic. It involved applying alternative leads or lags of up to six two-monthly periods to the national series in the equation, the resultant timing with the best relationship to the local series, being deemed to be the best representation of the process. All of the sub-regions of Britain, for both male and female series, were tested using this method. There was only one case, male unemployment on Clydeside, where an increase in the coefficient of determination resulted from any sort of phasing difference, and that was only for one period involving lagging the national series by two months.

The original studies themselves did only record small timing differences but these seem to have now almost totally disappeared. Certain questioning of the methodology has appeared in the literature of late, especially concerning the role of the national unemployment series in the equations (Johnston, 1979). However, it should be said that even when more sophisticated methods of analysis were employed the results showed little evidence to change the basic conclusion about timing differences.

The results of the research dealing with sensitivities and trends is again reported on in detail elsewhere (Frost and Spence, 1981b), and a brief summary will suffice here. The first point concerns the important influence of the national series in explaining the fluctuations in the local series. What little unexplained variation that does exist is highly ordered. This can be thought of as temporally consistent under- or over-response to national events. This finding is not out of line with other research results even compared to the original application by Brechling. However, the ordering in this case does seem to be a little more substantial than applications elsewhere in the world, and should be considered further.

The level of regional sensitivity is in the main closely linked to the level of regional unemployment. In general the development areas exhibiting high levels of unemployment are more responsive to the unemployment fluctuations of the national series than areas in most of the south-east of England. Table 10.3 illustrates this important feature for males isolating the industrial north-east, the South Wales valleys, north-west Wales and Glasgow as the extremes in high sensitivity. These are all assisted areas of high unemployment levels. But some of the areas represented in the table are not those of the highest unemployment levels. Areas in the West Midlands, much of Yorkshire and Lancashire together

Table 10.3 High unemployment sensitivities in male sub-regional unemployment

	Sensitivity coefficient	Changing sensitivity*
Industrial north-east: north	1.35	.24
Industrial north-east: south	1.54	−.09
North Humberside	1.37	−.12
South Yorkshire	1.14	−.05
Yorkshire coalfield	1.33	−.03
West Yorkshire	1.15	−.10
South Lancashire	1.10	−.19
Manchester	1.18	−.14
Merseyside	1.26	−.24
Fylde	1.12	.22
Lancaster	1.36	−.15
North-east Lancashire	1.37	−.09
West Midlands: conurbation	1.35	−.03
Coventry belt	1.18	.15
Kent	1.15	.10
South West: southern	1.20	.16
South West: western	1.34	.40
Industrial South Wales: C and E valleys	1.50	.24
North-west Wales: north coast	1.40	.31
North-west Wales: remainder	1.53	−.01
Glasgow	1.55	−.54
Falkirk/Stirling	1.10	−.59
Tayside	1.23	−.53
Scotland: south-west	1.14	.40
Highlands	1.33	.09

Note: * Sensitivity change between the first part of the series before April 1970, and after April 1970

with Kent have development-area-type sensitivities but with much lower rates of unemployment. The explanation is perhaps that it is the presence of certain sorts of volatile and highly sensitive industries such as textiles, metals, heavy engineering and coal that is crucial. The female sensitivity coefficients, interestingly, closely parallel those of males indicating that response sensitivity seems to apply to all sections of local economies.

The results from a changing sensitivity test, by dividing the period into two parts, are perhaps counter-intuitive. The purpose was to test whether development areas, for example, were becoming less sensitive over time to national economic fluctuations inferring that government policy was somehow broadening and strengthening their industrial bases.

Table 10.3 shows that there is no such overall tendency to decreased sensitivity. The industrial north-east: north and parts of South Wales are exceptions to this generalization. The results for Scotland are particularly disappointing, especially when taken in the context of the results for South East England. The female changes tend to follow the male with the contrast between the South East and Wales, as opposed to Scotland, important. Perhaps one explanation of this somewhat depressing conclusion is that the areas showing increased sensitivity in the second period are those that reacted sharply to the 1971–2 recession. This would focus heavily on the areas of basic industry in Scotland and the north of England. Reaction to this one deep recession seems to be critical. However, the simplicity of this conclusion is spoilt by the fact that many of the areas which showed a sharp reaction to the 1971–2 downturn in economic activity reacted only mildly to the deep recession in the economy from June 1974 to June 1976. Their increased sensitivity is thus the product of the averaging of these two contrasting responses.

What, then, are the main conclusions of the sensitivity analyses at this spatial scale? The first is that the influence of the national series is high in all regions and for both sexes. Second, this national effect is profoundly affected by the local economies in each area with the result that both male and female response rates are related both to the levels of unemployment and the industrial characteristics of the sub-regions (Thirlwall, 1966). As for changing sensitivities, there is little evidence of any positive policy effect overall for this period, the major development areas tending in the main to increase levels of sensitivity. Only the under-response to the 1975–6 major recession is in any way encouraging from a policy viewpoint. But even here the facts that the under-reaction is stronger for males than for females and is very sudden in character make for a doubtful positive industrial policy interpretation. Anyway, another policy interpretation may well be more valid. This concerns the influence of the doubling of the regional employment premium payments in August 1974 (from £1.50 per man-week to £3.00, half-rate for women). This favours male as opposed to female employment. It was paid only to manufacturing industry and was suddenly increased just when the residuals in this analysis began to fall. There is also some confirmation for this theory from the other sub-regions having some development area status. In the South West: western, central Wales, north-west Wales and south-west Wales large positive regression residuals are found, indicating that they appear to be reacting strongly to this downturn. This would correspond well with the dampening influence resulting from an effect on manufacturing industry alone. The only problem in accepting the regional employment premium explanation is that, in the whole of Wales, there is not one negative residual. In fact, South Wales behaves more like the South East than other development areas, which raises some interesting questions about industrial linkage in the spreading of cyclical responses. Finally, there seems to be little evidence for the notion that large metropolitan areas are relatively insensitive due to economic diversity (King and Clark, 1978). The structure of British labour markets appears to be more complex than this with more local diversity, and this is apparent if a comparison is made between the results of this study at a sub-regional spatial scale and Brechling's early results at a regional scale. In the arithmetically linear specification of his model there is a clear split between Scotland, the North and Wales and most of the remainder of the country – a clear sensitive/non-sensitive division. The sub-regional scale shows the spatial structure of responsiveness to be much more diverse than this and poses some intriguing questions for more local analysis. As the sensitivity results for the most part suggest a relatively stable pattern over time, it is useful to search next for the possible existence of trends in the levels of unemployment. Any such consistent movements may provide some evidence of changing employment behaviour, possibly reflecting a policy effect.

The trend component then was evaluated for three dates, June 1966, June 1971 and June 1975, and each was then subtracted from the initial value of the term for June 1963. In this way some measure of the changing unemployment trend can be specified in units of unemployment rate change. The statistics themselves should be interpreted as representing long-term tendencies to change in areal rates. For example, North Humberside with statistics (males) of 0.4, 0.9 and 1.1 for 1966, 1971 and 1975 respectively showed a long-term tendency to rise by these percentage points. By contrast, the Coventry belt with −0.1, −0.2 and −0.3 for 1966, 1971 and 1975 respectively showed a long-term tendency to decline, but on a much smaller scale. Figure 10.3 illustrates these evaluated trends for males and females in June 1975 for all the sub-regions of Britain.

Overall the results of these trend statistics are undramatic. In the main the patterns do not reflect any major long-term tendencies to change. The most obvious exceptions to this as far as tendencies to consistently increasing male unemployment is concerned are on North Humberside and South Lindsey. Figure 10.3 shows that these areas are joined by Merseyside, south-west Wales, north-east Wales and Lancaster with upward tendencies in much of the East and West Midlands becoming apparent by 1975. As for consistently decreasing rates of unemployment the clearest examples are the Highlands and north-east Scotland closely followed by north-east Lancashire. Significantly all areas in Scotland show, particularly by 1971, a tendency for decline in their rates of unemployment. Similarly, it is also noticeable that the three sub-regions of industrial South Wales all show, by 1975, tendencies for slight decreases in their male unemployment rates. The central and eastern valleys,

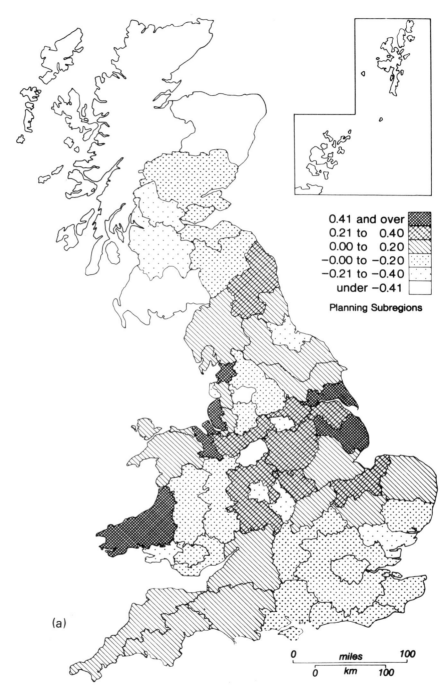

0.41 and over
0.21 to 0.40
0.00 to 0.20
−0.00 to −0.20
−0.21 to −0.40
under −0.41

Planning Subregions

(a)

0   *miles*   100
0   *km*   100

Figure 10.3 Evaluated trends from an analysis of bi-monthly sub-regional unemployment rates 1963–76 (a) males (b) females

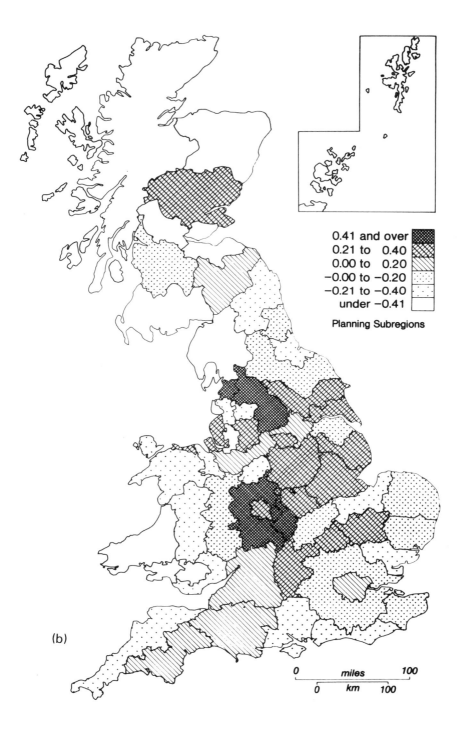

0.41 and over
0.21 to 0.40
0.00 to 0.20
−0.00 to −0.20
−0.21 to −0.40
under −0.41

Planning Subregions

(b)

0   miles   100

0   km   100

of course, clearly show the impact of coal-mining closures in the period from 1966 to 1971 with consequent rises in unemployment rates. Such a pattern can also be detected in most of the important coalfield areas; industrial north-east: north, the Yorkshire coalfield and to a lesser extent Nottingham/Derbyshire. In most of these areas, however, the effects of this tendency to increase have largely disappeared by 1975 (figure 10.3).

Although broadly following the same pattern as for males, the trends for females do illustrate some noticeable differences. There are certainly fewer upward trends in unemployment. Furthermore, those regions showing any major trend either upward or downward are not the same as their male counterparts. The main feature of the female patterns is a tendency for reduced unemployment in some industrial areas like Furness, south Lancashire, industrial South Wales and the Falkirk/Stirling sub-region. As with the male statistics, Scotland and Wales do not fare badly and show uniform relative unemployment declines, but in addition the female unemployment rates seem to show ubiquitous relative decreases across all the sub-regions of the northern region. However, this feature is not confined to the development areas as slight declining tendencies are to be seen throughout south-east England. As far as tendencies for upward trends in female unemployment are concerned, a broad belt of country in the centre of England seems to be most susceptible. The sub-regions of industrial Yorkshire and the East and West Midlands display the high upward values, the most notable occurring in the Coventry belt.

What then are the main conclusions of the unemployment trend analyses for this period at this spatial scale? One of the principal contexts for the study was the argued tendency for areas of the country to converge in unemployment terms perhaps primarily through the effects of government industrial policies. It must be said that the evidence for convergence of this sort is hardly reflected over this period. Perhaps the most encouraging results are found in Scotland, a part of the country benefiting from economic circumstances not wholly typical of the rest of Britain. If anything, the rest of the country shows evidence of unemployment tendencies the reverse of those hypothesized. For this period virtually all areas of the south-east of England and East Anglia, together with important areas in the West Midlands, show downward employment tendencies, although they are small. Conversely, virtually all of the assisted areas of England and Wales show slight tendencies for upward movement. Major exceptions to this generalization come from industrial South Wales and industrial north-east: south, where some long-term improvement is apparent. But against this the increasingly depressing picture on Merseyside, Deeside and Humberside must be kept in mind. The female results are, if anything, slightly more hopeful although still reflecting a rather mixed character.

These results, which certainly take into account a longer-term perspective than most, lead to the conclusion for the period 1963–76 that no great proliferation of unemployment into those areas which have been characterized by relatively low rates compared to the nation over the long period has occurred. What does seem to be apparent is a tendency for concentration of unemployment into certain traditional 'black spots' often still associated with decline of staple industries. Only in Scotland does there seem to be a convincing case for consistently declining unemployment rates. And it is doubtful here whether the government's regional industrial policy is the only or even a major causal factor.

Thus, the sub-regional results have raised a number of interesting questions. These centre upon the role of industrial structure in determining sensitivity levels, the apparent lack of change in regional sensitivities and the apparent stability of the 'system of unemployment' with few overall shifts in relative rates of unemployment between areas. To this list may be added the differences that exist between male and female patterns and, in particular, the poor female performance of the West Midlands.

Conclusion: the 1980–1 recession

All of the research reported on in the previous section, admittedly based on a reasonably lengthy time series, stops in 1976. What of the most recent recession? Does it constitute an unconformity with respect to the conclusions so far drawn?

A glance at figure 10.1 and tables 10.1 and 10.2 illustrates the depth of the most recent economic downturn in the economy. This has called forth some interesting commentary notably by Gillespie and Owen (1981a, 1981b). They claim and attempt to demonstrate that the latest recession is much different from anything experienced hitherto, and that this is having unprecedented spatial and sectoral effects. The argument advanced is that the recession is affecting those very industries upon which postwar expansion has been founded, notably in the engineering and metal-working sectors. And that the effects of this due to the concentrated location of such economic activity is affecting those very regions wherein postwar expansion has been found, notably in the West Midlands. The deep-rooted reasoning behind the argument lies in notions of phases of capital accumulation, currently in crisis and having both sectoral and spatial consequences in employment terms as industry restructures. The logic of the argument has much appeal, but what of the evidence? Over the relatively short term of the recession itself the evidence seems convincing. Gillespie and Owen (1981a) show that while Scotland has a 60 per cent change in unemployment between October 1979 and April 1981 the figure for the West Midlands is 135 per cent.

Although there are problems in using percentage changes in unemployment rates (Crouch 1982, Gillespie and Owen, 1982) similar results, at least at the extremes, are produced if a percentage point change system is adopted. However, perhaps once again the real question lies not so much in the method of calculating change as the period chosen over which to measure it.

As illustrated by the research reported on in the previous section, most recent studies conclude that the depressed areas of the nation seem to behave over the longer term with greater cyclical sensitivity to national economic fortunes. However, there were signs in some of this research that during the penultimate recession of 1974–5 some convergence of regional unemployment rates took place. This was apparent in the northern region as evidenced in detail by the Northern Region Strategy Team (1976). The plateau and trough which followed the downturn, however, seemed to show reversed tendencies (Frost and Spence, 1981a) where the rates for the depressed regions began to move apart from those elsewhere. As to whether the same will happen after the current downturn is of course a matter of conjecture. Much will depend on the permanency of the damage done by deep recession in regions like the West Midlands. But if the industry has been simply 'moth-balled' and not 'dismantled' it could well be that this region could be first out and benefit most from an improvement of economic fortunes.

Finally, a comment on policy. Gillespie and Owen (1981b) indicate that, at the time of writing, the most recent recession has done more for the equalization of employment rates across regions than three decades of regional policy. Although not substantiated, this may well be so, but what of the implications for policy. In August 1982 the government has stated that it will review areas eligible for regional assistance. Now while this may just be a simple exercise of confirming that certain planned de-scheduling of assisted area status can take place it is fascinating to conjecture what it might be, using the previous criteria of simple current unemployment rates. Paradoxically the de-scheduling of previous assisted areas may well be substantiated by the figures. In addition, much of the traditionally white (non-assisted) areas on the map could on the same logic become green (assisted). These are, indeed, confused times. It might now be possible to claim that the convergence of unemployment rates during the current recession is evidence of the positive effects of the government's regional policy as was claimed in the earlier period of such convergence between 1974 and 1976. However, at the time of writing, it must be argued that the clear instability of differences in unemployment rates for the last ten years provides an unreliable base on which to plan policies of regional assistance. This argument applies equally to the de-scheduling of traditionally depressed areas in the North, Wales and Scotland as to the inclusion of areas such as the West Midlands which have shown rapid recent deterioration of their economic fortunes. The main conclusion from this review of unemployment change is that an arbitrary choice of data can fundamentally influence the conclusions that may be drawn from comparisons between areas and that, until a better understanding can be achieved of the labour market processes which underlie these figures, they provide an inadequate and potentially misleading formulation for the operation of public policies.

Bibliography

Advisory Council for Applied Research and Development (ACARD) (1978) *The Applications of Semi-conductor Technology*, London, HMSO.

Advisory Council on Energy Conservation (1976) 'Passenger transport: short and medium term considerations', paper 2, London, HMSO.

Allen, K. and Yuill, D. (1978) *Small Area Employment Forecasting*, Farnborough, Saxon House.

Alonso, W. (1978) 'The current halt in the metropolitan phenomena', in C. Leven (ed.), *The Mature Metropolis*, Farnborough, Saxon House, 23–42.

Aronson, J. R. (1974) 'Voting with your feet', *New Society*, 29 August 1974, 545–7.

Australian Government (1977) 'Trends in non-metropolitan population growth and their relevance to decentralisation policy (draft)', Decentralization Policy Branch, Canberra, Department of Environment, Housing and Community Development.

Bacon, R. and Eltis, W. A. (1976) *Britain's Economic Problem: Too Few Producers*, London, Macmillan.

Bagwell, P. S. (1974) *The Transport Revolution from 1770*, London, Batsford.

Barlow Report (1940) *Report of the Royal Commission on the Distribution of the Industrial Population*, Command 6153, London, HMSO.

Bassett, K. and Haggett, P. (1971) 'Towards short term forecasting for cyclic behaviour in a regional system of cities', in M. Chisholm, A. E. Frey and P. Haggett (eds), *Regional Forecasting*, London, Butterworth.

Beale, C. L. (1975) 'The revival of population growth in non-metropolitan America', *ERS–605*, Economic Research Service, US Department of Agriculture.

Beale, C. L. and Fuguitt, G. V. (1976) 'The new pattern of non-metropolitan population change', *Working Paper 75–22*, revised 7–1976, Centre for Demography and Ecology, Madison, University of Wisconsin.

Beavan, K. S. O. (1977) *Central Place Theory: A Reinterpretation*, London, Longman.

Beesley, M. (1973) *Urban Transport: Studies in Public Policy*, London, Butterworths.

Bentham, C. G. (1978) 'Employment problems of male unskilled manual workers in London: an inner-city problem', *Area*, 10, 158–60.

Berry, B. J. L. (1967a) *Geography of Market Centres and Retail Distribution*, Englewood Cliffs, New Jersey, Prentice-Hall.

Berry, B. J. L. (1967b) *Functional Economic Areas and Consolidated Urban Regions of the US*, final report of the SSRC study of metropolitan area classification.

Berry, B. J. L. (1973) *Growth Centres in the American Urban System*, vol. 1, *Community*

Development and Regional Growth in the Sixties and Seventies, Cambridge, Massachusetts, Ballinger Publishing.

Berry, B. J. L. (1975) 'The decline of the ageing metropolis: cultural bases and social processes', in G. Sternlieb and J. W. Hughes (eds), *Post Industrial America: Metropolitan Decline and Inter-Regional Job Shifts*, Centre for Urban Policy Research Rutgers, State University of New Jersey.

Berry, B. J. L. (1976) 'The counter-urbanization process: urban America since 1970', in B. J. L. Berry (ed.), *Urbanization and Counter-Urbanization*, Urban Affairs Annual Review, 11, London, Sage, 17–30.

Birch, D. (1979) *The Job Generation Process*, Cambridge, Massachusetts, MIT.

Blake, P. (1978) 'Some temporal aspects of commercial movement in Inner Liverpool between 1964 and 1974', *Reading Geographer*, 6, 54–72.

Boal, F. W. (1968) 'Technology and urban form', *Journal of Geography*, 67, 229–36.

Bourne, L. S. and Simmons, J. W. (1979) 'Canadian settlement trends: an examination of the spatial pattern of growth 1971–76', *Major Report 15*, Centre for Urban and Community Studies, Toronto, the University.

Bradford, D. F. and Kelejian, H. H. (1973) 'An econometric model of the flight to the suburbs', *Journal of Political Economy*, 81, 566–89.

Bradford, D. F., Malt, R. A. and Oates, W. E. (1969) 'The rising cost of local public services: some evidence and reflections', *National Tax Journal*, 22, 185–202.

Bradford, D. F. and Oates, W. E. (1974) 'Suburban exploitation of central cities and governmental structure', in H. Hochman and G. Peterson (eds), *Redistribution through Public Choice*, New York, Columbia University Press, 43–90.

Brechling, F. (1967) 'Trends and cycles in British regional unemployment', *Oxford Economic Papers*, 19, 1–21.

Broadbent, T. A. (1977) *Planning and Profit in the Urban Economy*, London, Methuen.

Bruton, M. J. (1975) *Introduction to Transport Planning*, 2nd edn, London, Hutchinson.

Buchanan, C. D. (1963) *Traffic in Towns*, London, HMSO.

Buck, T. W. and Atkins, M. H. (1978) 'Social class and spatial problems', *Town Planning Review*, 49, 209–21.

Bull, R. J. (1978) 'The spatial components of intra-urban manufacturing change: suburbanization in Clydeside, 1958–1968', *Transactions of the Institute of British Geographers*, new series, 3, (1), 91–100.

Burke, P. (1972) *Culture and Society in Renaissance Italy*, London, Batsford, reprinted as *Tradition and Innovation in Renaissance Italy*, London, Fontana.

Burrows, E. M. and Town, S. (1971) *Office Services in the East Midlands*, East Midland Economic Planning Council, Nottingham.

Burt, E. J. (1961) 'Changing labour supply characteristics along Route 128', *Research Report 17*, Boston, Federal Reserve Bank.

Buswell, R. and Lewis, E. W. (1970) 'The geographical distribution of industrial research activity in the UK', *Regional Studies*, 4, 277–306.

Cairncross, A. (1979) 'What is de-industrialization?', in F. Blackaby (ed.), *De-industrialization*, London, Heinemann, 5–17.

Cambridge Economic Policy Review (1980) *Urban and Regional Policy with Provisional Regional Accounts 1966–78*, 6, (2), Aldershot, Gower.

Carmichael, C. (1978) 'Local labour market analysis: its importance and a possible approach', *Geoforum*, 9, 127–48.

Caulcott, T. (1977) in *Local Government Chronicle*, 29 July 1977.

Central Policy Review Staff (1974) *Energy Conservation*, London, HMSO.

Central Statistical Office (1977) *Economic Trends* (February).

Centre for Environmental Studies (1978) 'Introduction', *CES Review*, 3.

Centre for Urban and Regional Studies (1968) 'The migration of elderly people to retirement areas', *CURS Annual Report 1967/8*, Centre for Urban and Regional Studies, Birmingham, the University.

Champion, A. G. (1976) 'Evolving patterns of population distribution in England and Wales, 1951–71', *Transactions of the Institute of British Geographers*, new series, 1 (4), 401–20.

Champion, A. G. (1981) 'Counterurbanization and rural rejuvenation in rural Britain: an evaluation of population trends since 1971', *Seminar Paper*, 38, Department of Geography, Newcastle upon Tyne, the University.

Cheshire, P. C. (1973) 'Regional unemployment differences in Great Britain', *Regional Paper*, 2, NIESR, Cambridge University Press.

Cheshire, P. C. (1979) 'Inner areas as spatial labour markets: a critique of the inner areas studies', *Urban Studies*, 16, 29–44.

Chisholm, P. C. (1976) 'Regional policies in an era of slow population growth and higher unemployment', *Regional Studies*, 10, 29–44.

Christaller, W. (1966) *Central Places in Southern Germany*, trans. C. W. Baskin, Englewood Cliffs, New Jersey, Prentice-Hall.

Civil Service Inter-Departmental Working Party (1972) *Unemployment Statistics*, London, HMSO.

Clark, D. (1979) 'The spatial impact of telecommunication', in 'Impacts of telecommunications on planning and transport', *Research Report*, 24, London, Departments of Environment and Transport.

Clark, G. (1980) 'Critical problems of geographical unemployment models', *Progress in Human Geography*, 4, 157–80.

Clarke, J. I. (1960) 'Rural and urban sex ratios in England and Wales', *Tijdschrift voor Economische en Sociale Geographie*, 51, 29–38.

Coates, B. E. and Rawstron, E. M. (1971) *Regional Variations in Britain*, London, Batsford.

Collins, M. F. and Pharoah, T. M. (1974) *Transport Organization in a Great City: The Case of London*, Hemel Hempstead, George Allen & Unwin.

Collura, J. and Schuster, J. J. (1971) 'Accessibility of low income residential areas in Philadelphia to regional industrial parks', Institute for Transportation Studies, Villanova, Pa., the University.

Coombes, M. G. (1979) personal communication concerning classification of MELAs.

Coombes, M. G., Dixon J. S. and Openshaw, S. (1979) 'A user's guide to the CURDS definitions of functional regions for the 1981 Census of Britain', *Discussion Paper*, 30, Centre for Urban and Regional Development Studies, Newcastle upon Tyne, the University.

Coombes, M. G., Dixon, J. S., Goddard, J. B., Openshaw, S. and Taylor, P. J. (1979) 'Daily urban systems in Britain: from theory to practice', *Environment and Planning A*, 11, 565–74.

Coombes, M. G., Dixon, J. S., Goddard, J. B., Openshaw, S. and Taylor, P. J. (1982) 'Functional regions for the Population Census of Great Britain', in D. T. Herbert and R. J. Johnston (eds), *Geography and the Urban Environment*, (5),

Progress in Research and Applications, London, Wiley, 63–112.

Cordey-Hayes, M. and Gleave, D. (1973) 'Migration movements and the differential growth of city regions in England and Wales', *Research Paper*, 1, London, Centre for Environmental Studies.

Craig, J. (1975) *Population Density and Concentration in Great Britain 1931, 1951 and 1961*, Studies on Medical and Population Subjects No. 30, London, HMSO.

Craig, J. (1980) *Population Density and Concentration in Great Britain 1951, 1961 and 1971*, Studies on Medical and Population Subjects No. 42, London, HMSO.

Crouch, C. S. (1982) 'Trends in unemployment', *Area*, 14, 56–59.

Crum, R. E. and Gudgin, G. (1977) 'Non-production activities in UK manufacturing industry', Collection Studies, *Regional Policy Series*, 3, Brussels, Commission of the European Communities.

Damesick, P. (1979a) 'Service employment and office location change in Britain', unpublished Ph.D. dissertation, University of Cambridge.

Damesick, P. (1979b) 'Office location and planning in the Manchester conurbation', *Town Planning Review*, 50, 346–66.

Daniels, P. W. (1970) 'Employment decentralisation and the journey to work', *Area*, 1 (3), 47–51.

Daniels, P. W. (1972) 'Transport changes generated by decentralised offices', *Regional Studies*, 6, 273–89.

Daniels, P. W. (1977) 'Office location in the British conurbations', *Urban Studies*, 14, 261–74.

Das, M. (1978) 'Travel to work in Britain: a selective review', *TRRL Laboratory Report* 849, Crowthorne, Transport and Road Research Laboratory.

Davidson, R. N. (1976) 'Social deprivation: an analysis of intercensal change', *Transactions of the Institute of British Geographers*, new series, 1 (1), 108–17.

Davies, W. K. D. and Musson, T. C. (1978) 'Spatial patterns of commuting in South Wales, 1951–71: a factor analysis definition', *Regional Studies*, 12, 353–66.

Deakin, N. and Ungerson, C. (1977) *Leaving London: Planned Mobility and the Inner City*, London, Heinemann.

Department of Employment (1975) *The Changing Structure of the Labour Force*, London, Unit for Manpower Studies.

Department of Employment (1976) 'The changed relationship between unemployment and vacancies', *DoE Gazette*, 84, 1093–99.

Department of Environment (1971) 'Long-term population distribution in Great Britain', study report prepared by inter-departmental study group, London, HMSO.

Department of Environment (1975) 'Study of the inner areas of conurbations', parts 1, 2 and supplement, Analysis of 1971 Census Indicators, London, DoE.

Department of Environment (1976a) 'British cities: urban population and employment trends, 1951–71', *Research Report* 10, London, HMSO.

Department of Environment (1976b) *Transport Policy: a Consultative Document*, 2 vols, London, HMSO.

Department of Environment (1977a) 'Policy for the inner cities', White Paper, Command 6845, London, HMSO.

Department of Environment (1977b) 'Inner London: policies for dispersal and balance', final report of the Lambeth Inner Area Study, London, HMSO.

Department of Environment (1977c) 'Change or decay', final report of the Liverpool Inner Area Study, London, HMSO.

Department of Environment (1977d) 'Unequal city', final report of the Birmingham Inner Area Study, London, HMSO.

Department of Health and Social Security (1976) 'Sharing resources for health in England', report of the Resource Allocation Party, London, HMSO.

Department of Trade and Industry (1979) 'Government announces "more selective" regional policy', *Trade and Industry*, 36, 99–102.

De Vise, P. (1976) 'The suburbanisation of jobs and minority employment', *Economic Geography*, 52 (4), 348–62.

Dicken, P. and Lloyd, P. E. (1978) 'Inner metropolitan industrial change, enterprise structures and policy issues: case studies of Manchester and Merseyside', *Regional Studies*, 12, 181–98.

Dicken, P. and Lloyd, P. E. (1980) 'The contribution of foreign-owned firms to regional employment change: a components approach with particular reference to North West England', *Environment and Planning A*, 12, 1405–26.

Drewett, J. R. (1967) 'The definition of Standard Metropolitan Labour Areas', *Working Paper* 1, Urban Growth Study, London, Political and Economic Planning.

Drewett, J. R., Goddard, J. B. and Spence, N. A. (1975) 'What's happening to British cities?', *Town and Country Planning*, 43, (12), 523–30.

Drewett, J. R., Goddard, J. B. and Spence, N. A. (1976a) 'What's happening in British cities?', *Town and Country Planning*, 44, (1), 14–24.

Drewett, J. R., Goddard, J. B. and Spence, N. A. (1976b) 'Urban Britain: beyond containment', in B. J. L. Berry (ed.), *Urbanisation and Counterurbanisation*, Urban Affairs Annual Review, vol. 11, London, Sage, 43–80.

Dugmore, K. (1975) 'The migration and distribution of socio-economic groups in Greater London: evidence from the 1961, 1966 and 1971 Censuses', *Intelligence Unit Research Memorandum* 443, Greater London Council.

Dunning, J. H. and Norman, G. (1979) 'Factors influencing the location of offices of multinational enterprises', *L.O.B. Research Paper* 8, London, Economists Advisory Group.

Dyos, H. J. (1955) 'Railways and housing in Victorian London', *Journal of Transport History*, 2, 14.

Dyos, H. J. (1961) *Victorian Camberwell: A Study in Urban Growth*, Leicester University Press.

The Economist (1978) 'Devolving London', 8.7.78, p. 14.

Erlandsson, U. (1979) 'Contract potentials in the European system of cities', in H. Folmer and J. Oosterhaven (eds), *Spatial Inequalities and Regional Development*, The Hague, Martins Nijhoff Publishing.

Evans, A. W. (1973) 'The location of headquarters of industrial companies', *Urban Studies*, 10, 387–95.

Eversley, D. (1972a) 'Old cities, falling populations and static incomes', *GLC Quarterly Bulletin*, 18, 5–17.

Eversley, D. (1972b) 'Rising costs and static incomes: some economic consequences of regional planning in London', *Urban Studies*, 9, 347–68.

Eversley, D. (1975a) 'Who will rescue our cities?', *Built Environment Quarterly*, 2 (2), 94–8.

Eversley, D. (1975b) 'Reform of local government finance: the limitations of a local income tax, evidence submitted to committee of inquiry into local government finance (chairman: Layfield)', *RP16*, London, Centre for Environmental Studies.

Ewers, H. J. and Wettmann, R. (1979) 'Innovation-oriented regional policy', final report, *Research Project MFPRS 77/19*, Berlin, International Institute of Management.

Fielding, A. J. (1971) 'Internal migration in England and Wales', *UWP 14*, London, Centre for Environmental Studies.

Firn, J. R. and Swales, J. K. (1978) 'The formation of new manufacturing establishments in the central Clydeside and West Midlands conurbations, 1963–72', *Regional Studies*, 12, 199–214.

Forbes, J. and Robertson, I. (1978) 'Intra-urban migration in Greater Glasgow', paper presented to IBG Population Studies Group, Durham.

Fothergill, S. and Gudgin, G. (1978) 'Long-term trends in the regional distribution of service activity in the UK', *WN 560*, London, Centre for Environmental Studies.

Fothergill, S. and Gudgin, G. (1979a) 'In defence of shift-share', *Urban Studies*, 16, 309–19.

Fothergill, S. and Gudgin, G. (1979b) 'Regional employment change: a sub-regional explanation', *Progress in Planning*, 12, 155–219.

Fothergill, S. and Gudgin, G. (1979c) 'Regional differences in service sector employment growth: further analyses', *WN 560*, London, Centre for Environmental Studies.

Fothergill, S. and Gudgin, G. (1982) *Unequal Growth: Urban and Regional Employment Change in the UK*, London, Heinemann.

Freeman, C. (1979) 'Technical innovation and British trade performance', in F. Blackaby (ed.), *De-industrialisation*, London, National Institute of Economic and Social Research, 56–73.

Frost, M. E. and Spence, N. A. (1980) 'A more selective regional policy', *Town and Country Planning*, 49, 252–5.

Frost, M. and Spence, N. A. (1981a) 'Policy responses to urban and regional economic change in Britain', *Geographical Journal*, 147, 321–49.

Frost, M. and Spence, N. A. (1981b) 'Unemployment, structural economic change and public policy in British regions', *Progress in Planning*, 16, 1–103.

Frost, M. and Spence, N. A. (1981c) 'The timing of unemployment responses in Britain, 1963–1976', in R. Martin (ed.), *Regional Wage Inflation and Unemployment*, London, Pion, 208–30.

Fuchs, V. R. (1968) *The Service Economy*, New York, National Bureau of Economic Research.

Ganz, A. (1968) 'Emerging patterns of urban growth and travel', *Highway Research Record*, 229, 21–37.

Gershuny, J. I. (1977) 'Post-industrial society: the myth of the service economy', *Futures*, 9 (2), 103–14.

Gershuny, J. I. (1978) *After Industrial Society: the Emerging Self-Service Economy*, London, Macmillan.

Gillespie, A. E. (1977) 'Journey to work trends within British labour market areas,

1961–71', *Working Report*, Urban Change Project, Department of Geography, London School of Economics.

Gillespie, A. E. (1980) 'Transport and the Inner City', *Working Report 3*, Inner City in Context Working Party, London, SSRC.

Gillespie, A. E., Drewett, J. R., Goddard, J. B., Kennett, S. R. and Spence, N. A. (1978) 'British cities: work travel trends', part 2 of the final report to the DoE, Urban Change Project, Department of Geography, London School of Economics.

Gillespie, A. E., Frost, M. E. and Spence, N. A. (1979) 'London's inner city residents: their industrial, occupational and work travel characteristics', IBG Annual Conference, University of Manchester, January 1979.

Gillespie, A. E. and Owen, D. (1981a) 'The current recession and the process of restructuring in the British space-economy', paper presented at the European Regional Science Association meeting, August 1981.

Gillespie, A. E. and Owen, D. (1981b) 'Unemployment trends in the current recession', *Area*, 13, 189–96.

Gillespie, A. E. and Owen, D. (1982) 'Trends in unemployment: reply', *Area*, 14, 59–61.

Glaister, S. (1976) 'Transport pricing policies and efficient urban growth', *Journal of Public Economics*, 5, 1–14.

Gleave, D. and Palmer, D. (1977) 'Labour mobility and the dynamics of labour market turnover', *WN 460*, London, Centre for Environmental Studies.

Gleave, D. and Palmer, D. (1979) 'The relationship between geographic and occupational mobility in the context of regional economic group', in J. Hobcraft and P. Rees (eds), *Regional Demographic Development*, London, Croom Helm, 188–210.

Goddard, J. B. (1975) *Office Location in Urban and Regional Development*, Oxford University Press.

Goddard, J. B. (1976) *The Communications Factor in Office Decentralisation*, Oxford, Pergamon.

Goddard, J. B. (1978a) 'The location of non-manufacturing occupations within manufacturing industries', in F. E. I. Hamilton (ed.), *Contemporary Industrialisation: Spatial Analysis and Regional Development*, London, Longman, 62–85.

Goddard, J. B. (1978b) 'Trends in the intra and inter urban location of economic activity in the UK', paper for the CREST Working Group on Location of Economic Activities, Brussels.

Goddard, J. B. (1980) 'Technology forecasting in a spatial context', *Futures*, 12, 90–105.

Goddard, J. B. and Morris, D. (1976) *The Communications Factor in Office Decentralisation*, Oxford, Pergamon.

Goddard, J. B. and Pye, R. (1977) 'Telecommunications and office location', *Regional Studies*, 11, 19–30.

Goddard, J. B. and Smith, I. J. (1978) 'Changes in corporate control in the British urban system, 1972–77', *Environment and Planning A*, 10, 1073–84.

Goddard, J. B. and Spence, N. A. (1976) 'A national perspective on employment changes in urban labour markets and questions about the future of the provincial conurbations', paper presented to CES Conference on Employment in the Inner City, University of York.

Goddard, J. B., Thwaites, A. T., Gillespie, A. E., Nash, P. A., James, V. Z., Smith,

I. J. and Oakey, R. P. (1979) 'The Mobilisation of Indigenous Potential in the UK', report to the Regional Policy Directorate, EEC, Centre for Urban and Regional Development Studies, Newcastle, the University.

Goddard, J. M., James, V. Z., Marshall, N. and Waters, N. (1980) *Telecommunications, Industrial Organisation and Regional Development*, Chichester, Wiley.

Goering, J. M. and Kalachek, E. M. (1973) 'Public transportation and black unemployment', *Transaction-Society*, 10 (5).

Gold, N. N. (1972) 'The mismatch of jobs and low income people in metropolitan areas and its implications for central city poor', in the Commission on Population Growth and the American Future, (5), Population distribution and policy, Washington.

Goldthorpe, J. H. and Hope, K. (1974) *The Social Grading of Occupations*, Oxford, Clarendon Press.

Goodman, J. F. B. (1970) 'The definition and analysis of local labour markets: some empirical problems', *British Journal of Industrial Relations*, 8, 179–96.

Gray, W. (1978) 'The S.D.A's contribution to urban renewal', *Housing*, 14, 24–6.

Greater London Group (1969) 'The socio-geographic enquiry', *Research Studies* 1, Local Government in South East England, Royal Commission on Local Government, London, HMSO.

Gripaios, P. A. (1976) 'The loss of jobs in London', *Working Paper*, London, Thames Polytechnic.

Gripaios, P. A. (1977) 'The closure of firms in the inner city: the South East London case', *Regional Studies*, 11, 1–6.

Gudgin, G. (1979) *Industrial Location Processes and Regional Employment Growth*, Farnborough, Saxon House.

Gudgin, G., Crum, R. and Bailey, S. (1979) 'White collar employment in the UK manufacturing industry', in P. W. Daniels (ed.), *Spatial Patterns of Office Growth and Location*, Chichester, Wiley, 127–58.

Guest, A. M. (1975) 'Journey to work, 1960–70', *Social Forces*, 54, 220–25.

Guest, A. M. (1976) 'Night-time and daytime population of large American suburbs', *Urban Affairs Quarterly*, 12, 57–82.

Gujurati, D. (1972) 'The behaviour of unemployment and un-filled vacancies in Great Britain, 1958–71', *Economic Journal*, 82, 195–204.

Haggett, P. (1971) 'Leads and lags in inter-regional systems: a study of cyclic fluctuations in the South West economy', in M. Chisholm and G. Manners, *Spatial Policy Problems of the British Economy*, Cambridge University Press, 69–95.

Hall, C. B. and Smith, R. A. (1968) 'Socio-economic patterns of England and Wales', *Urban Studies*, 5, 59–65.

Hall, P. (1971) 'Spatial structure of metropolitan England and Wales', in M. Chisholm and G. Manners, *Spatial Policy Problems of the British Economy*, Cambridge University Press, 96–125.

Hall, P. (1977) 'The inner cities dilemma', *New Society*, 39 (748), 223–5.

Hall, P. (1978) 'Marshall plan', *New Society*, 45 (823), 76.

Hall, P. (1980) 'Issues for the eighties', *The Planner*, 67, 4–5.

Hall, P., Thomas, R., Gracey, H. and Drewett, R. (1973) *The Containment of Urban England*, 2 vols, London, George Allen & Unwin.

Hamilton, F. E. I. (1976) 'Multinational enterprise and European Economic Community', *Tijschrift voor Economische en Sociale Geographie*, 67 (5), 258–78.

Hamnett, C. (1976) 'Social change and social segregation in Inner London', *Urban Studies*, 13, 261–72.

Hannah, L. (1976) *The Rise of the Corporate Economy*, London, Macmillan.

Hannah, L. and Kay, J. A. (1977) *Concentration in Modern Industry*, London, Macmillan.

Harris, D. F. and Taylor, F. J. (1978) 'The service sector: its changing role as a source of employment', *Research Series* 25, London, Centre for Environmental Studies.

Harris, G. and Kennett, S. (1978) 'The use of local authority areas in studies of urban change: a local perspective on decentralisation from Manchester and Birmingham', *Discussion Paper* 73, Graduate School of Geography, London School of Economics.

Harris, M. (1973) 'Some aspects of social polarization', in D. Donnison and D. E. C. Eversley (eds), *London: Urban Patterns, Problems and Policies*, London, Heinemann, 156–89.

Harris, M. and Lyons, J. (1971) 'Social polarization', *Research Memorandum* 324, Department of Planning and Transportation Intelligence Unit, Greater London Council.

Harvey, D. (1973) *Social Justice and the City*, London, Edward Arnold.

Heggie, I. A. (ed.) (1976) *Modal Choice and the Value of Travel Time*, Oxford University Press.

Hicks, Lady U. (1973) 'Experiments in the organisation and finance of metropolitan areas (the future of conurbations)', *Publication no.* 10, London, Institute of Fiscal Studies.

Hill, S. J. and Martin, T. K. (1976) 'Consumer preference in transportation', *Highway Research Record* 197, Washington DC.

Hillman, M. (1978) 'The social consequences of the decline in public transport', in K. Grime (ed.) *Discussion Paper* 10, London, Regional Studies Association.

Hillman, M., Henderson, I. and Whalley, A. (1973) 'Personal mobility and transport policy', *PEP Broadsheet* 542, London, Political and Economic Planning.

HM Government (1978) Inner Urban Areas Act, London, HMSO.

Holland, S. (1979) 'Foreign manufacturing by UK firms: a comment', in F. Blackaby (ed.), *De-industrialisation*, London, National Institute of Economic and Social Research, 95–101.

Howard, R. S. (1968) *The Movement of Manufacturing Industry in the UK, 1945–65*, Board of Trade, London, HMSO.

Hudson, R. (1978) 'Spatial policy in Britain: regional or urban?', *Area*, 9, 3–8.

Hughes, J. T. and Price, S. F. (1977) 'Urban services: locational dynamics and sectoral stability', paper at CES conference on Urban Economics, July 1977, Keele University.

Hyman, G. and Gleave, D. (1978) 'A reasonable theory of migration', *Transactions of the Institute of British Geographers*, new series, 3 (2), 179–201.

Independent Commission on Transport (1974) *Changing Directions*, London, Coronet Books.

Jackman, R. and Sellars, M. (1977) 'The distribution of RSG: the hows and whys of the new needs formula', *Review* 1, London, Centre for Environmental Studies.

James, V. Z. (1978) 'Office employment in the Northern Region: its national, regional and organisational context', *Discussion Paper* 14, Centre for Urban and Regional Development Studies, Newcastle, the University.

Jarvis, J. (1976) 'The changing composition of London's workforce and the effects on journey to work', DoE internal paper, LTP Division, London.

Jeffery, D. and Webb, D. J. (1972) 'Economic fluctuations in the Australian regional system', *Australian Geographical Studies*, 10, 141–60.

Johnson, J. H., Salt, J. and Wood, P. A. (1974) *Housing and the Migration of Labour in England and Wales*, Farnborough, Saxon House, Lexington Books.

Johnson, P. S. and Cathcart, D. (1979) 'The founders of new manufacturing firms: a note on the size of incubator plants', *Journal of Industrial Economics*, 28, 219–24.

Johnston, R. J. (1979) 'On urban and regional systems in lagged correlation analysis', *Environment and Planning A*, 11, 705–14.

Joint Unit for Research on the Urban Environment (JURUE) (1979) 'Industrial renewal in the inner cities: an assessment of potential and problems', JURUE, Birmingham, University of Aston.

Kain, J. F. (1967) 'Urban travel behaviour', in L. F. Schnore and H. Fagin (eds), *Urban Research and Policy Planning*, Beverley Hills, Sage Publications, 161–92.

Kasarda, J. (1976) 'The changing occupational structure of the metropolis: selective redistribution', in B. J. L. Berry and J. Kasarda (eds), *Contemporary Urban Economics*, New York, Macmillan.

Keeble, D. E. (1976) *Industrial Location and Planning in the United Kingdom*, London, Methuen.

Keeble, D. E. (1977) 'Spatial policy in Britain: regional or urban?', *Area*, 9, 3–8.

Keeble, D. E. (1978) 'Industrial geography', *Progress in Human Geography*, 2, 318–323.

Keeble, D. E. (1980) 'Industrial decline, regional policy and the urban–rural manufacturing shift in the United Kingdom', *Environment and Planning A*, 12, 945–62.

Kennett, S. (1975) 'A classification of the components of intra-urban and inter-urban population change in England and Wales, 1961–71', *Discussion Paper* 54, Graduate School of Geography, London School of Economics.

Kennett, S. (1977) 'Migration and "Million City" labour markets, 1966–71', *Working Report* 52, Urban Change in Britain Project, Geography Department, London School of Economics.

Kennett, S. (1978a) 'Exploding the myth of rapidly expanding urban systems in Britain: implications for the adoption of functional areas in the 1981 Census', *Discussion Paper* 70, Graduate School of Geography, London School of Economics.

Kennett, S. (1978b) 'Census data and migration analysis: an appraisal', paper at SSRC conference on Census Data, April 1978, London.

Kennett, S. (1979) 'Migration within and between the Metropolitan Economic Labour Areas of Britain, 1966–71', in J. Hobcraft and P. Rees (eds) *Regional Demographic Development*, London, Croom Helm, 165–87.

Kennett, S. (1980) 'Local government fiscal problems: a context for inner areas', *Working Report* 6, Inner City in Context Project, London, SSRC.

Kennett, S. and Randolph, W. (1978) 'The differential migration of socio-economic groups, 1966–71', *Discussion Paper* 66, Graduate School of Geography, London School of Economics.

Kennett, S. and Spence, N. (1979) 'British population trends in the 1970s', *Town and Country Planning*, 48 (7), 221–4.

Kidder, A. E. and Saltzman, A. (1973) 'Mode choice among auto workers in auto-oriented cities', first International Conference on Transportation Research, proceedings, 642–5, Transportation Research Forum, College of Europe.

Kiernan, K. (1979) 'Characteristics of young people who move inter-regionally: a longitudinal study', in J. Hobcraft and P. Rees (eds), *Regional Demographic Development*, London, Croom Helm, 211–27.

King, L. J. and Clark, G. L. (1978) 'Regional unemployment patterns and the spatial dimensions of macro-economic policy: the Canadian experience, 1966–75', *Regional Studies*, 12, 283–96.

Labour Party (1978) *Regional Authorities and Local Government*, London, Transport House.

Law, C. M. and Warnes, A. (1975) 'Life begins at sixty: the increase in regional retirement migration', *Town and Country Planning*, 43, 531–34.

Law, C. M. and Warnes, A. (1976) 'The changing geography of the elderly in England and Wales', *Transactions of the Institute of British Geographers*, new series, 1 (4), 453–71.

Lawton, R. (1963) 'The journey to work in England and Wales: forty years of change', *Tijdschrift voor Economische en Sociale Geographie*, 44, 61–9.

Lawton, R. (1968) 'The journey to work in Britain: some trends and problems', *Regional Studies*, 2, 27–40.

Lawton, R. (1974) 'England must find room for more', *Geographical Magazine*, 46, 179–84.

Lawton, R. (1977) 'People and work', in J. W. House (ed.) *The UK Space: Resources, Environment and the Future*, 2nd edn, London, Wiedenfeld and Nicholson, 109–213.

Layfield Report (1976) *Local Government Finance: Report of the Committee of Enquiry*, Command 6453, London, HMSO.

Leicester, C. (1978) 'Future employment trends', *The Planner*, 64, 103–5.

Leigh, R. and North, D. (1978a) 'Regional aspects of acquisition activity in British manufacturing industry', *Regional Studies*, 12, 227–45.

Leigh, R. and North, D. (1978b) 'The spatial consequences of takeovers in some British industries and their implications for regional development', in F. E. I. Hamilton (ed.) *Contemporary Industrialisation: Spatial Analysis and Regional Development*, London, Longman, 158–81.

Lever, W. F., Danson, M. W. and Malcolm, J. F. (1979) 'Manufacturing and service industries in inner cities', Stage 2, report to DoE, Inner Cities Directorate, Department of Economic and Social Research, Glasgow, the University.

Lever, W. F., Danson, M. W. and Malcolm, J. F. (1980) 'The inner city employment problem in Great Britain, 1952–76: a shift-share approach', *Urban Studies*, 17, 193–210.

Liepmann, K. K. (1944) *The Journey to Work: its Significance for Industrial and Community Life*, London, Kegan Paul.

Lloyd, P. E. and Mason, C. M. (1978) 'Manufacturing in the inner city: a case study of Greater Manchester', *Transactions of the Institute of British Geographers*, new series, 3, 66–90.

Lloyd, P. E. and Mason, C. M. (1979) 'Industrial movement in North West England, 1966–75', *Environment and Planning A*, 11, 1367–85.

Lock, D. (1976) 'Planned dispersal and the decline of London', *The Planner*, 62, 201–4.

Losch, A. (1967) *The Economics of Location*, trans. W. H. Woglom, Chichester, Wiley.

Lowry, I. S. (1966) *Migration and Metropolitan Growth: Two Analytical Models*, University of California, Chandler.

Manley, P. and Sawbridge, D. (1980) 'Women at work', *Lloyds Bank Review*, 135, 29–40.

Manners, G. (1976) 'Reinterpreting the regional problem', *The Three Banks Review*, 111, 33–5.

Manpower Research Group (1980) 'Occupational changes in the British economy', *DoE Gazette*, 88, 1204–8.

Marquand, J. M. (1979a) 'The service sector and regional policy in the United Kingdom', *Research Series* 29, London, Centre for Environmental Studies.

Marquand, J. M. (1979b) 'A locational analysis of the UK service sector', *Occasional Paper* 9, London, Centre for Environmental Studies.

Marquand, J. M. (1980a) 'Measuring the effects and costs of regional incentives', *Working Paper* 32, Government Economic Service, London, Civil Service College.

Marquand, J. M. (1980b) 'Spatial change and economic divergence in the EEC', *Journal of Common Market Studies*, 19, 1–20.

Marquand, J. M. (1980c) 'The role of the tertiary sector in regional policy: comparative report, collection studies', *Regional Policy Series*, Commission of the European Communities.

Marshall, Sir F. (1978) *Inquiry into Local Government*, Greater London Council.

Marshall, J. N. (1977) 'Business travel and regional office employment', *Discussion Paper* 6, Centre for Urban and Regional Development Studies, Newcastle upon Tyne, the University.

Marshall, J. N. (1979a) 'Organisational and location factors associated with the performance of manufacturing establishment', *Discussion Paper* 26, Centre for Urban and Regional Development Studies, Newcastle, the University.

Marshall, J. N. (1979b) 'Corporate organisation and regional office employment', *Environment and Planning A*, 11, 553–63.

Marshall, J. N. (1979c) 'Ownership, organisation and industrial linkage', *Regional Studies*, 13, 531–58.

Massey, D. B. (1979) 'In what sense a regional problem?', *Regional Studies*, 13, 233–44.

Massey, D. B. and Meegan, R. A. (1978) 'Restructuring versus the cities', *Urban Studies*, 15, 273–87.

Massey, D. B. and Meegan, R. A. (1982) *The Anatomy of Job Loss*, London, Methuen.

McDermott, P. (1977) 'Overseas investment and industrial geography of the UK', *Area*, 9, 200–7.

Metcalf, D. and Richardson, R. (1972) 'The nature and measurement of unemployment in the UK', *The Three Banks Review*, 93, 30–45.

Meyer, J. R. (1968) 'Urban transportation', in J. Q. Wilson (ed.) *The Metropolitan Enigma*, Cambridge, Massachusetts, Harvard University Press, 41–69.

Mogridge, M. and Eldridge, D. (1970) 'Car ownership in London', *Research Report* 10, Greater London Research Intelligence Unit, Greater London Council.

Moore, B. C. and Rhodes, J. (1973) 'Evaluating the effects of British regional economic policy', *Economic Journal*, 83, 87–110.

Moore, B. C. and Rhodes, J. (1976) 'Regional economic policy and the movement of manufacturing firms to development areas', *Economica*, 43, 17–31.

Moore, B. C. and Rhodes, J. (1980) 'Employment, unemployment and labour supply in Great Britain and the inner cities, 1951–76', paper at conference in Industry in the Inner City, Civil Service College, Sunningdale (mimeo).

Moore, B. C., Rhodes, J. and Tyler, P. (1977) 'The impact of regional policy in the 1970s', *Review No.* 1, London, Centre for Environmental Studies.

Moore, B. C., Rhodes, J. and Tyler, P. (1980) 'New developments in the evaluation of regional policy', paper at SSRC conference on Urban and Regional Economics, May 1980, Birmingham.

Morrison, P. A. and Wheeler, J. P. (1976) 'Rural renaissance in America?', *Population Bulletin*, 31 (3), 1–27.

Muller, P. O. (1976) 'Social transportation geography', *Progress in Geography*, 8, 208–31.

Munt, P. W. and Woodhall, R. (1967) 'A study of travel times by private and public transport in Greater London', *Research Memorandum* 44, Department of Highways and Transport, Greater London Council.

National Institute for Economic and Social Research (1972) Summaries, *National Institute Economic Review*, nos 59–62.

Northern Region Strategy Team (1975) 'Cyclical fluctuations in economic activity in the Northern Region', *Technical Report* 1, Newcastle upon Tyne, NRST.

Nunn, S. J. (1980) 'Openings and closures of manufacturing establishments, 1966–75', *Regional Research Series* 1, London, Department of Industry.

Oakey, R. P., Thwaites, A. T. and Nash, P. A. (1980) 'The regional distribution of innovative manufacturing establishments in Britain', *Regional Studies*, 14, 235–53.

Office of Population Censuses and Surveys (OPCS) (1970) *Classification of Occupations*, London, HMSO.

OPCS (1978a) 'Demographic review 1977', *Series DR 1*, London, HMSO.

OPCS (1978b) 'Population estimates, 1971–77', *Population Trends*, 13, 10–12.

OPCS (1981) 'Census 1981: preliminary report, England and Wales', *CEN 81 PR(1)*, London, HMSO.

Ogilvy, A. A. (1980) *Inter-regional Migration since 1971: an appraisal of data from the National Health Service Central Register and Labour Force Surveys*, London, OPCS Occasional Paper 16.

Ogilvy, A. A. (1982) 'Population migration between the regions of Great Britain, 1971–79', *Regional Studies*, 16, 65–73.

Openshaw, S. (1978) 'An empirical study of some zone-design criteria', *Environment and Planning A*, 10, 781–94.

Ornati, O. A. (1969) *Transportation Needs of the Poor: a Case Study of New York City*, New York, Praeger.

Osborne, R. H. (1964) 'Population', in J. W. Watson and J. B. Sissons (eds) *The British Isles: a Systematic Geography*, London, Nelson, 331–57.

Pahl, R. E. (1978) 'Will the inner city problem ever go away?' *New Society*, 45, 678–81.

Pavitt, K. (1979) 'Technical innovation and industrial development', part 1, *Futures*, 11, 458–68.

Pavitt, K. (1980) 'Technical innovation and industrial development', part 2, *Futures*, 12, 35–44.

Pinch, S. P. (1981) 'Urban growth and social change', in C. M. Mason and M. E. Witherick (eds), *Dimensions of Change in a Growth Area: Southampton since 1960*, Aldershot, Gower, 121–45.

Pollins, H. (1964) 'Transport lines and social divisions', in R. Glass (ed.), *London: Aspects of Change*, London, Macgibbon and Kee, 29–61.

Pounce, R. (1981) 'Movement of manufacturing industry in the UK since 1965', Department of Industry, London, HMSO.

Prais, S. J. (1976) *The Evolution of Giant Firms in Britain*, Cambridge University Press.

Pred, A. (1971) *City Systems in Advanced Economics*, London, Hutchinson.

Quarmby, D. A. (1967) 'Choice of travel mode for the journey to work: some findings', *Journal of Transport Economics and Policy*, 1, 1–42.

Redcliffe-Maud (1969) *Report of the Royal Commission on Local Government in England*, Command 4040, London, HMSO.

Rees, P. (1976) 'The measurement of migration from census data and other sources', *Working Paper* 162, Department of Geography, Leeds, the University.

Rees, T. L. (1978) 'Population and industrial decline in the South Wales coalfield', *Regional Studies*, 12 (1), 69–77.

Registrar General Scotland (1981) *Census 1981: preliminary report*, Edinburgh, HMSO.

Rhodes, J. and Kan, A. (1971) 'Office dispersal and regional policy', *Occasional paper* 30, Department of Applied Economics, Cambridge, the University.

Richardson, H. W. (1971) *Urban Economics*, Harmondsworth, Penguin Educational.

Roberts, K., Cook, F. G., Clark, S. C. and Semeonoff, E. (1977) *The Fragmentary Class Structure*, London, Heinemann.

Robertson, J. (1982) *The Structure and Employment Prospects of the Service Industries*, Research Paper No. 50, London, Department of Employment.

Robinson, J. F. F. and Storey, D. J. (1981) 'Manufacturing employment change in Cleveland, 1965–76', *Regional Studies*, 15 (3), 161–72.

Roos, D. (1973) 'An overview of demand-responsive transportation systems', first International Conference on Transportation Research, proceedings, 324–36, Transportation Research Forum, College of Europe.

Routh, G. (1965) *Occupation and Pay in Great Britain*, Cambridge University Press.

Sammons, R. and Hall, P. (1940) 'Urban activity patterns and modal split in the journey to work', *Geographical Paper* 2, Department of Geography, Reading, the University.

Schaeffer, K. H. and Schlar, E. (1975) *Access for All: Transportation and Urban Growth*, London, Pelican.

Sleigh, J., Boatwright, B., Irwin, P. and Stanyon, R. (1979) *Manpower Implications* of Micro Electronic Technology, Department of Employment, London, HMSO.

Smart, M. W. (1974) 'Labour market areas: uses and definitions', *Progress in Planning*, 2 (4), 239–353.

Smith, I. J. (1979) 'The effects of external takeover and manufacturing employment change in the Northern Region, 1963–73', *Regional Studies*, 13, 421–37.

Smith, I. J. (1980) 'Some aspects of direct inward investment in the UK', *Discussion Paper* 31, Centre for Urban and Regional Development Studies, Newcastle upon Tyne, the University.

Spence, N. A., Gillespie, A., Goddard, J., Kennett, S., Pinch, S. and Williams, A. M. (1982) *British Cities: Analysis of Urban Change*, Oxford, Pergamon.

Steinherr, A., De Souza, E. and Lemaitre, J. P. (1977) 'Factor contents can explain West Germany's foreign trade', *Working Paper* 7711, Institut des Sciences Economiques, Université Catholique de Louvain.

Sternlieb, G. and Hughes, J. W. (1975) 'Prologue', in G. Sternlieb and J. W. Hughes (eds), *Post Industrial America: Metropolitan Decline and Inter-Regional Job Shifts*, Centre for Urban Policy Research, Rutgers, State University of New Jersey.

Stone, P. A. (1978) 'The implications for the conurbations of population changes', *Regional Studies*, 12 (1), 95–123.

Taafe, E., Garner, B. and Yeates, M. (1963) *The Peripheral Journey to Work: a Geographical Consideration*, Evanston, Illinois, Northwestern University.

Thatcher, A. R. (1979) 'Labour supply and employment trends', in F. Blackaby (ed.), *De-industrialisation*, London, Heinemann, 26–48.

Thirlwell, A. P. (1966) 'Regional unemployment as a cyclical phenomenon', *Scottish Journal of Political Economy*, 13, 205–19.

Thomas, R. (1968) 'Journeys to work', *PEP Broadsheet*, 504, 335–419.

Thomas, R. and Potter, S. (1977) 'Landscape with pedestrian figures', *Built Environment Quarterly*, December, 286–90.

Thwaites, A. T. (1978) 'Technological change, mobile plants and regional development', *Regional Studies*, 12, 445–61.

Town, S. W. (1977) 'Access to employment opportunities: outline strategy', project application from Access and Mobility Division, TRRL to Department of Employment.

Townsend, A. R. (1977) 'The relationship of inner city problems to regional policy', *Regional Studies*, 11, 225–52.

Townsend, A. R. (1980) 'Unemployment geography and the new government's regional aid', *Area*, 12, 9–18.

Townsend, A. R. (1981) 'Geographical perspectives on major job losses in the UK', *Area*, 13, 33–8.

Vernon, R. (1970) *The Technology Factor in International Trade*, Irvington, NY, Columbia University Press.

Vining, D. R., jun., and Kontuly, T. (1978) 'Population dispersal from major metropolitan regions: an international comparison', *International Regional Science Review*, 3 (1), 49–73.

Wabe, J. S. (1969) 'Commuter travel in Central London', *Journal of Transport, Economics and Policy*, 3 (1), 48–68.

Warnes, A. M. (1972) 'Estimates of journey-to-work distances from census statistics', *Regional Studies*, 6 (3), 315–26.

Warnes, A. M. (1977) 'The decentralisation of employment from the larger English cities', *Occasional Paper* 5, Department of Geography, King's College, London University.

Webber, M. E. (1973) 'Post-automobile transport', first International Conference on Transportation Research, proceedings, 289–92, Transportation Research Forum, College of Europe.

Westaway, J. (1973) 'Contact potential and the occupational structure of the British urban system, 1961–66: an empirical study', *Geography Discussion Paper* 45, Graduate School of Geography, London School of Economics.

Westergaard, J. (1957) 'Journeys to work in the London region', *Town Planning Review*, 28, 37–62.

Westergaard, J. and Resler, H. (1975) *Class in a Capitalist Society*, Harmondsworth, Penguin.

Wettmann, R. *et al.* (1979) 'Deglomeration policies in the European Community: a comparative study', International Institute of Management, Berlin, for the EEC Commission, DG XVI.

Willeke, R. and Baum, H. (1971) 'Theory and practice in road pricing', in *Techniques of Improving Urban Conditions by Restraint of Road Traffic*, Paris, OECD.

Willis, K. G. (1974) *Problems in Migration Analysis*, Farnborough, Lexington Books.

Wilson, F. R. (1967) *Journey to Work*, London, Maclaren and Sons.

Wood, P. A. (1979) 'Priorities in industrial location research', *Area*, 11 (3), 253–56.

Index